Oswald Crawfurd

Travels in Portugal

Oswald Crawfurd

Travels in Portugal

ISBN/EAN: 9783337209346

Printed in Europe, USA, Canada, Australia, Japan

Cover: Foto ©Andreas Hilbeck / pixelio.de

More available books at **www.hansebooks.com**

TRAVELS
IN
PORTUGAL.

BY

JOHN LATOUCHE

WITH ILLUSTRATIONS
BY
THE RIGHT HON. T. SOTHERON ESTCOURT.

SECOND EDITION.

London:
WARD, LOCK, AND TYLER, WARWICK HOUSE,
PATERNOSTER ROW.

PREFACE TO FIRST EDITION.

These Travels were published in consecutive Numbers of "The New Quarterly Magazine," under the title of Notes of Travel in Portugal. The favourable reception they met with from the public press has induced me to revise them, to enlarge them considerably, and to republish them in book form. Although, at my publisher's suggestion, I have altered the title to the more convenient one of Travels in Portugal, I desire to say that they are nevertheless nothing more than notes—mental notes, for I travelled without any design of future publication, and kept no single written memorandum of what I did or saw. This I say in apology for the somewhat discursive style of my work, and in mitigation of critical judgment. Furthermore, I did not travel continuously. My travels were interrupted by periods of residence; both of which extenuating circumstances may, I pray, when I come to be reviewed, be taken into consideration.

In looking over the proof sheets, it has struck me that I may have unconsciously magnified the difficulties in the way of pleasure travelling in Portugal. I have, therefore, somewhat modified my original statements, and in one place I have added a long explanatory note.

I would wish my dissuasion from Portuguese travel to be accepted only by the mere tourist—the ignorant, conceited, incurious, moneyed tramp, for whom so much deserved contempt has been expressed in current literature. Those who go to Portugal to enjoy a pleasant winter climate will, as a rule, I think, do well to go. Those who go to see a strange people with a famous name in European history, to watch the successful working of a representative Constitution, to study archæology, ecclesiology, or natural history; or, again, those who simply desire to take a month's holiday and a month's relaxation in spring, summer, or winter, in a quite new country (with no intention to " do " the country in ordinary tourist fashion) will, I think, not regret a visit to Portugal.

For the illustrations to this volume I am indebted to the kindness of the Right Honourable Thomas Sotheron Estcourt, who has allowed me to choose from among a valuable series of finished sketches in pen and ink and in sepia, made by him in the course of a visit to the Peninsula. These sketches were in every case made upon the spot, and to their perfect fidelity I can myself testify. After attempting in vain to get the delicacy and finish of the drawings reproduced by the engraver, I had to fall back on photography; and they appear in the shape of reduced facsimiles by means of the Woodbury Type process.

JOHN LATOUCHE.

PREFACE TO SECOND EDITION.

AFTER recording the pleasing circumstance that a very large First Edition has been exhausted in rather more than two months, I have little to say in this Preface to a Second Edition beyond expressing my gratitude for the friendly and—what is as important to an author—the early reviews of my book in the leading journals. By no other means can a comparatively unknown and quite unrecommended writer bring his literary wares to market; for the very fastidious reading public of Great Britain follows the great social law observed by our countrymen everywhere, and will make no acquaintance with a strange author till he be first formally introduced to their notice by the critics, the indispensable fuglemen of the press, and masters of the ceremonies in the society of letters.

Exception has been taken by the "Times," in the course of a full and favourable notice of the "Travels," to my apparently "implacable" feelings against the

Tourist class. It is perhaps true that I have expressed my objection to one section of this class rather freely; but be it understood that I, no other than a tourist myself on many occasions of my life, should be, and am the very last person to speak ill of tourists generally. I did, indeed, draw a distinction between the idle and luxurious tourist and the traveller who is in pursuit of something beyond the mere killing of his time. The first, I urged, after a considerable knowledge of Portugal, would find that country quite unsuited to him; the true traveller, on the other hand, prepared for rough travelling, and willing to pay the price of much discomfort for an increase of his knowledge of a curious country and a little-known people, would find Portugal very well worth travelling in. Again, I have recommended the two chief towns of Portugal as health resorts, under some circumstances and with some limitations.

As evidence that I have no desire whatever to dissuade the more intelligent class of travellers from visiting Portugal, I will even do my utmost to induce them to go thither. I hereby confirm the opinion expressed in the "Times" review as to the ease with which the country can be reached from England. "Imagination," says my critic in the "Times," "invests the little western kingdom with all the vague terrors inspired by the long-continued disturbances of the rest of the Peninsula." All of which terrors the reviewer shows to be groundless. The "Times" writer might have gone further, and said that imagination plays more pranks than this with travellers. It would be safe to say that nine intending sea-travellers to Portugal out of every ten expect to have to cross the "ever-vexed" Bay of Biscay; this is, as any map will show them, a geographical error, seeing that their steamer's true course from Ushant to Finisterre never once brings them within a line drawn between these two points, inside of which line only are the turbulent waters of this much-feared bay.

From all this it may be concluded that this said quality of imagination is a very troublesome sort of commodity for a traveller—fatal to enterprise. It is, indeed, the bane of travellers; and the Scotch, the most daring of all adventurers by sea and land, possess either least of this unheroic quality, or have, more than other people, the power of suppressing its excess. As to which fact, I beg to relate a pleasant and appropriate instance which chanced to come under my own observation. It happened that a Scotch lady, residing in a distant land, desired to take a favourite native servant home with her. "Oh, madam," objected the woman, "I would willingly go with you, but for the sea—I am so terribly afraid of it." "The sea!" said her kindly and energetic mistress; "what do you think you will have to do with the sea? You are simply put into a steamer here and taken out at London. Pray, what does the sea matter to you?" The girl went, and found that her mistress had been right, and she altogether wrong; and this I think proves what a foolish thing is this same imagination, which, for this poor girl, had clearly summoned up mountains of waves which she personally was to do battle with, sea-devils, whales with their huge mouths gaping at her, monstrous spear-nosed fish tilting at her weak body, and heaven only knows what beside; and, compared to these horrors, all the nasty realities of steam-boat travel, the hot, stuffy, oily smells, the closeness, the noise, the nausea, the stewardess—appeared, no doubt, quite endurable evils.

To right-thinking, non-tourist travellers contemplating a visit to Portugal, I commend this anecdote. I say to them, "Pray, let your imagination lie in abeyance. What have rebellious Carlists, or the rough waves of the Bay of Biscay to do with you? You are put into a steamer at London, Liverpool, or Southampton, and taken out, in due time, at Lisbon or Oporto, safe and sound."

JOHN LATOUCHE.

LONDON,
  September 20, 1875.

CONTENTS.

CHAPTER I.

                                                                PAGE

Vigo—Real Travel and Holiday Travel—Choice of a Horse—Lies of a Spanish Horse dealer—Vigo Bay, in connection with British Naval History—Serious Quarrel between Guide and Innkeeper's Family—Boorishness and Virtues of the Galicians—Story of a Zarzuela Actress—Bed and Board of Travellers in Portugal—Tuy; its Gothic Cathedral 1

CHAPTER II.

Spanish and Portuguese on the Frontier Line—Travel Southward—Banks of Minho—Caminha—Sea Coast—Hospitable Farmer—Ghost Stories—The *Lobis-homem*; a Grisly Tale—Farm Work in Northern Portugal—Land Tenure and Peasant Farms—Undescribed Druidical Remains—A District Peopled by Women—Anecdote in Testimony of their Good Conduct—Timoléon of Cossé 19

CHAPTER III.

Vianna—Costume and Looks of the Women—Cheerfulness of the People—Their Dances; their Improvised Singing—River Lima—Unsupported Tradition—Funeral Customs—Surrounding Scenery Overpraised—Raptures over Scenery make poor Reading—Home of Miranda, the Poet—Reflections on Ill-directed Travel, suggested by Misadventures of Two British Tourists—Abundant Traces of the Moors—Wrong Construction put upon the Author's Motives—Belief in Hidden Treasure—Stories in Proof—Precious Stones in Portugal—The Crown Jewels; the Braganza Diamond. 44

CHAPTER IV.

Visit to the Gaviarra—Prudery of Portuguese Writers—Decay of Literature—View from the Top of Gaviarra—Early Portuguese History—Advantages of Travelling on Horseback—Ride through the Gerez Mountains and along Spanish Frontier—Wild Birds, Beasts and Flowers—Fishing and Shooting not Good in Portugal—Hill Forts—Legends Connected with One—Mild Religious Exercises—Pilgrimages to Shrines 73

CHAPTER V.

The Castle of Braganza—Hebrew Type of Face in Braganza—Important Part Played by Jews in Portuguese History—Conversation with a Jewish Traveller—His Story of Spinosa—Mirandella—Monotonous Cuisine of Well-to-do People in Portugal—Legend of the Bruxas—Villa Real; its Architecture—Return of Enriched Adventurers from India and Brazil—Dull Life in Portuguese Country Towns—Curious System of Courtship—Anecdote—Description of Port Wine Country—Sketch of the History of Port Wine—Has a Literature of its Own—The Pass over the Marão Mountains 99

CHAPTER VI.

Luxuriance of Vegetation on Western Slopes of Marão Hills—A Large Cactus—Affair between General Loison and Portuguese Troops at Amarante—Cinque-cento Ornamentation of Church of San Gonçalo—Sketch of Progress of Christian Architecture in Portugal—Legend of Saint Gonçalo—Undeserved Ill Repute of People of Amarante—An Unlucky and Foolish Mining Company—Curious Waterproof Cloak—Portuguese Peasantry Lineal and Unchanged Descendants of Conquerors of the Saracens and Castilians—Old Charters—Breed of Horses Crossed with Arab Blood in Moorish Times—Vallongo—Its Ancient Gold Mines—A Toy Mine at Work—Mining Prospects of Portugal—Oporto—Its History—Its Famous Siege—Is the Centre of Political and Commercial Movement in Portugal—The Douro; its Dangerous Bar—An Old Roman Beacon 127

CHAPTER VII.

Foz, the Brighton of Oporto—Sea Bathing—Douro Boats—The Portuguese a Trafficking People, but not Commercially Adventurous—Churches of Oporto—Remarkable Historical Picture—The Douro Passage of, in 1812—Curious Reputation of the Douro in Spain—Fish and Fishing in the River—Ethnology of Portugal—Variety of Races—Appearance of the People—Gold Ornaments of Moorish Design—Railway to Lisbon—Places on the Way—Marsh Scenery—Coimbra—Erroneous Tradition about Inez de Castro—University of Coimbra; its Connection with George Buchanan—Pombal—Marquis of Pombal the Bismarck of Portugal—His Life and Character—Alcobaça—Batalha, the Battle Abbey of Portugal—Its Plateresque Style of Architecture—"Tanias El Rey," meaning of—Objection to "Interviewing" Respectable People, and Reporting their Conversation—Conversation of Chance Acquaintances very Poor—An Instance 146

CONTENTS.

CHAPTER VIII.

Lisbon—Cintra Overpraised—Monserrat, and the Author of *Vathek*—Moorish Palace Fort at Cintra—Pariah Dogs of Lisbon have Ceased to Exist—Dog Hunts—Humanity of the Portuguese—Mild Bull Fighting Practised in Portugal—Singular Tameness of Domestic Animals—Native Newspapers—Their Timidity and Scanty News—Curious System of Avowedly Paid Literary Criticism—Modern Art Progress in Portugal disappointing—Repoussé Work—Point Lace—Ancient Furniture—Caldas Faience—Paintings Deplorable—The Academy Exhibition—Gran Vasco and his supposed School 187

CHAPTER IX.

From Lisbon to Evora—Lost Fertility of Great South Tagus Plain—Fine Roman Remains at Evora—Abundance and Triviality of Roman Inscriptions—Elvas—Wrong Choice of a Guide—His Blunders, his Ghost Stories, and General Imbecility—Legend of the Seven Whistlers—The Guide's Terror—Benighted in a Forest—Recovery of Horses and Guide 207

CHAPTER X.

Hostess at Monsaras a Shrew—Her Volubility and Use of Proverbs—Spanish Frontier—Line of Demarcation Distinct between Spanish and Portuguese Character—The Portuguese Language—Affectation of the Brazilians—Portuguese Share in "Pigeon English"—Portuguese a Living and Growing Language—An Instance; Origin of Word, *Fajardismo*—An Intelligent Swindle—Olivença, once Portuguese, now Spanish—Radical and Important Difference between Spanish and Portuguese National Character and Institutions 225

CHAPTER XI.

Juromenha—Desolate Country—Last Stand of Moors of Portugal Made in this Region—Final Wars of Moors and Portuguese Treacherous and Bloody—Sketch of History of the Great Portuguese Home Crusade—Names of Different Sorts of Christian Marauding Expeditions Preserved in Charters to Towns and Convents—Mertola—Final and Crowning Misadventure of the Guide Francisco 246

CHAPTER XII.

Boat Journey down the Guadiana to Villa Nova—Scenery and Botany of Province of Algarve—The Locust Tree—Boatmen's Stories—The Ginet—Mr. Mason's Successful Mining at San Domingo—Embark for Lisbon in a Trading Schooner—The East Wind; its Bad Reputation—Proverbs—The "Rock" of Lisbon; Why so called—Viseu—Its Famous Pictures—Gran Vasco—Discussion as to his Authorship of Pictures ascribed to him—The Province of Beira—Its Unsophisticated Inhabitants—Their Singular Dress —Their Probable Origin—Remarks on Travel Writing—Culture and Good Manners and Nature of the People—A Theory Unsupported by Facts—A Portuguese Priest—His Stories about Wolves—Diminution of Wolves in the Country—Good and Inoffensive Character of the Priest—His Views on Sport—Through Oporto Northward—Monastic Church of Leça do Balio—Description of a Pine Forest—Barcellos—A Portuguese School Inspection—Farming—Strong Traces of Roman Farm System—"Green Wine;" its Taste and Good Effects—Recapitulation of Impressions of the Portuguese, as a People 259

SUPPLEMENTARY CHAPTER.

Reasons for Writing a Supplementary Chapter—Influence of the Moon in Portugal—The Planting of Cabbages—Spade and Hoe Cultivation—Women's Work—Superstitious Notions—The Fattening of Pigs—The Priests' Influence—Non-Secular Education—Cheap Substitute for Newspapers—Hints to Tourists—Climate—Language—Anecdote—Philistinism—Anecdote—Manners and Morals—Management of Forests and Orchards—A Secret in Forestal Science—Flower Gardens—A Problem in Agriculture—Farm System of Portugal 324

LIST OF ILLUSTRATIONS.

Tuy and Valença.   Ponte de Lima.
Vianna.   Amarante.
            Batalha.

TRAVELS IN PORTUGAL.

CHAPTER I.

Vigo—Real Travel and Holiday Travel—Choice of a Horse—Lies of a Spanish Horse-dealer—Vigo Bay, in connection with British Naval History—Serious Quarrel between Guide and Innkeeper's Family—Boorishness and Virtues of the Galicians—Story of a Zarzuela Actress—Bed and Board of Travellers in Portugal—Tuy its Gothic Cathedral.

LANDING at Vigo, in the ancient kingdom of Galicia, the traveller is only nine leagues from the northern frontier of Portugal; and he may make his preparations for a journey into that country with as great advantage in Vigo as in any of the larger towns of Portugal itself. If he is in haste, and wants rather to have seen the country and the people than to see them, let him take the diligence, which will hurry and jolt him along a road leading due south, over the Spanish frontier, through the town of Vianna, and the city of Braga, to Oporto. At this latter city he may take the train, and, still going due south, will make for Lisbon; stopping for a day, perhaps, to look at the architectural splendours of Batalha and Alcobaça. From Lisbon he will visit the cool retreats of Cintra. He will take a hasty railway trip south of Lisbon, through a hideously barren country, to Setubal; another to the west, through an uninteresting country, to Evora; and he will, on finding himself at Lisbon again (and, if I am not mistaken, with no small satisfaction), take his passage in the first steamer for London or Southampton, and his report upon the country he thinks he has seen will be—"Portugal is thoroughly uninteresting; the country in parts is pretty but not remarkable, in parts it is a barren wilderness. The people are inaccessible from the difficulties of a language which does not appear worth learning, and therefore of their manners, habits, or customs, it is difficult to say anything."

Now, a man needs not to be of that order of traveller who will journey from Dan to Beersheba, and say, "all is barren," to arrive very honestly at this conclusion; and yet the country is not in fault, only his mode of trying to see it wrong; and I hope to show, in the following pages, that the verdict of my supposititious traveller is unjust in every particular.

Portugal is as yet virgin soil, so far as the British tourist is concerned. No preparations have as yet been made for him, hardly any one speaks his language, no inn-keeper expects to see him, no guide is ready to show him the lions.

There is a large class of travellers who should avoid Portuguese travel—those who are impelled to foreign journeying less because they care for it than because all their friends travel, and who, driven from England by that "*œstrum*" which flies abroad in the autumn months, not unreasonably like to find all the comforts of home during their holiday in foreign lands. Let not any of the migrant tribe who propose to travel in established tourist fashion, visit Portugal. Even Spain has greater, nay, along beaten tracks, great facilities for the luxurious tourist. Yet the obstacles to profitable travelling in Portugal—profitable in the sense of learning something of the people and of their ways—are, after all, but few. Unfortunately, first among them stands the language, and, without a fair command of it, let no traveller venture. It is a language which few people think it worth while to acquire; moreover, it is a difficult language, easy enough to learn to read, but far harder to speak than either Spanish or Italian. This is the chief obstacle; another is the extraordinary badness of food and lodging along the road. Sour wine, stale oil, black bread, and dried fish are the staples in the less frequented districts. Another is the absolute necessity, if it is desired to see the real beauty of Portuguese scenery and to study the lives and manners of the people, that the traveller should journey chiefly on horseback; for the few carriage roads, as a rule, pass through the least picturesque and interesting parts of the country. I know of no other difficulties, and, on the other hand, Portuguese travel has its good side; there are no brigands, and the people are well-tempered and well-mannered, very obliging and very hospitable.*

The present writer does not propose to write a regular itinerary of his travels in Portugal; for, in truth, he has journeyed over many dreary leagues of road on which he would be sorry to ask for the reader's company. His object will be to carry him rapidly from one point of interest to another, and tell him what he has learned in his travels of the ways of life of a very singular and interesting people. Nevertheless, the reader who shall follow him will have quite enough of the usual incidents of horseback travel, of roadside inns, of good landlords and bad ones, of kind welcomes and of cold ones.

There is now, I am told, an excellent hotel at Vigo, kept by a German with a French wife. There is, therefore, the less occasion for me to dwell on

* This warning, be it observed, applies only to tourists: not, as shall hereafter be set forth, to persons intending to reside—permanently or temporarily—in the country.

the fact that no excellence of the kind existed at the time of my visit, which was made several years ago.

Since that time a French scientific expedition has taken up its quarters at Vigo. The work they have before them is the recovery of the treasure believed to have sunk with the Spanish galleons which had taken shelter in Vigo, in the year 1702, during the War of the Succession, when the combined French and Spanish fleets were attacked by Sir George Rooke, in command of a Dutch and English squadron, and the town was stormed by three thousand men, under the command of the Duke of Ormond.

My first and, in fact, my only object in remaining even a single hour in Vigo was to buy a horse for my journey. With this view, and without mentioning my purpose at the inn, for landlords are only too apt to be in league with roguish horse-dealers, I sallied forth to discover for myself the equine capabilities of the place. I had made the tour of the town and was coming back, without seeing anything desirable, when I perceived a gentleman in high boots with immense silver spurs, a well-used velveteen jacket, and a dirty red sash wound several times round his waist. This person was leaning against the wall of a dark entry leading from the street, and had so evident an expression in his face, attitude and bearing, of some sort of proprietorship in horseflesh, that I instantly accosted him.

I was correct in my surmise. He told me that he was the possessor of about twenty of the very finest mares in Spain; "every one of which," said the horse-dealer, taking off his hat and making me a bow, "is at your Excellency's service."

I followed the man along the vaulted passage into a large stable. My eyes getting in time used to the gloom of the place, I could perceive the indistinct forms of some twenty or thirty under-sized ponies; some tied up to mangers running round the walls, and some fastened to the numerous stone pillars which supported the roof. I looked with some dismay at their diminutive bodies and generally "weedy" appearance.

Horse-dealing is a serious matter in all countries, but in none more so than in Spain, where a bargain, even for the hire of a pack mule or a guide's pony, is approached with the utmost circumspection and gravity.

"Sir," I said, addressing the horse-dealer, with a suitable solemnity; "pray look well at me, and having done so, inform me to which of these animals you recommend me to confide my person for a journey of some three or four hundred miles."

My companion gravely and politely removed his hat for the purpose of the desired inspection, and having concluded it, he replied—

"Caballero, I perceive that you are a person

not to be imposed upon. These animals you have seen are certainly not worthy nor indeed capable of carrying your distinguished person." And thus he went on with a blarneying speech of great length and volubility, ending by telling me that he possessed one horse of quite superlative excellence. Descanting on the way upon the merits of this particular animal, he led me to its stable.

Knowing the ways of horse-jockeys—knowing that a horse is praised by them generally in inverse ratio to his merits—I was not a little surprised to find, in a small separate stable to which the dealer conducted me, a strong, good-looking horse of the Andalusian breed, apparently sound in wind and limb.

The dealer led him out into the street, saddled him with the cumbrous saddle of the country, and put a bridle in his mouth. He mounted him. The horse's action was as good as his looks. I asked the price with some anxiety, for I saw that the performance of my journey on horseback was dependent upon getting this horse. After a great deal of tedious bargaining, I obtained him for twenty-five pounds; no doubt much more than the horse's market value, but he was a fairly good one, and did me very good service.

My plans were to make at once for Tuy, on the River Minho, which is the northern boundary of Portugal, and there or at Valença, the Portuguese town which is on the opposite side of the river, to procure an active servant to accompany me upon the Portuguese portion of my journey. My preparations were soon made. A good English saddle I had brought with me; also a pair of regulation cavalry pistols, and holsters for them. At Vigo I bought a true Spanish cloak of stout broadcloth, a saddle-cloth, a pair of capacious saddle-bags, and I was ready. I might have carried all my baggage on the stout Andalusian, and ridden to Tuy in a day by the high road; but I had a reason for wishing to keep along the sea-shore. Asking the horse-dealer for a guide over the mountains by the sea, he proposed to accompany me himself, remarking, however, that the road was bad, and the people along it no better than the road.

At daybreak the following morning we made our start. Skirting the magnificent Bay of Vigo for a mile, we soon began the ascent of a steep mountain, and continued, till the sun was pretty high, ascending a good deal, and now and then descending a little. Presently the whole bay was spread out like a map beneath our feet. The day was calm, and the steep hills and white houses, with their verandahs and projecting eaves, were reflected as in a looking-glass.

Fine as the scene before me was, there was a certain human interest about this bay which far outweighs any admiration for it as scenery. Some very momentous episodes of our own history have been transacted within sight of these hills, and evidences thereof cannot but be lying at this moment beneath the quiet waters of the bay. If, by a miracle, they could be lifted for an instant, we should see such a sight as would realize Clarence's dream. We should look upon

> " Wedges of gold, great anchors, heaps of pearls,
> Inestimable stones, unvalued gems,
> All scattered in the bottom of the sea."

Looking from the hill-side on the bay, I forgot all about its beauties in the fancy of how many brave deeds might have been witnessed from the hill-side on which I was standing. From this spot a spectator might have seen the entry of Drake's squadron in Elizabeth's reign, and have counted the men on the decks—seen them work their guns upon the town, and felt the earth shake to the booming of the heavy artillery from the castles overhead. I suspect that our tiny English ships, moving quickly about, ran no great risk from the plunging fire of the Spanish gunners, and that the affair was rather a one-sided one. A far better show must have been the capture of the galleons by Rooke and the Dutch, when five of the huge treasure vessels of Spain were set on fire, and eleven borne away by their captors. It must have been a very gallant sight, and be sure that the traces of that fight still lie under the waves of Vigo Bay, and that there is a rich prize there well worth the seeking for.

The rocky island which is seen from where I stand, and which, with its sister island, not now visible, commands the entrance to the bay, is Bayona; and, high up on its southern face, I make out what my guide assured me are the remains of ancient fortifications. There is an infinitesimally small literary difficulty connected with Bayona which caused me to choose to ride along the sea-shore to Tuy, rather than along the high-road.

The question is whether it is this Bayona to which Milton refers in the lines—

"Where the great vision of the guarded mount
Looks towards Namancos and Bayona's hold;"

or whether it is the little seaport of Bayona, lying a few miles farther south. My own strong impression, after seeing both places, is that Milton meant the islands, "Bayona's hold" being equivalent to "Bayona's fortress," and being taken to signify Vigo Bay, its castle and its fortified islands. I do not see how such a place as Bayona, the town, could even have been heard of by Milton; while, when he wrote "Lycidas," events had taken place near "Bayona's hold" which, though they occurred some fifty years before, would have made its geography familiar enough to British ears.

I now turned my face southwards, and in a few hours we saw the white houses of Bayona on one side of a little bay. It is a place, as I had been led to believe, of little importance, and my bird's-eye view of it quite satisfying me, I left it to the right, and, against the advice of my guide, made across the mountains south-eastward, in order to strike the high-road which I knew ran due north and south from Vigo to Tuy. I trusted to a pocket compass when I should have listened to the guide; nevertheless, after a weary ride, and after entangling ourselves more than once in a labyrinth of steep hills, we did, at last, suddenly come upon the high-road.

Shortly afterwards the diligence from Vigo overtook us, and I recognized two French gentlemen inside whose acquaintance I had made at the hotel at Vigo, and whom I had earnestly besought not to entrust themselves to the abominable conveyance in which they were imprisoned. They looked supremely miserable as they passed by in a stifling cloud of dust, jolted, jammed, and deafened by the rattle of the ill-fitting box on wheels.

"That is not the fitting way for gentlemen to go through the country," said the horse-dealer, ranging his little mare up to my side.

"You are right," I said, for the proverb says, "'A good man on a good horse is a servant to no man.'"

"It is a good proverb," said the horse-dealer, "though I never heard it before, for these gentlemen who saluted your worship will soon find that they are no longer their own masters; they must eat, sleep, get down and up, not when they please, but when they are told by the coachman; whereas the Caballero here does what he likes, stops where he pleases, and eats and lodges when, where, and how he chooses."

The horse-dealer could not better have summed up the advantages of travelling on horseback in Portugal.

We had rested once in the hills at a farmhouse, and begged a little straw and water for our horses, and now again we looked about for the bush hung over the house door, the old conventional sign of an inn. Houses of any kind were scarce, however, and night was coming on, and we were within a few miles of Tuy before we found what we wanted, a little one-storied inn where we could bait the horses.

"The people in these parts," said my companion, sententiously, "are a bad lot."

Certainly those we had had to do with to-day were as surly and sullen a set of peasants as I ever encountered; but, as virtue is commonly reported to reside in a rough exterior, I will not undertake to endorse the opinion of the horse-dealer.

Asking for horse provender at the inn, we got

monosyllabic answers and black looks; not a finger was stirred to help us. Finally, we tied up our own horses, and, discovering a secret store of corn, helped them liberally thereto. The inn-keeper found his tongue, as we were leaving, to ask an exorbitant payment; but, having given what we knew was just, we would not yield an inch, whereupon the whole family set up a chorus of execration. The man, his wife, and apparently countless brothers, sisters, and children, flocked into the stable to bellow, and yell, and scream in all keys at us. Amid this fearful outcry we composedly mounted our horses, and charged through the family at a fair cavalry trot. The enemy was routed, but re-formed outside the gate, and fired a parting volley of abuse as we rode off; whereupon the horse-dealer, losing the temper and equanimity which he had hitherto preserved, turned short round, and, standing up in his stirrups, raised his right hand threateningly, and, spurring his mare hither and thither in his wrath in front of the hostile lines, execrated and defied them.

So, it is related, did that redoubtable Moorish champion, Ibn-l-Walid, in like hostile and defiant manner, prick forth upon his charger before the long-drawn lines of Christian warriors, and, by the mere vigour of his speech and fierceness of his gesture, carry consternation into the ranks of the Christian host.

The Moorish champion, however, had the advantage over the horse-dealer in this respect, for the latter seemed to carry no consternation whatever into the ranks of the inn-keeper's family; and the encounter might have lasted far into the night, if I had not gently led away my champion by the arm. We rode off, but it was some time ere he recovered his serenity. He had, however, given me an opportunity of learning that a horse-dealer in Galicia, like persons of the same profession in England, excels all his countrymen in his command of strong language.

The Galician peasant is, in truth, an uncouth being; but he can take a certain amount of polish. It is a good material. The Galician is the Auvergnat of the Peninsula, and especially of Portugal. Of a hundred men-servants, coachmen, grooms, porters, and water-carriers, in the larger towns of Portugal, ninety-nine are Galicians. The rusticity, awkwardness, and slowness of the Galician have become proverbial. Of an ill-bred man the Portuguese say all when they say, "What a Galician!" A coarse expression is a "*Gallegada*"—a Galicianism. The epithet "Galician" is even used as an equivalent of wild, common, or uncultivated: the crab-apple is, with the Portuguese, the Galician apple; the common cabbage of Portugal, which grows a yard or more in height, is the "*Couve Gallega*"—the Galician cabbage; and so forth.

I remember once, in Lisbon, seeing an exceedingly pretty young Spanish lady, the prima donna of a Zarzuela troupe, assume the character of a Galician servant with great success. The Zarzuela actors are chartered buffoons, by no means tied down by any of the traditions or prescriptions of the legitimate drama. Their only object is to entertain; and they sing, dance, and declaim their burlesque operettas with the greatest spirit. On this particular occasion, however, the piece dragged; the audience would not be amused; the songs were stale, the dances old, the dialogue known by heart—when suddenly, with true histrionic inspiration, the pretty prima donna advanced to the foot-lights, and began a serio-comic remonstrance with the audience in the character of a Galician servant who has been found fault with.

It was really an admirable improvisation. As she came forward, her step lost the graceful firmness of the true Zarzuela dancer; her movements became stiff, angular, and slouching; her voice changed the quick ring of the Andalusian tongue for the drawl of the Galician brogue; her face assumed the semi-idiotic stare of a stupid servant. The effect was magical. We all had our Galician servant; we all recognized that drawl, that slouch, and that expression. In theatrical phrase, *it brought the house down.* After this, the piece went on swimmingly; and if, for a moment, the audience seemed not sufficiently responsive to the efforts of the actors, one look of remonstrance, in character, from the fair actress, or one of those familiar gestures, was enough to bring back its gaiety and its attention in an instant.

Now, all this is one side of the picture. If the Galician is rough, he is honest; if he is a boor, he is a faithful one. Better men-servants can hardly be found; clean, sober, attentive, good-tempered, and hard-working, they very soon learn to accommodate themselves to the ways and habits of the family. A very little intercourse with better-mannered people than themselves serves to rub off their native asperities. They grow attached to masters who treat them well, and it is common enough for a Galician servant to grow white-headed in faithful service with the master who engaged him as a boy.

It was quite dark before we reached Tuy, and therefore we had to put up at the inn there for the night; having travelled no more than nine or ten leagues, in a straight line, since daybreak.

At Tuy I had not, at any rate, to begin any sort of commissariat troubles. Almost everywhere in Spain there is good bread, and Tuy is celebrated for its hams and for its wine.

When the tired and hungry traveller in Portugal is nearing his resting-place for the night, two thoughts sufficiently prosaic are apt to engross his attention—his board and his bed. As to the former, there is room for speculation. There is immense variety; he may arrive late at night, and find black bread, sour wine, and sourer looks. On the other hand, his senses may be pleasantly assailed, as he crosses the threshold of his inn, by the steam of the simmering stew; and he may be gladdened by friendly looks, and a kind invitation to partake of the family supper.

As to the other point—his bed—let the traveller not speculate. Here there is no variety. A Peninsular bedroom is a fearful thing. A door that will not fasten, windows that were never intended to open, a floor, through the chinks of which the mules and horses, which invariably have their lodging beneath, can be seen and heard, and an atmosphere composed of the emanations of their stables. A bed, of which it is enough to say that the experienced traveller will instantly throw all its coverings to the further end of the room, and recline upon it involved in his own cloak, plaids, or rugs.

Tuy possesses a small Gothic cathedral, which, so far as I could judge from the outside, is of very early date. The building is remarkable for its enormous solidity, and the small size of the windows and their height from the ground. The original work is pure Romanesque, pointing to a date early in the twelfth century; a period when some fears might be entertained of an irruption of the Saracens, and Christians might look to having to defend themselves on a sudden. I was disappointed at not being able to get inside the cathedral, which promised from its exterior to be interesting. Gothic buildings are so scarce in Portugal that one hardly likes to leave one behind unvisited on the confines of that kingdom.

CATALOGUE OF

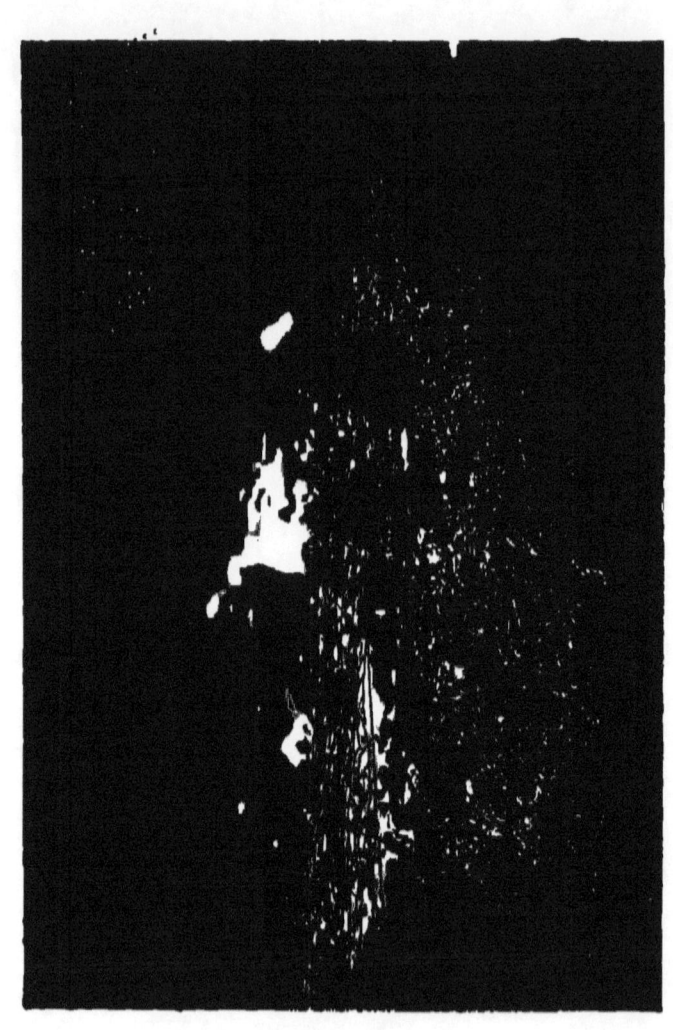

CHAPTER II.

Spanish and Portuguese on the Frontier Line—Travel Southward—Banks of Minho—Caminhá—Sea Coast—Hospitable Farmer—Ghost Stories—The Lobis-homem; *a Grisly Tale—Farm Work in Northern Portugal—Land Tenure and Peasant Farms—Undescribed Druidical Remains—A District Peopled by Women—Anecdote in Testimony of their Good Conduct—Timoléon of Cossé.*

THERE are few things which seem so strange to a British traveller, the boundary of whose country is the sea, and who has, fortunately, no experience of arbitrary frontier lines, as to see how an invisible line of demarcation can as completely separate one nation from another, so far as any identity of manners and customs is concerned, as long miles of ocean or impassable mountain ranges.

The Spanish town of Tuy is divided only by the river Minho from the Portuguese town of Valença. Looked at by the traveller going southwards, the houses of the two towns seem to form but one. A good swimmer would cross from the Spanish to the Portuguese bank in a few minutes; a stone thrown from the streets of Tuy might fall among the houses of Valença. And yet, though they are such near neighbours, the inhabitants of either town are, in customs, habits, manners, and dress, almost as distinct as the people of Dover and those of Calais. What makes the present distinction the more remarkable is, that it is almost certain that the races are identical. Perhaps it would be safer to say that they contain the same constituents, though probably in different proportions. So nearly identical, indeed, are they, that the frontier line of Portugal and Galicia shifted continually during the Middle Ages.

The reason why Portuguese life flows up to Valença, and no further, and why Spanish life is suddenly arrested at Tuy, is of course easy enough to find. If the people of the one town had had free access to those of the other, and had bought and sold with them; if the old men and women had had full liberty of gossiping with each other; if the youths of one town could have wooed the maidens of the other;—then it would have been different. But to all this there have always been two barriers—the conscription and the customs duties. To cross the frontier, it is necessary to be provided with a pass, and all who do so cross are, of course, subjected to examination for contraband goods. It is these restrictions, acting through many hundred years, which have worked the results we see, in spite of race and in spite of propinquity.

At those points where the Portuguese and Spanish

races are conterminous, the Portuguese is, at least as far as my observation goes, the better looking, better dressed, and better mannered of the two. Nowhere is this so conspicuous as on the Minho. The contrast here, however, is heightened by the fact, that the Portuguese of *Entre Douro e Minho*—the province, that is, lying between the Douro and the Minho—are as far superior in the above respects to other Portuguese as the Galicians fall short—in the same matters—of men of the other provinces of Spain.

Leaving Valença early in the morning, we followed the course of the Minho to the sea, passing on the way the fortified town of Villa Nova da Cerveira, and the little harbour and town of Caminha, surrounded by flats and marshes, with its outlying island fortress; then, again striking southward by the sea-shore, through a half-cultivated region which in former times was a Royal forest, we reached a gloomy-looking fortress, close to the sea; the first of a series which continues along the whole coast-line of the province of the Minho.

Towards nightfall we overtook a farmer on horseback, and when, after riding on in friendly conversation with him for a mile or so, I asked him how far off I might be from an inn and shelter for the night, he good-humouredly laughed at the idea of my condescending to put up at any place nearer than Vianna.

On my telling him that I was by no means particular, and that my guide's horse was too tired for further travelling, he drew up his horse to a stand-still, and looked hard at me.

"There is a house about one mile from here," said the farmer; "you will get poor fare and poor shelter, but none better, I think, on this side of Vianna. I will show you the way," he added.

So saying, he trotted on, and soon turning aside from the main road, guided us along a vile ox-cart road, the worst of all roads to ride over in a bad light. For about a mile we travelled up a narrow valley. On each side of the road grew pollarded oaks and chestnuts, whose branches were twisted so as to join overhead; and on these trees were trained vines, whose foliage, though it was only May, already gave a dense shade.

Presently this narrow road opened out into a square walled enclosure, which was also perfectly embowered and shaded by vines, carried on stout rafters of wood, the whole supported by the side walls, and by five or six stone pillars in the centre; so that the place was like a huge room, the ceiling of which was of vine leaves. It was, in fact, the court-yard of a good-sized farm-house.

The farmer stopped at the door of the house which opened on to this yard.

"Why," I said to him, "this is a private house."

"It is the house of your Excellency," said the farmer, as he stood uncovered, with the true courteous hospitality of an old-fashioned Portuguese.

It was, in truth, his own house; and presently a man appeared, to take our horses, a dog came and licked the master's hand, children issued from the house and greeted their father, and the wife stood in the doorway and welcomed us.

"Cea! cea!" the farmer called out cheerfully, which, interpreted, is supper, a pleasant sound to a belated traveller. "Here is a gentleman who has eaten nothing since he was in Spain."

Looking round the room we entered, I saw much that I should have seen in a farmer's kitchen at home: the old single-barrelled gun slung on the wall, the English willow-pattern plates ranged on the shelves, the well-polished high-backed chairs, the sides of bacon hanging from the rafters. What was not like England was the quaint collection of coloured prints of sacred subjects—pious daubs, fearful to the artistic eye—which hung about the walls.

Presently our supper was on the table, and let the reader take note that the table was not decked with a cloth " coarse, but of snowy whiteness." Indeed, for the matter of that, we did not even indulge in plates, but before each of us was placed a good-sized earthenware bowl and a wooden spoon. And if the reader should ask of what the meal consisted, let him know that there was one dish and a *remove*. The dish, *Sopa secca*, literally "dry soup," made of wheaten bread, beef, cabbage, and mint, almost a national dish in Portugal; and the remove, *Bacalhau*, dried codfish, boiled—which is quite a national dish—and the man who objects to such a bill of fare, must, indeed, be an epicure.

I praised the fish for its tenderness, and my hostess explained to me that to make it so it was essential that the dried fish—which, indeed, is often, when cooked, as hard as a board—should be previously soaked for exactly eighteen hours in running water.

Then the host filled me a large tumbler of country wine, his own vintage, assuring me that wine never tastes so well as after *Bacalhau*. It is a very remarkable drink, this "green wine," as it is called. I have tasted the country wines of many lands, but never yet such a one as this. Perfectly sound, but possessing a fruitiness, astringency, and sharpness enough to take one's breath away, it has yet little more alcoholic strength than claret. So full is it of what may be called vinous matter, that it is hardly ever clear; it is apparently, however, not liked the less for being quite thick and muddy. To an exhausted man, on a summer's day, I know no greater restorative than a full draught of this Minho wine.

When we had eaten and drunk, the dishes were pushed "below the salt," and one or two of the farm servants fell to on the plentiful remainder; whilst we, wrapping ourselves in our cloaks, and leaning our elbows on the table, lighted our cigarettes, and proceeded to hold grave discourse.

Knowing that my host must be curious to be told where I came from, and the purpose of my travelling, I thought it due to his hospitality to offer him a sketch of my proceedings, in which I was assisted by the horse-dealer, who, after the manner of such squires, added fancy details illustrative of the magnificence, wisdom, and so forth, of his master. I ended by saying that I was going to travel through Portugal at my pleasure, and to see whatever was curious, or worthy to be seen by a foreigner.

The farmer nodded his head slowly once or twice, as I finished. The idea was too strange to him to be taken in at once; at last he got firm hold of it.

"Your country, I dare say, is very different from Portugal," he said.

"Very different," I answered. "You may understand how much so when I tell you that our farmers neither grow maize nor make wine?"

"Coitadinhos!" (poor devils!) said the man; "then what do they eat and drink?"

"Well," I said, "it is not so difficult as you may think. We can make all sorts of things in England, and sell them to all countries, and then buy what we want from them. For instance—there is the shirt you wear—it was made in England, and that gun, it was made there, too; so, you see, if we wanted to eat maize, or drink wine, we should have something to offer in exchange."

"Wonderful!" cried the farmer, quite delighted. It was clear that he had never been lectured before on political economy.

We talked on many matters. At last I thought of questioning the farmer on a subject which has always had a great interest for me—the superstitious beliefs and tales of the peasantry.

I have long held a theory, that wherever the Romans have left permanent marks of their stay, there the superstitions have the peculiar gloomy stamp of the legendary mysteries of ancient Italy. If this is true anywhere, it must be true in Portugal, where these people have left their vestiges not only in the language, which is nearer to Latin than any other known tongue, but even in the manner of cultivating the soil, which, to this day, is done in accordance with the precepts of Cato and Columella.

The type of Latin legend to which I refer, is that well-known and most grisly and hideous of all ghost stories, the tale of the soldier in Petronius

Arbiter. Now the belief in the "*Lobis-homem*" is very prevalent in parts of Northern Portugal. It is the legend of the Loup-garou—the Wehrwolf—the periodical transformation of human beings into wolves, with all the savage instincts of that animal. It is a superstition whose existence in many countries has been too well investigated to need further description from me; suffice it to say, that nowhere is this belief invested with so many peculiar and gloomy circumstances as in Portugal.

I began to sound the farmer on the subject of folk-lore and popular superstitions rather cautiously, for people are apt to be reticent in talking of these matters to strangers, but the farmer was not shy at all.

"Yes," he said; "he had known some strange things to happen, and in that very neighbourhood, too."

"Would he tell me what?"

"Well, he would," he said, "and with great pleasure; he would tell me one of the most singular things he ever heard of; but," looking at me doubtfully, "you will hardly bring yourself to believe it; and, to tell the truth, no more should I, if it had not been related to me by one who saw it—no other than my own brother's son.

"You must know," said the farmer, with a grave air, "that not many miles from this is a river, in which are vast quantities of fish. Now, every year there comes a stranger to this river; he stands upon the bank, and holding in his hand a magical fly—*uma mosca encantada*—tied to the end of a very long thread, he blows the fly away from him as far as a man can throw a stone; it falls upon the water, and no sooner does it touch the surface than a fish seizes it, and the stranger draws both fly and fish ashore by the thread which he holds in his hand. Now, what do you think of that?"

My host had given me this fancy description of fly-fishing with so very serious a face, that I was almost afraid to laugh, till I observed a sympathetic twinkle in his own eyes; but he nodded towards his servants as if to hint that I was not to betray the secret of the mysterious fisherman to them.

Then the farmer, perceiving that I was an attentive and by no means a captious listener, began another story.

"We are all good Christians here, and ought not to fear the malice of the evil spirit; nevertheless, we know that power is given him sometimes to work mischief in some mysterious manner, which all the priests put together do not understand. In proof of this, I will tell you of an event that happened not twenty years ago; and, moreover, I was myself a witness of what I am going to relate, for I was then a young man, living at a farm near Cabrasam, among the mountains of the Estrica, which is, as you know, as wild a country as any in Portugal."

The farmer filled up his own and my glass, and his wife and children and the servants gathered round us and stood, with solemn faces, to listen to a tale which they had probably already heard more than once.

"The farmer with whom I served was a young man, and his wife a young woman. He had just come on to the farm. Two or three other men besides myself worked with him, but there was no other woman in the place than his wife. Now, she being about to give birth to a child, desired to get another woman into the house, to do such work as she would shortly not be able to perform herself. So the master went about the country to engage a woman, but, for some reason or other, he could not succeed. As time pressed, he sent me to the nearest town, Ponte de Lima, with directions to inquire along the way, and engage the very first likely looking young woman I should meet with.

"I started next morning before daylight, and I had not gone more than a mile on the road before I saw, sitting by the wayside, one of the queerest looking girls my eyes ever fell on. She was wrapped up, head and all, in a brown cloak, such as we never see in this part of the country. The sun had just risen, and she was stretching out her hands as if to warm them in its rays. The oddest thing about her was that her hair was cut close to her head, like a man's. Now, this is common enough with our women when they get old and do not care to be troubled with long hair; but for a young and handsome girl like her to be '*chamorra*' (crop-haired), was a thing I have never seen before or since. So I stood still and stared at her, like a fool as I was.

"'Well, Santinho,'* said the girl, 'you are wondering to see me warm my hands in the sunbeams?'

"'I think you would get warm quicker,' I answered, 'if you went on your way, instead of sitting still in this cold wind.'

"'And what if I am tired, as well as cold?' she said, sharply.

"'Have you been travelling all the night?'

"'Indeed, I have,' said the girl, 'and many a one before that.'

"'Then you come from a long way off?'

"'I come from Tarouca, in the mountains of Beira, and that is a long journey from here.'

"'And if it is not a secret, what have you come so far from home for?'

---

* Literally, "Little Saint"—a common form of address, among the peasantry, from one stranger to another.

"'No secret at all,' she replied. 'My name is Joana, and I am looking for a place as servant at a farm. Do you know any one who requires one?'

"Now, it struck me here was the very thing I was looking for—a strong, hearty-looking girl, who wished to be a servant; so I told her I was out with the object of engaging such a person as herself, and if she would come with me to my master's, she might find the place she wanted. The girl expressed her readiness, and we started homewards.

"I left her outside the house while I went in. The farmer did not much like the idea of having so strange a being for a servant; but his wife, hearing that she was a 'chamorra,' insisted upon engaging her—for we have a saying that 'chamorras' make the best of workers.

"Very soon after this the child was born, and the new girl took the mistress's place—cooked for us and so forth.

"Now, the newly-born infant was a remarkably fine and healthy one. Everybody said so, except one old woman—a neighbour—who was thought to be a 'wise woman.' This person looked rather put out the moment she saw the child, and said it was bewitched. The father and mother laughed heartily at this, seeing how well the child looked. Then the woman said she was mistaken if the child had not the devil's mark somewhere on its skin; and. sure enough, so it had—a mark on its shoulder, exactly as if the pattern of a small crescent or half-moon had been pricked upon the skin with a pin. Then we all began to get frightened, but the woman said there was no cause for alarm, except during the time of the new moon, and then the child must be watched all the night through.

"When the old woman passed out of the house, the new servant was sitting on the floor with her brown cloak pulled right over her face, and though the old woman spoke to her, she made her no answer, pretending to be asleep.

"Nothing particular occurred for some months. The servant, Joana, was very useful in the house, and both master and mistress congratulated themselves on having engaged a 'chamorra' to work. However, we, her fellow-servants, did not much like her. She was very sharp in her speech; and whenever she was angry, her eyes, which were long and narrow in shape, seemed almost to emit fire and gave her a terribly savage aspect. However, when not out of temper, she was a handsome girl. She seldom spoke much, but she very soon got into the confidence of her master and mistress, and one day, when the latter mentioned to her what had been told her by the old woman, she said—

"'Ah, yes! I have known it a long time, but I was afraid to tell you. Children with that mark grow into *lobis-homems* before they get to be sixteen, unless something is done to stop it.'

"'And what can be done?' said my mistress.

"'You must cover the evil mark with the blood of a white pigeon, strip the child naked, and lay it on a blanket on the mountain side the very first time the moon rises in the heavens after midnight. Then the moon will draw the mark up through the blood, just as she draws the waters of the sea up at full tide, and the child will be saved.'

"The farmer and his wife agreed to do this, to save their child from becoming a *lobis-homem*, and it happening to be a new moon late in the night, a day or two afterwards, the needful preparations were made, and when the night came the child was laid out on the mountain side near the house, while the moon was still below the horizon. This done, we all returned to the house, for it was essential that no eye should be upon the child until the moon had risen. The farmer began to be uneasy, thinking that there might be wolves near, but the men reassured him, saying that a wolf had not been seen in the neighbourhood for many years. Nevertheless, he loaded his gun, putting into it, for want of other ammunition, five or six rusty nails.

"He had hardly done so when, to our horror, we heard the most piercing screams from where the child was lying. In an instant we had all rushed out—the screams increasing as we neared the spot. At this very instant the moon rose, and we saw a huge brown wolf standing over the body of the child, his fangs bloody and his eyes looking like fire. Seeing us come up he slunk off, but the farmer fired at him before he could reach the wood close by, and he fell and rolled over. I ran up to finish him with the heavy stick which I had in my hand, but I could only give him one stroke before he rose to his feet and made off. The blow was a heavy one, and struck him on the foreleg, and he went off into the wood, howling and limping.

"We found the poor child quite dead; its throat was frightfully torn by the wolf's teeth, and the blanket was soaked with blood.

"Now, it was noticed almost immediately that the girl, Joana, had not been seen since the child had been put out, nor was she in the house when we got back. Then for the first time did the truth flash upon us—the woman had been an accursed *lobishomem*, and had murdered the child, and in wounding the wolf we had in truth wounded the girl who had assumed his form. The next morning we followed the traces of the wounded wolf, and, inside the wood, not ten paces from where he had been seen to enter it, we found Joana lying on the ground covered with blood. She immediately began to explain to us that she had crept into the wood when we had left the child, fearing that some mischief might happen to him; that she had heard screams and had run towards the child in the darkness; that just as she was getting to the outside of the wood the moon rose, she saw us coming, saw the wolf run towards her, heard the gun fired, immediately felt herself to be wounded in the side, and fell to the ground, where she had lain ever since.

"Of course we knew that these were lies suggested by the devil, so we sent for the priest, but before he came she had died. They buried her where she lay, and the 'wise woman,' who came to look at her, said she had the mark of the *lobis-homem* on her breast quite plain, and was evidently a servant of the Evil one. The woman said that if she had seen the girl's eyes she could have told at once what she was, for the *lobis-homems* all get to have the long, narrow eyes and savage look of the wolf. She also explained to us that if a *lobis-homem* can murder and drink the blood of a newly-born child, the enchantment ceases, and they are *lobis-homems* no longer."

"And what did the priest say?" I asked.

"He said," replied the farmer, "that we were fools to have had anything to do with a woman from Tarouca, for it was a nest of witches and warlocks."

"And you are quite sure this girl was a real '*lobis-homem*'?"

"I never doubted it for a moment. Did I not see Joana's own eyes in the wolf, as he turned round when I struck him? How can I doubt? Besides," said the farmer, after a pause, "there was the mark of a heavy blow on her right arm—exactly where I struck the wolf. She never accounted for that."

The next morning at daybreak we were all afoot, late hours being by no means compatible with the economy of a Portuguese farm. A piece of "broa" (black bread) and a drink of fresh milk was breakfast enough. I asked the farmer to let me accompany him afield. The farm consisted, as I should judge, of not more than twenty-five acres, all in arable land, and every inch of it cultivated and cared for like a garden. He had five men and three women labourers, and he kept five yoke of oxen. The farm was divided into many little fields, each of them formed terrace-wise on the hill sides, and bounded either by a streamlet or by a row of vine plants, borne aloft on stout trellis-work, or trailing up the limbs of low-growing oak or chestnut trees. Here and there a dozen olive trees formed a little grove, or a spreading, oak-like cork tree stood at the corner of a field.

There was plenty for the farmer to see to. Some of the men were set to turn the water on to the fields, and guide it with their hoes over the roots of the growing maize-crop; others to hoe up the earth between the young plants. The women cut grass for the cattle with quaint little reaping-hooks; a pair of oxen was yoked to the cart, and went to the hill side to cut gorse for the stabling of the cattle. A prettier rustic scene never was—with the rich green of the crops, the abundant shade of the trailing vines, and the drip and murmur of the trickling waters, joined to the chorus of singing birds. A man might have fancied himself carried back eighteen hundred years, and transported to that famous farm among the Sabine hills. Barring the maize, I fancy Horace would have seen nothing outlandish on this Portuguese farm. The ploughs, the ox-carts, the sickles, the pruning-hooks, are of the ancient Latin patterns; and all the operations of farming absolutely the same.

The farmer told me that the land was his own, and had been his father's and grandfather's; being *afforado*, or held as a copyhold estate, on payment of a trifling rent of one or two shillings to a nominal landlord. But so absolutely was the land his own, he told me, that even if he were to fail to pay the rent for several years, the landlord would not be entitled to re-enter, but only to sue him for debt; so that, as tenant or holder, he is, to all intents and purposes, the actual proprietor of the estate.

This is the tenure by which a great deal of the

land of North Portugal is held. It is, of course, not conducive to high farming; but it results in this, that the length and breadth of the land is cultivated like a market-garden. The extreme sub-division of land which takes place in France, where there is also peasant proprietorship, and which is so incompatible with good farming, is obviated here by the fact that, on the death of the holder of the estate, it is not divided among the children, but devolves upon one of them only, at the father's option. The legatee has then to pay his brothers and sisters their portions of the estate, which are fixed by law.

This system has created, in the Northern Provinces of the kingdom, a population of hardy, independent, contented yeomen. There are no great territorial possessions, no accumulation of agricultural wealth in one man's hands; but then, again, there is no pauperism. If we cross into some of the Southern Provinces, we find, however, the reverse of this picture of prosperity and content—great estates ill-farmed, rich absentee landlords, and crowds of ill-looking, poverty-stricken, and woe-begone day-labourers.

It was in riding along with my host towards Vianna that he gave me the particulars of the tenure of his estate.

The day being hot, and our ride a long one, we

got down at a wine-house, and had a delicious drink of country wine.

If it had not been for an accident, I should have missed seeing a curious sight. I had been talking to the farmer of the number of castles along the sea-shore, and he maintained that they were built to protect the Portuguese littoral from the attacks of the Spaniards.

This, in point of fact, is not the case; but, of course, I did not dispute the assertion.

The landlord of the wine-shop confirmed the farmer's opinion, and added, in corroboration of it, that there was a building of stone, some little way inland, which was expressly made to light a beacon fire upon, whenever the Spaniards came in sight. As it was not half-an-hour's walk, I immediately got a boy to guide me, and started for the place, after having taken a thankful leave of the hospitable farmer.

To my great surprise I found a very perfect specimen of a Cromlech, or so-called Druidical altar; a number of flat stones, set in a semicircle open to the west, and covered at top by either one or two (I forget which) huge slabs of stone. It was large enough to hold twenty or thirty men, and high enough for a tall man to stand upright in.

It could clearly never have served for a beacon or a watch station, situated as it is on low-lying land with hills rising north and south of it, and commanding therefore only a glimpse of the sea, and it would itself be visible from only a small extent of country.

The Cromlech stands in the centre of a wood, and I was therefore unable to see whether there were any tumuli near at hand. These remains, from their size and general appearance, are unquestionably such as we commonly call Druidical. Such remains have been found in Northern Spain, but I have never yet seen any record of their existence in Portugal; nor, in my travels in the country, have I ever come across another instance of such a stone monument.

For the benefit of any future traveller, I will add that the Cromlech lies about a quarter of a mile northeast of the bridge at Ancora, which again is about ten or twelve miles north of the town of Vianna; and, unless I have forgotten, the boy who showed me to it, said it was known in the neighbourhood as "A Casa do Diabo"—the Devil's house.

Travelling on southwards we soon came to a range of steep mountains, running parallel to the coast line, between which and the hills passes the high road. On either side of the road are fields of great fertility. The whole conformation of the land has a general resemblance to the Undercliff in the Isle of Wight; but what is most singular about the district is, that its population seems to be chiefly composed of women, and, let it be remarked, of remarkably handsome, smartly-dressed women. The explanation is that the male owners of nearly all the pretty little tree-shaded cottages on the hill side are artisans, who, enjoying the monopoly in Portugal of the trade in stucco-working, spread themselves over the whole kingdom and earn very high wages, but are only very seldom able to sit down by their own hearthstones.

Now the uncharitable reader may expect that the ladies of this community, in the continued absence of their natural guardians, would to some degree not resemble their neighbours across the Minho, whom Lord Carnarvon in somewhat pompous phrase styles "the virtuous but unbenevolent Galicians." This, I am glad to report, is not the case. Their good looks and smart appearance co-exist with the best of characters. Indeed, they have earned for themselves, in this respect, a somewhat formidable reputation. A long time ago, a lady of this district, feeling herself to be aggrieved by the addresses of a person, who presumably omitted some of the formulas proper to such advances, called a meeting of her female friends, who proceeded forthwith to execute so complete a vengeance upon this unfortunate person, that the deed has acquired for the ladies of this district a sobriquet which commemorates at once their virtue and the nature of their revenge.

My Galician guide, who had beguiled the way with this anecdote in illustration of the morality of the neighbourhood, now plainly gave it to be understood that, having eaten nothing since five o'clock in the morning, he was both hungry and thirsty. Agreeing with him on both points, I proposed that we should stop at the first inn. Presently we came to a hamlet a little off the road, but the only house not a private one was a barber's, a circumstance which roused a little indignation and some mirth on the part of the horse-dealer.

"What can they want with barbers here," he said, "where only every tenth face wears a beard?"

Perhaps business was slack on this account, for the barber did not hesitate to deal in a jug of wine and a loaf of bread. Then we went on, refreshed.

The trade of a barber is a thriving one all over the Peninsula. If a village has three houses, one, be sure, is a barber's. The sign is a basin; sometimes, as theatre people say, "practicable," and dangling from a chain over the door; sometimes, painted in vermilion on the whitewashed wall.

The Portuguese, like the Spaniard, is never full dressed unless he is well shaved, and, unlike the celebrated De Cossé, Duke of Brissac, he never shaves himself; and, in truth, I would not undertake to say, that the admirable motive which drove the aforesaid peer to this daily task would, under any circumstances of high rank or idleness, have similar sway with the lazy Peninsular. "Timoléon de Cossé," the French noble was often heard to soliloquize of a morning, with the open razor in his hand: "God has made thee a gentleman, and the King has made thee a duke. It is, nevertheless, right and fit that thou shouldst have something to do; therefore thou shalt shave thyself." A conclusion which, from similar premises, would never be arrived at in the Peninsula, where the ruling axiom is—Never to do for oneself what others can do for one.

CHAPTER III.

Vianna—Costume and Looks of the Women—Cheerfulness of the People—Their Dances; their Improvised Singing—River Lima—Unsupported Tradition—Funeral Customs—Surrounding Scenery Overpraised—Raptures over Scenery make Poor Reading—Home of Miranda, the Poet—Reflections on Ill-directed Travel, suggested by Misadventures of Two British Tourists—Abundant Traces of the Moors—Wrong Construction put upon the Author's Motives—Belief in Hidden Treasure—Stories in Proof—Precious Stones in Portugal—The Crown Jewels; the Braganza Diamond.

I LEFT Vianna, an uninteresting town, passing over the curious bridge, said to be a mile and a quarter in length, which crosses the broad estuary formed by the river Lima. It was my first intention to keep the high road to Oporto; but this road looked so uninviting that after travelling along it some ten miles, till I reached a range of bare hills whence I could still look back upon the town of Vianna, and seeing in front of me a country that did not promise to be more interesting, I turned north-eastwards, towards Ponte de Lima, which lies on the same river as Vianna, about ten or fifteen miles above it, and I was rewarded by coming upon a very rich and picturesque country.

CATHOLIC UNIVERSITY OF AMERICA

It was a " festa,"—a holiday—and the peasantry were all in their holiday dresses; the women very gaily attired, with embroidered muslin kerchiefs on their heads, over which is worn the heavy, black Spanish-looking hat, with ornaments of floss silk made to curl and to look like a black ostrich feather. The costume of the women varies slightly in almost every parish of the kingdom; but it generally consists of an ample serge petticoat, descending to the ankle, and gathered round the waist into innumerable pleats, a close-fitting bodice (either black or gaily-coloured) over a linen shirt showing white on the shoulders and the arms, with a bright-coloured kerchief, commonly red, or orange, or blue, crossed over the breast. All this makes a picturesque costume which well suits the comely, buxom, black-haired peasant women of the Minho Province, with their rich olive complexions and fine eyes. The women have retained their national dress, and in the remoter parts, the men also; but in many places the latter are less conservative, and wear *wide-awake* hats, trousers, and short jackets, in lieu of the old national costume.

The women use their peculiar peasant jewellery of ancient Moorish design, on feast days only. Heavy necklaces of complicated pattern suspend huge, heart-shaped lockets on their breasts; in their ears are heavy pendent earrings. One woman will often wear three or four such necklaces of gold, of a standard of not less than twenty carats; and I have been assured that many of the peasant women carry about them not less than twenty or thirty pounds worth of gold ornaments.

Coming from Galicia, where the natives are so exceedingly boorish, I was much struck by the kindly, cheerful manners of the people. In every little hamlet by the road side—and the frequency of such hamlets and the density of the population are marvellous—in every village I passed to-day, there was a gathering of the inhabitants: the men busy with a game of bowls, the youths and girls dancing, with a crowd of lookers-on; the twanging of guitars mingling pleasantly with the sound of laughter and cheerful voices.

Up among the mountains, some kind of "Bolero" is danced, that is, a "pas de deux" between a male and female dancer; but in this part of the country, I have seen only one kind of dance, certainly a very singular one. Each person dances by himself or herself, to a slow and monotonous jig tune, following the person in front in a circle. The music often accompanies—in the most literal sense—the dancers: it is generally a fiddle, and an amusing sight it is to see the man who plays it fiddling gravely away as he cuts the queer little steps of the dance. There are usually one or two guitar players among the spectators, who join the fiddle and make up an orchestra. These monotonous dances will last for hours, the tired dancers falling out and fresh ones taking their places.

Often on a holiday evening, the villagers assemble to listen to extemporary singing; one lad will challenge another lad or maiden to sing against him in alternate rhymed verse; or a champion will saunter up, with his guitar, from a neighbouring village, and throw down the gauntlet to a whole hamlet. This is called singing *ao desafio*, singing to a challenge. There is, of course, as in Italian extemporary recitation, some trust to the performer's memory, and when his invention is at fault, he may often interpolate some stock rhyme; but as the Portuguese improvisor has to find a rhyme to his opponent's verse, there must be far less dependence on memory, and more on quickness of fancy, than in Italy. The rule is, as far as I can understand, that the singer who begins, goes on plying the other with verses, to which the second has to find rhymed answers; when he hesitates or stops, the bout is concluded, the parts reversed, and the improvisation recommences.

It must not be supposed that this feat is quite so difficult as it might appear. The verses are half sung, half recited, in a peculiar, slow, drawling tone, and plenty of time is given to find a ryhme in a language like the Portuguese, which is very full of them. Moreover, practice makes perfect, and this alternate verse singing is to be heard all day among the fields and hill sides of the Minho. The shepherd lad, keeping his flock on the hill, will serenade his friend across the valley, perhaps a quarter of a mile away. A girl cutting grass will shout out her remarks to her lover, two fields from her, and these two will go on singing to each other the live-long day, like cicadas in the sunshine. I have heard a man, when no companion was at hand, actually whistle each second verse in a higher key, to represent, I presume, the sweet strains of some absent mistress.

This alternate song is not common except in the Northern Province of the Minho; the most populous, the most fertile, and the most beautiful province of the kingdom. In the mountainous district of Beira, the singing is of quite a different character; and in the poverty-stricken provinces of the south, there is neither singing nor cause for singing.

I am not disposed to construct a theory to account for this most curious custom; but a man given to theorize might easily build up a very plausible one. It is difficult to convey an accurate impression of the actual song, so utterly unlike any kind of vocal music in use among civilized or uncivilized men. The tone is a peculiar nasal drawl, audible very far off, and, it must be admitted, very much improved by distance. The verse is metrical in a high degree, and often takes the form of a rough hexameter. Considerable licence is allowed in the number of feet, but I have heard ten or twenty consecutive lines which were as perfect hexameters as Virgil ever wrote. Whatever licence is taken, a dactyl and spondee invariably terminate the line. Its original character was, I have no doubt, that of a love song—one verse being chanted in a bass voice, and the answering line coming in a higher key; even if two men or two women sing together, this difference of key is maintained; but it is as often, or oftener, used for satirical purposes. The harvest and the vintage are the times when the song can be studied to most advantage, and then it is to be heard in its full luxuriance and, it must be added, in its full licentiousness.

It has often occurred to me, that the origin of this Amœbæan song may be sought for among the Italian nations which colonized Portugal. Looking to the tenacity with which, as I have shown, the Minhotes have kept to the old rules of husbandry of their Roman masters, to some of the old Italian myths, and to the Latin tongue, might it not be that they retained as well, in this ancient form of song, another vestige of their first civilizers? To those who have heard the Minhote peasant chanting (for it is a chant, rather than a song) "with eager thought his Doric lay," it is not difficult to believe that its origin dates from a remote antiquity. May it not be lineally derived, and (except for the addition of verse borrowed from the Moors, the monks, or the troubadours) be almost identical with the rude Fescennine verses which Horace says were sung in his day, by the country people at harvest time? I propound this not as an opinion, but as a suggestion.

The River Lima passes Ponte de Lima in a rapid stream. There is a tradition that the Roman colonists named it Lethe, the River of Oblivion. I know no solid reason for supposing that this was so; but the old Portuguese poet, Diogo Bernardes, mentions it, and the untrustworthy historian Florus asserts that the Roman troops on reaching its banks, hesitated to cross a river with so ill-omened a name, until their general had set them an example, by plunging into the stream with the standard in his hand.* If any Portuguese river was

---

* The editor, or rather compiler, of Murray's "Handbook for Portugal," relates this fable as an actual historical fact, citing as his authority, "The Historian," so that the unwary reader might suppose that Livy or Suetonius was responsible for it. The hero is also made to be Lucius Junius Brutus—the avenger of Lucretia and expeller of the Tarquins—who, of course, if he lived at all did so several centuries before any Roman soldier set foot in the Peninsula.

ever known as Lethe, it was, I suspect, the little River Leça, near Oporto; but the whole story is almost certainly a myth.

Ponte de Lima is a plain-looking town, with a broad Praça, or square, in the centre. It contains about three thousand inhabitants, of whom apparently two-thirds were in temporary mourning for a much respected resident, whose funeral had taken place a day or two before. The house of the deceased gentleman was besieged by a crowd of sympathetic friends, who not only thronged the stairs and passages, but had formed themselves outside, six or seven deep, to wait their turn for admittance.

It is customary throughout Portugal, on the occurrence of a death, for the friends of the deceased person to pay visits of condolence to the relations

The fact is that the editor has "cribbed" the story from a foolish Portuguese compilation, and copied the blunder as well as the story.

Murray's "Handbook for Portugal" is not only the worst handbook in that eminent publisher's series—for that might still be high praise—but probably the very worst handbook that ever was printed. The compiler would seem to be possessed of strong reactionary opinions, both in politics and religion. He sympathises with the miserable cause of Dom Miguel, and deplores the suppression of the convents. All that has hindered Portugal on the road to progress, all that would make arbitrary government possible, helped on by priestcraft and ignorance, finds favour in his eyes. This gentleman would seem to be on an intellectual level with a certain Mr. Smith, a reverend tourist who has recently written a book on Portugal, and who, while mildly disapproving of the Inquisition, highly commends the uniformity and absence of all Dissent consequent upon the former activity of the Holy Office!

two or three days afterwards. The bereaved relatives sit in a half-darkened room, and receive all those acquaintances who may think fit to pay this token of respect. The more distant friends, entering the room with grave and gloomy countenances, bow or curtsey to each of the relations present, with all the expression of sympathy they can command, sidle off towards the doorway, and "exeunt bowing." It is to be observed that in the upper and middle classes, this ceremony is performed by men in black tail-coats, white ties, and white gloves; and by ladies in black silk dresses, with more, less, or no crape, according to circumstances. While the more distant acquaintances are let off thus easily, the nearer friends of the family have to sit about the room, all lugubriously dressed in the deepest mourning, none of them venturing to speak above a whisper; and as each new arrival enters, a little chorus of sighs and groans is heard. This mournful ceremony is often repeated during three or four days. In the case of a widow, particularly a young widow, she is required to "renew her grief" to all her acquaintances for weeks after her loss; and this mild form of *suttee* is sometimes known seriously to affect the health of an unfortunate woman, already broken, perhaps, by a long course of sick-bed nursing and watching.

The different funeral observances of different nations are surely very singular. The Chinese, when their relations die, dress themselves in bright yellow; the bereaved of another nation shave their heads; in another, they cut and slash their bodies; we ourselves, when we mourn, let down white window-blinds for a week; but I think this custom of the Portuguese, of allowing themselves to be bowed to and sighed at, is the least rational of all ways of showing grief and respect for the dead.

The country about here has been praised by all travellers, as being beautiful above everything else to be seen in Portugal. Lord Carnarvon says of the banks of the Lima that he had never gazed on lovelier scenes. Beautiful as it unquestionably is, I should not be inclined to set it above much scenery of the same kind in the Minho; and after hearing so much of Ponte de Lima, I was, in truth, inclined to find the neighbourhood rather tame than otherwise.

The fact is, that travellers do wrong to go into raptures over a particular scene, seeing that so very much depends upon the light and shade, the time of day and of year, the discernment of the individual, and the popular notions about scenery prevalent at the time. At the present day, persons of the most approved taste seem to be in favour of rugged foregrounds; for the middle distance, a jumble of craggy rocks, well coloured with lichens and mosses; and for the far distance, a Turneresque effect of mist, caught in the tops and clefts of far-off mountains. Some time ago, critics of scenery of the very highest judgment thought mountains barbarous and "horrid," and set no store on a scene without a picturesque ruin, a river, a lake, a dance of maidens and, of course, the inevitable dark-brown tree in the foreground. Further back, again, the artistic and poetic instincts combined into an æsthetic appreciation of what was perfectly regular and smooth. The poet Marvel, wishing to describe a beautiful scene, shows how the land was shaped into a perfect hemisphere. "The stiffest compass," he says—

"could not strike
A line more circular or like."

Now, I maintain that, seeing how general opinion on such matters varies from day to day, travellers should be cautious how they praise any scenery at all. No author is bound to be wiser or more consistent than his readers. Rhapsodies over scenery make the worst " padding," and a traveller is sure to provoke criticism from the majority of his readers, if he indulges in anything but the very mildest eclecticism on the subject. I therefore limit myself to observing of this highly extolled district, that what seems to me chiefly worthy of attention about it, is the contrast of bold, rocky hill with valleys teeming with vegetation of a luxuriance of growth which can be seen hardly anywhere else in Europe.

The neighbourhood of Ponte de Lima is classic ground to the student of Portuguese literature. Not far from the town is the Quinta de Tapada, the country-house of the great poet, Sá de Miranda, who holds the second place among the poets of Portugal, even if he does not deserve to rank with Camoens himself. Miranda was the father of Portuguese poetry, and was hardly less distinguished as a traveller, an accomplished courtier, a philosopher and a patriot, than as a poet; and yet his fame in Portugal is almost nothing. A man whose name, if he had lived in any other country, would never be allowed to die on the lips of his admirers, is all but forgotten in the land of his birth. His works are ill-edited, and ill-printed, his life unwritten; and no other monument of the great poet exists among his countrymen than a cold acknowledgment of his excellence.

For what inscrutable reasons do men—chiefly our own countrymen and Americans—visit countries of whose language they know no syllable? Not contenting themselves, even, with keeping upon the beaten tourist tract, where French and English will serve them, but plunging recklessly into by-paths, where they are utterly unintelligible, and where the unsophisticated inhabitants regard them, not without reason, as beings of perverse mind and crass stupidity; for it takes some grasp of intellect to look upon a foreigner who speaks one's own language imperfectly as anything but an idiot. Travellers of this idle, ignorant and ridiculous class, bring great disparagement upon all our race, and, as I fully believe, do more to lower our national prestige, than the respectful contemplation by foreigners of all the accumulated wisdom of our Ambassadors, Ministers, and Consuls does to elevate it.

A man's home must be very desolate, a man's mind very barren, or his love for solitude very great, if he wilfully puts himself into that most complete of all solitudes, a foreign crowd, whose language is unknown to him. It is like a man going to a concert with his ears stopped, or to a picture-gallery and blinded. What can a man gain in return for the fatigues and troubles of travel, if he is never to perceive more than the outside of things, if he is never to be able to ask a question or understand an answer, never to get at the inner life of the people? What avails him painfully to cultivate the tenth muse, the Muse of Travel, with "wisdom at one entrance quite shut out?"

These reflections and this mild indignation were

called forth by the presence of two English tourists, who had come to Ponte de Lima by carriage from Oporto, and who wished to be taken down the river to Vianna in a boat. An altercation, pitiful to behold, was going on between them and their driver; neither party understanding a syllable spoken by the other. The Englishmen were condemning—I might use a shorter word—the stupidity of the natives, while they overlooked their own. Both sides got more and more puzzled, angry, and red in the face. The crowd laughed. The driver turned round to the natives, and made his view of the question quite clear to them. The Englishmen, speaking in their own tongue, put their meaning equally plainly to each other. It was a melancholy exhibition. After looking on for a little time, I intervened and made things straight; with the feelings of a man who has seen a fly fall into the cream-jug, and, for a time, thinks him well served for his greediness, then pities his struggles and helps him out, watching him crawl ridiculously away with clogged wings and legs; so did I help out these two foolish tourists, and watched them for a while crawling as it were on their way, laughed at, ashamed, contemptible.

Throughout my ride to Ponte de Lima it had been striking me how many traces of the Moors were still to be observed in the rural parts of Portugal. To any one who has been in Eastern countries, the impress of Orientalism in many of the customs and habits of the people of Portugal is very perceptible. A hundred little circumstances in daily life, insignificant in themselves, are constantly reminding the traveller how much the people around him must have learnt from the singular race who were their masters for so many centuries, and with what curious tenacity these lessons have been retained.

The "*Socco*" or wooden-soled slipper, worn by both men and women—by women only on gala days—is precisely the foot covering to be seen in the bazaars of Cairo or Damascus; and the Portuguese will shuffle off these slippers, in token of respect, as they enter a house or a church, just as an Oriental will leave his at the entrance of his mosque.

If the gold ornaments which I have mentioned as being worn by the women, are closely examined, their admirable form and pattern will be found to be of pure Arab type and origin. The crescent and the circle are the prevailing "motives" of the work, combined and intertwined with all the elaborate intricacy of Eastern artifice. The patterns never change; and the ornaments are repaired, but never re-cast. The parish priest, at a place near Barcellos, assured me that the ornaments which covered a Madonna in his church dated from the time of the Moors. They had every appearance of great antiquity, even if they were not quite so old as the priest believed; nevertheless, except that the work was a little more delicate than that of the present day, these ornaments were identical in design with those now worn.

Although the jewellery is delicately worked, yet considering the absolute indestructibility of gold, except by actual violence, and considering also the rare occasions on which they were worn, I see no improbability in some of the ornaments worn by the Portuguese women at this day, having been actually the work of Moslem artificers.

Another instance of the prevalence and enduring character of Moorish art-forms is found in the "cangas," or yokes of the oxen. While the ox-cart itself is purely Roman in shape and appearance, without having undergone the smallest change in its construction during fourteen centuries, the yoke is Oriental. It is, in shape, a single board set edgewise upon the necks of the oxen, and is ornamented on each face, sometimes profusely and very beautifully, with characteristic Moorish incised designs.

The common earthenware vessels, the cooking pots and water-jars, might many of them have been turned on a potter's wheel in Morocco or Algiers; so, likewise, the whole economy of the kitchen, in peasant households, is conducted on simple Eastern principles.

I amused myself to day by watching, from the

commencement, the preparation of a stew. Having arrived, at about three o'clock, at a solitary wayside inn, the sun being overpoweringly hot and the air sultry, I rode my horse through the inn-door, and tied him up in a cool and lofty stable communicating with the kitchen. No one was about, and I walked into the kitchen. It was a room with a mud floor, raised one step higher than the stable, and divided from it only by a wooden partition. The sleeping-room was again separated from the kitchen by another slight partition, so that the construction of the house was simple, consisting of an oblong square building, having a kitchen in the centre, with a stable on one side of it and a bed-room on the other.

Having surveyed the establishment at my leisure, and, perceiving that its inhabitants were taking advantage of the holiday to indulge in a siesta, I woke them up, and asked for something to eat and drink; then, sitting down on a stool, I watched the preparation of my meal. First, a fire was kindled upon the hearthstone, which consisted simply of a huge slab of stone in the middle of the room. Looking up to see what was going to become of the smoke, I saw that more or less of it was finding its way into a peculiar wooden contrivance, like an immense square extinguisher, suspended from the ceiling at a height of about two feet above our heads, and passing through the roof. In the meantime, a *levée en masse* of the family was pursuing a solitary chicken that I had seen outside, and, before the fire was well lighted, he had found his way into an earthenware pot, with a little water, a piece of bacon, a little rice, beans, bread, and about five or six other ingredients. I have watched the making of these stews often since, and I believe the only secret is to put in some of everything eatable in the house. The result is always successful.

Now, all this that I have described is purely Eastern. The flat stone for a fireplace, the wooden chimney, the covered earthenware cooking-pot, with the hot cinders raked up round it, even to the variously compounded stew, have all their prototypes in the tents of the Bedouin or the dwellings of semi-Arab tribes on the northern shores of Africa; and if one were to address the old woman watching the simmering pot, like a witch her cauldron, and express a hope that her cooking might turn out well, ten to one but that she would reply, "Oxalá, meu amo,"—"Pray Heaven it may, my master!" *Oxalá*, being a pure Moslem adjuration, meaning, "Would to Allah!" quite unsuspectingly employed by orthodox Portuguese Christians.

The traces of Arabic in the Portuguese language are by no means so many as might have been expected. So far as I can ascertain, the Arabic words in Portuguese amount to about two hundred in number; but they are, for the most part, words in very common use by the lowest as well as by other classes, and two hundred words form a large proportion of the whole vocabulary of an illiterate peasant. The civilization superimposed by their Moorish invaders upon a people already educated to some extent by the Romans, is clearly evidenced by the character of the words which are taken from the Arabic. What the people already knew they retained the old names for. New ideas and new things they expressed in the language of the race which introduced them. If we had no other evidence than that of language, we might have gathered that it was the Moors who extended and improved the art of healing, and taught the use of many medicinal herbs and chemical substances; who invented a new system of numeration; who developed commerce and established customs' dues; who taught the use of the Eastern water-wheel; who first showed how water could be made to flow upwards in jets and fountains; who taught the art of glazing pottery, and how to fabricate decorative tiles; and who first made known the ingenious arts of sugar-making and distilling spirit. Record of all these inventions and discoveries exists in such Arabic words as—"Almofariz," a chemist's mortar; "Alfazema," lavender; "Alzebre," aloes; "Algarismo," a numeral; "Alfandega," a custom-house;

"Nora," a water-wheel; "Chafariz," a fountain; "Azulejo," a glazed tile; "Alcatruz" a drain-pipe; "Azucar," sugar; "Alembico," a still; and "Alcool," spirit.

Of all marks of the former ascendency of the Moors, the most striking to a foreigner is to be found in the manners of the people themselves. The contrast in this respect is very strong between the northern races of the Peninsula, where there was little or no contact with the Arabs, as in the case of the Galicians, the Asturians, the Biscayans, and the Catalonians; and those where that contact was long continued and intimate, as in Portugal, Murcia, Valencia, and Andalusia. The ceremonious courtesy observable among these latter races is unquestionably due to the bygone influences of the Moors and Arabs, races of men who derive their institutions, their religions, and some, in many cases most of their blood, from the most courteous and high-bred nation that the world has ever seen—a spirited and accomplished people, who, in their wars with the Christians, set the example of that generosity and courtesy which grew into our Christian chivalry.

The extreme importance of good breeding, and what may be called educated manners, has always been inculcated by the Moslem as part of their religion, and is apparent enough to anyone who has had opportunities of observing the daily life, either of the Arabs themselves, or of peoples brought strongly under the influence of their religious and social customs. Very rough manners probably prevailed among the mediæval Portuguese and Castilians, and a Moorish farmer of the twelfth century in Andalusia or Algarve would probably have had nothing to learn in propriety of demeanour—possibly much to impart—at the Christian Courts of Toledo or Guimaraens. This good influence of the Moors continues to this day, and in Portugal it is very apparent. Nowhere in the Peninsula, not even in Andalusia, where the vestiges of the Moors are supposed to be stronger than elsewhere, have I found such an observance of the old ceremonious habits of speech as in Portugal. To say of a Portuguese that he is *mal creado*—ill brought up, ill-bred—is still the greatest of reproaches. The exceptions to this universal good breeding are to be seen among the lower middle classes, with whom liberal ideas are happily become common, but who appear to think, with liberals elsewhere, that discourtesy is equivalent to an assertion of equality. It has frequently been noticed that, in Portugal, the best manners are to be found in the very highest and the very lowest classes. The middle classes, as a rule, however, sin rather from an excess than from a want of manners; they are, like some vulgar people at home, far too anxious to show that they know how to behave. They are too ceremonious to be perfectly courteous.

That such lasting effects should have resulted from collision between the two races, and that the Christians should have preserved their religion, and much of their liberty, under the sway of their Moslem conquerors, are circumstances which should have seemed utterly unaccountable, according to the theories of those who have written the history of Mahometan rule in the Peninsula with the preconceived notion that the Moslem invader invariably offered to the conqueror the alternative of the sword or the Koran; the fact being that the cruelty, intolerance, rapine, and injustice ascribed to the Saracens are, to a great extent, the fables of monkish chroniclers. Incompatible as these allegations are with the known respect shown to Christian churches—in some cases the mosque and the church stood side by side—and with the proved prosperity of many Christian cities under the rule of Islam, it was not until history, as told by the monks, came to be compared with the writings of Arabian annalists, that the truth came fully out; and that the government of the Saracens was proved to be, on the whole, just, tolerant, and even beneficent. Gayangos, in Spain, and the historian, Herculano,* in Portugal, are the two

* I hardly know a greater service to letters than would be

men to whom this rectification of history is chiefly due.

Coming back to my inn at Ponte de Lima after a walk about the town and near the river, I found the public room pretty full of towns-people. A little very mild gambling was going on, and a great deal of conversation. From the sudden cessation of talk as I entered the room and saluted the company, and from the curiosity with which I was regarded, I was led to gather that I had myself been the subject of both conversation and curiosity. That a foreigner on horseback should have come among them, and that that foreigner should be travelling without a servant to allay any of their natural inquisitiveness, for I had left my Spanish guide at Vianna, was no doubt, doubly puzzling to the citizens. In former days, my business would have been thought to be political, and as they had reason to know it was not commercial, I was probably set down as a person

accomplished by the translation into English or French of the three volumes of the "History of Portugal," by this most eminent of living Portuguese writers. Herculano is perhaps, on the whole, the first historian of the present age. His pure style, unequalled in Portugal since the days of Barros—the so-called Livy of Portugal—is a pleasant contrast to the rhetorical writings of many of his contemporaries. His acumen and judgment in the appreciation of authorities, his lucidity, and the art with which he satisfies the reader of his learning without importing into his narrative any of the dryness of the chroniclers among whom his researches have lain, are qualities in a historian which the world has not seen since the death of Gibbon. Unfortunately, Herculano's history only reaches to the end of the thirteenth century.

connected with mines; but as this part of Portugal has little mineral wealth, such a supposition was not likely to be very strong; so when I came to enter into conversation with these gentlemen, I had evidence that their minds were by no means made up. I knew well that they were far too clever to believe me if I had told them the plain truth, namely, that I was travelling to see the country and the people: therefore I said nothing.

In the course of conversation it was mentioned that when the French army fled northward, after the passage of the Douro and capture of Oporto by Wellington, the military chest of the French was secretly buried, to avoid risk of capture somewhere in this neighbourhood. When I remarked that I had not before heard of this circumstance, I observed a look of incredulity upon the face of my informant; and I have very little doubt that what would appear to them as my affected ignorance of a well-known fact, taken in conjunction with the French expedition, then talked of for the recovery of the lost treasure at Vigo, convinced those present that this military chest, and nothing else, was the object of my mission!

It is hardly to be believed with what childish credulity stories of hidden treasure are told and accepted in all parts of Portugal. There is more time and labour wasted in searching for imaginary concealed riches, than would earn real wealth if properly directed. Some small foundation, indeed, for this general credulity exists in the hoarding propensities necessarily produced in former times of insecurity and danger; and one or two well-attested instances of the discovery of hidden treasure have come to my own knowledge. An English merchant having occasion to make some repairs in a house rented by him, in or near the town of Regoa, the workmen, either in pulling down a wall or in taking up a floor, came upon a receptacle containing about two hundred milreis, in gold and silver coin—about £40 or £50. A goldsmith of Viseu told me that the garden-wall of a neighbour threatening to fall, it was ordered to be pulled down; and that on one very heavy stone in it being removed, an earthen pot was laid bare in a little hollow behind where it had stood, and in this pot were found no less than seven golden moidores! These discoveries were not magnificent ones, and it is not likely that the few which now and again are made, are more so; but they serve to keep up the prevailing appetite for treasure-seeking.

There has always prevailed a belief that an immense treasure was hidden away—I have never heard under what circumstances—in the uninhabited royal palace of Queluz, near Lisbon; and ineffectual efforts have from time to time, been made to find it. A few years ago, great interest was suddenly created by the announcement that an old sergeant of artillery had sent, on his death-bed, for a high officer of the court, and had confided to him that he—the sergeant—was the sole survivor of the party which had been entrusted with the concealment of the treasure in question. He then proceeded to describe accurately the situation in which it was to be found. There was, as may be imagined, prodigious excitement among the lords and ladies of the court; and on a certain day, a large party of them went to the deserted palace. The particular plank designated by the sergeant, in the particular room which he mentioned, was found. The workmen brought for the purpose forced it up with their tools, and between it and the ceiling below was found a space, in which there was—nothing at all! Then more planks were pulled up, then the floors of other rooms, then holes were made in likely-looking places in the walls; but still no treasure, and the courtly party had to return without it: but the palace of Queluz has been left in a state the reverse of what is known to lawyers as "tenantable repair."

Another instance of credulity is of so astounding a nature that, if I had not heard the account on unexceptional authority, I should not venture to relate it. In the city of Oporto, a society or club has been formed, for the sole purpose of seeking for the hiding-place of a fabulously large diamond, concealed, under I know not what circumstances, either in the city or in its near neighbourhood. I am ignorant of the rules and regulations of this club—whether the entrance is heavy, the subscription high, or how many black balls exclude. I should imagine that the search for a single gem, among the streets and squares, and suburbs of a large city, must be very much like looking for a needle in a bottle of hay; nor do I well see how such a search could be set about without exciting comment and suspicion. I presume the members perambulate each other's gardens after nightfall, with dark lanterns. They must, of a truth, be men of a solemn and earnest temperament if they can meet together and preserve their gravity. Perhaps the club is broken up now, and for this very reason, and that *solvuntur risu tabulæ,* they could not look each other in the face without laughing.

I am not aware that the belief of the members of the Diamond Club in the hidden stone rests upon anything resembling evidence, or upon anything at all, except the fact that a great number of fine gems, particularly diamonds, do exist in the country. The Portuguese obtained many precious stones of great value from India during the palmy days of their connection with that country; and more still, chiefly diamonds, from their Brazilian dependencies. I have seen, at evening parties in Lisbon and Oporto, a far greater show of good diamonds than would be seen, on similar occasions, in London or Paris; the stones, indeed, mostly ill-cut and ill-set, but representing an immense money value.

The crown jewels of Portugal are, for so small a kingdom, marvellous, and if the huge Braganza diamond—which is one of them—is a true " brilliant," the Portuguese regalia must be quite unequalled. The Braganza stone was found in the Caethé Minim Mine in Brazil, in 1741, and was frequently worn by King John VI. The lowest estimate of the weight of this stone is sixteen hundred and eighty carats, while the Kohinoor weighs but a hundred and six; the Star of the South a hundred and twenty-five; and the great Orloff diamond a hundred and ninety-four carats. The Orloff is, however, "rose-cut," *i.e.*, not the true " brilliant " shape. The Braganza diamond, from its unusual size, has been suspected to be nothing more than a fine white Brazilian topaze; but the fact that it has been publicly worn by the king, at a court whose frequenters are particularly good judges of diamonds, must go some way to make us believe it to be what it professes. I have never seen it. A person who had the opportunity of examining it closely, told me it was as large as a hen's egg, and was badly cut, having but few facets. My informant had no doubt but that it was a true diamond; but an ordinary observer's evidence on such a point goes for little. If the stone is uncut, or imperfectly cut, the marvel of its size is lessened, but not removed. To cut such a rough stone into true "brilliant" shape could only be effected by reducing its weight to nine hundred or a thousand carats. It would, even then, be five times as large as the largest diamond in existence.

CHAPTER IV.

Visit to the Gaviarra—Prudery of Portuguese Writers—Decay of Literature—View from Top of Gaviarra—Early Portuguese History—Advantages of Travelling on Horseback—Ride through the Gerez Mountains and along Spanish Frontier—Wild Birds, Beasts and Flowers—Fishing and Shooting not Good in Portugal—Hill Forts—Legends Connected with One—Mild Religious Exercises—Pilgrimages to Shrines.

LEAVING Ponte de Lima I rode along a fair road to Arcos, intending to examine the Gaviarra—the loftiest mountain in Portugal—whose height is nearly eight thousand feet. Although I have given reasons for avoiding description of scenery, it is impossible not to notice the exquisite beauty of the whole country hereabouts—a beauty which appeals to the eye of the artist, rather than to that of the ordinary scenery-hunter: craggy hills, with their wealth of lichen growth, of a colour beyond the daring of any landscape painter; valleys rich with the luxuriance of a half-tropical vegetation, and richer still in their association with the best idyllic poetry of Portugal. It is this very country which the poets Miranda and Bernardes describe in their poems; and certainly these green dells and stream-watered valleys with their hanging vineyards, rich in waving crops of maize, and alive with the songs of birds, the peaceful lowing of cattle, and the chants of peasant girls and youths, might well seem to a poet's fancy to contain all that is delightful of rustic life. Passing along the narrow roads in the early morning, when the sun had just risen, and with its slanting rays sparkling on the leaves, grass and wild flowers, and drawing up the thin vapour from among the clefts and gorges of the distant hills, I thought that I had never seen a country so various and so rich in its attractions; and this I say after having premised, in a previous chapter, that I am a reluctant admirer of " fine views," and very unwilling to describe them.

It is a pity that the ancient Greeks and Romans were not acquainted with the maize plant. The nations which have said so many fine and grateful things of the vine, the olive tree, and the wheat plant, consecrating each of them to a different god or goddess, would assuredly have said still more for this most kindly boon of a beneficent Nature. The rapid growth of the maize, its size and noble appearance, the value of all its parts, and the immense returns it makes to the cultivator in comparison with any other cereal, would certainly, in their eyes, have placed it at the head of all products of nature. As it is, I hardly think a civil word has ever been said for it by the poets of a country which it has so much benefited. It is true, indeed, that maize was not introduced, or at least, did not begin to thrive, in Portugal, until after true poetry had ceased to do so; and since then, a spirit of such fastidiousness and false refinement has taken possession of the nation—both verse-makers and others—that so commonplace and vulgar a subject as maize could hardly be brought into verse. The prevailing delicacy on such a point is, in fact, like that which actuated the Dublin clergyman who had to preach a sermon upon the Potato Famine, and succeeded in not pronouncing the word "potato" once in his whole discourse. A preacher of this fastidious sort would be applauded in this country; and there is many a word quite as good as or better than "potato," that a Portuguese would not dream of saying outright in good company. In some parts of the country, it is a positive solecism to talk of a dog; the animal must be named apologetically as a puppy, a "*cachorro*." No Portuguese of any class will name that shocking animal the pig. If he must be alluded to—and it is necessary sometimes, seeing that the Portuguese are very fond of him cooked, he is called "the fat animal," "*cevada;*" and if a Portuguese is driven into a corner and absolutely forced to employ the word, he will use the diminutive "*porquito,*" a little pig, and even that only under his breath, and with the phrase, "by your leave."

I have been amused by reading the translation into Portuguese of a French savant's account of a fossil bone cave, in which had been found, among other remains, abundant bones of swine. The Portuguese translator ingeniously eluded all direct mention of the animal; and as often as science clearly demanded the plain word "pig," he would have recourse to some ingenious paraphrase, such as, "a familiar mammal, which we still employ as food," and so forth!

If this foolish prudery applied only to the two animals held abominable by the law of Islam, it might be traced to the influence of the Moors; but it applies to a hundred other words, things and ideas, which the Moors never dreamt of interdicting; for instance, no one in Portugal ventures to speak of a certain migratory bird, which both Shakespeare and Molière have mentioned allusively, although I believe no other nation in Europe thinks it wrong to speak familiarly and even lovingly of the bird in question. Moreover, the modern Portuguese dislike of calling a spade a spade by no means prevailed during the best period of Portuguese literature, which was two centuries after the Moors had left the country. The present fastidiousness dates from a time when letters, as well as morals, began to degenerate; a period in literature which is, oddly enough, as Mr. Matthew Arnold may think, designated "Culturismo" which would probably, by its admirers, be translated "culture;" a period during which it was thought well to stimulate an over-sensibility of emotion and an over-refinement of expression. This grew into effeminacy and ended in absolute decadence. These influences have, unfortunately, never ceased to have sway in Portugal. Among the prose writers of the present day are many unmanly sentimentalists, or rhetoricians; and any true poetical utterance in the land of Camoens and Ferreira, of Miranda and Bernardes, is rare, if not altogether absent :—

"The languid strings do scarcely move,
The sound is forced, the notes are few."

I had a long day's journey before me, for I had determined to reach the mountain of the Gaviarra before nightfall. I rode as fast as the boy I had engaged at Ponte de Lima could keep up with on foot, and the result was that upon reaching Arcos where I had determined to breakfast, he was dead tired, and I had to send him back. Taking a new guide, I followed a fair road up the course of a trout stream, which has its sources in the Gaviarra itself. To my left, as I ascended, was the wild range of the Estrica; on the right rose the taller mountains of the Soajo range among which towers the lofty, Outeiro Maior, the Great Hill, properly called the Gaviarra.

The ascent is gradual, and as the cultivation of the valley is left behind, the mountain becomes bleak and its scenery comparatively tame. I had, too, the common bad luck of a mountain ascent. Though the day had been clear and fine in the morning, a suspiciously misty appearance had hung all day about the summits of the mountain, and towards noon had turned into a drizzling rain, which gradually descending the sides of the hill, blotted out all the features of the landscape. I rode on for several hours, skirting the side of the hill with a continuous ascent, the view never extending more than a hundred yards around me. It was late evening before we reached a shepherd's house, or hut, where my guide had promised that we could pass the night. Two men occupied the house, whose solitary room served for kitchen, dining-room, and bed-room. There was no stable or out-house of any kind, and as we were high enough up on the mountain to feel a considerable change of temperature, I was in some difficulty about my horse. However, the shepherds soon settled the matter by building up a little lean-to of green branches against the sheltered side of the house; and in this improvised stable he passed the night, probably as agreeably as his master himself did on a bundle of rye straw on the floor of the cabin.

We had bought an "odre," or skin, of Monçao wine at Arcos; and with this, some black bread, goat's-milk cheese, and a large bowl of ewe's milk, the two shepherds, my guide, and myself, made, at any rate, a cheerful meal—for the Monçao wine is the best in this province, and my hosts enjoyed it amazingly. One of them after supper sang a good Spanish song, recounting the adventures—of a very "picaresque" and rascally description for the most part—of one Don Spavento; the hero of the song being supposed to sing in his own person, and to be so overcome by the enjoyment of his recollections as to break out, at the end of each stanza, into a laughing refrain of "Ha! ha! ha! Dice Don Spavento," and this being taken up in chorus by the whole strength of our company, so shook the walls of the cabin as to startle my horse outside, and to raise a second chorus of bleating in the flocks of goats and sheep which had crowded round the building. The man told me that in his youth he had been a mule-driver, and had learnt this song on the Spanish frontier. The song was so successful that, at my particular request, it was repeated, and then, the singer's repertory being exhausted, and feeling very tired, I got some fresh straw, and spreading it upon the floor slept fairly well till daybreak. The morning was misty again, but it did not rain, and I started at once up the mountain. The summit was, I should imagine, about two thousand feet above our heads, and the early morning air was exceedingly cold. The slope was stiff, but the ascent by no means difficult.

I am one of that minority who hold that mountains were not exclusively formed for the purpose of being ascended. I even go so far as to think a writer owes some apology to his reader for taking him into the clouds, either by means of a mountain or otherwise; and I, for one, shall not be sorry when we see the end of a great deal of printed enthusiasm on the subject of Alpine climbing.

The mist began to lift, as the shepherds had foretold that it would, when the sun rose; and continuing my ascent, I had presently spread out before me a vast panorama to the south and to the east, with a radius of probably not less than a hundred miles. The greater part of the Province of the Minho lay immediately to the south-west, with its innumerable white villages dotting the dark green of the landscape. The province is a hilly one, but in comparison with the more mountainous regions within my ken, it looked, from this great height, almost like a fruitful wooded plain. To the south, about ten miles off, but appearing from the clearness of the air to be almost within rifle shot, lay the ranges of the Gerez Mountains, looking as if they were cast in steel, so sharply did their barren peaks and ridges stand out in the transparent atmosphere.

Beyond the hills of the Gerez, the eye ranges over a confused mass of hills of a lesser elevation, which compose the Province of Traz-os-Montes, beyond which the River Douro flows; and the sight, passing thence over the hill country of Beira, is limited to the south by the noble range of the Estrella Mountains, which stretch nearly across the whole central part of Portugal. The hill country between the Gerez and the Estrella is drained by the Douro, whose sources lie to the eastward, and much farther than the eye can now reach, in the heart of Leon. To the north-east, the eye ranges across the Spanish frontier towards the Asturias, in the direction of Astorga and Leon.

The traveller who has looked over this stretch of country from the Gaviarra, has seen the very cradle of the Portuguese nation, which is an offshoot of the vigorous race which in the eighth, ninth, and tenth centuries inhabited the great basin and watershed of the Douro, from the heights of the Asturias, of Leon and of Old Castile, as far as the mountain ranges of Beira and Traz-os-Montes; the race of men who, in the Asturias, preserved some sort of independence, when the rest of the Peninsula was overrun by the Arabs, who were the first to rise against the enemies of their faith and of their country, and by whose efforts the Moslem was finally thrust from the soil in all parts of the Peninsula. When the long war between Christian and Mahometan commenced and the Christians first began to hold their ground, it was in the region we are now surveying that some of the earlier struggles took place. One of the finest passages in the "Cid" relates the siege of Zamora, on the Douro, by the Campeador himself and the King of Leon; and the hills about Zamora are the eastern limit of the view from the Gaviarra. The northern portions of the fertile province of the Minho were early wrested from the Moors; and here, in 1095, Count Henry as Viceroy of the Leonese king, established his court in the centre of this province, at Guimaraens—whose battlemented castle walls, thirty or forty miles away, due south from us, are distinctly visible.

At Guimaraens the son of Count Henry was born —Affonzo Henriquez—the most heroic figure in Portuguese history; whose adventures and conquests, authenticated by Christian and Moorish chroniclers, are hardly less romantic than those which go to make up the great epic of the "Cid." It was in the wild country at the foot of the Gaviarra that he fought, while still a mere boy, the Galician Count who had stirred up a civil war in Portugal, and finally defeated him at San Mamede, near Guimaraens. Then turning his arms against the Saracens, he routed them utterly at the battle of Ourique, on the field of which he assumed, for the first time, the title of King of Portugal.

In reading the history of the extraordinary race of men which sprang from the wild hill country below my feet, and whose subsequent exploits by land and by sea fill such an important page of the world's history, the story of their early vicissitudes and adventures has always seemed to me more surprising than even the discoveries, conquests, and colonizations of after years, in foreign and distant lands. Surely it is a marvel that so numerically small a tribe—for they hardly amounted to a nation—should have had the energy and the constancy to hold their independence against the attacks of powerful nations of their own race, commanded by leaders accounted the most accomplished captains of their day; that they should have done this when their efforts were hampered by a civil war, and when the whole of their southern frontier was occupied by a warlike race in never-ceasing hostility with them; that having disposed of their Christian enemies, they should have turned upon the Mahometans, and won upon them the greatest Christian victory which had yet been obtained in the Peninsula. It might, perhaps, not be so strange that such a series of successes and victories should have resulted from the genius of one great sovereign and commander, or the accident of weakness or division among their enemies; but that these successes should have continued for long centuries after the death of the first monarch, and that after many battles and many victories over their two powerful enemies, the Moors should finally have been crushed at the decisive battle of Salado and the Castilians at Aljubarrota,—this, I think, proves a loyal fortitude and, perhaps as much as anything else, a faithful devotion to their independence as a people, almost beyond example.

Moreover, it is to be remembered that this maintenance of Portuguese independence under so many circumstances of difficulty, was owing in no case to the inaccessibility of their territory, as with the Swiss, or, to some extent, with the Greeks; for I can recollect no instance of the Portuguese having owed victory to the accident of a strong position; nor, again, was the coherence of the Portuguese ranks due to any sort of feudalism or servile compulsion. The rallying to the standard of their chiefs resulted from a feeling, partly of clanship, and partly of loyal and dutiful devotion of each private interest to the public good. The noble motto of one of the earliest and greatest of the Portuguese kings was " Polla ley e pollo grey "—" We rule by law and by our people's will."

On returning to the shepherds' house, I found them away on the mountain side with their flocks. The guide was still asleep on the floor, and my horse had eaten all the bundle of rye-straw I had put before him in the morning—the poorest horse-provender there is. I had ridden him not far from thirty miles, over hilly roads, the day before; and though not in any condition, he had carried me admirably. He had now passed the night on a cold hill-side, in a draughty shed, and with scanty food; but he was as fresh as ever—an example to travellers to make sure of a good horse at the beginning of their work. Nothing is so tiring to the body nor so wearing to the mind, as to be compelled to ride a weak, stumbling horse on a long day's journey. The pleasure of travel is quite spoiled by it; whereas to ride a strong and willing beast through a pleasant country is the *summa felicitas* of travelling—the healthiest, the most exhilarating, and the most independent mode of progression that human ingenuity has yet invented.

I have recounted, in a previous chapter, how I accidentally fell in with this horse at Vigo, and how I gave the unusual price of twenty-five pounds for him—he being of the Andalusian breed, and not likely to meet with appreciation so far from his home as Galicia. He was hardy, untiring, easy in his paces, gentle, and very sure-footed. His only fault was one shared by many Andalusian horses—a delicate appetite. He was what English grooms call "a shy feeder." During my connection with him, he has certainly made acquaintance with some exceptional kinds of horse-food. He has had to eat green fern-fronds; once I had to employ a boy to gather the leaves of a neighbouring ash; and often I have eked out his "feed" with slices of black bread: and these varieties of provender he seemed to prefer to ordinary horse-food.

I descended the hill on the Spanish side, and followed the border line between Spain and Portugal for several hours along one of the very worst bridle-paths it was ever my fortune to travel over. Crossing the River Lima near Flervael, I had hoped, by a very long ride, to reach the city of Chaves the same day; but my route lay through the passes of the Gerez, over which my guide had only a very faint notion of the road, and I fully believe that I had ridden over forty miles before reaching the fortified city of Montalegre, which is only half-way to Chaves.

Montalegre is perhaps the smallest cathedral city or fortified place in the world. At the most, eighty to a hundred inhabitants are contained in its ruined and tumble-down houses. Its *raison d'être* is clearly the strongly placed castle on the hill above the city, which guards a path through the frontier.

The walls of the town are still in fair condition, and its position, in the extreme north-east corner of the kingdom, would obviously give Montalegre considerable military importance, so long as war with Spain was possible. The tiny cathedral is of poor Renaissance work, and possesses no architectural interest whatever.

Leaving my useless guide at this place, I followed an average road through the mountains to Chaves, situated on an extensive and fertile tableland. Chaves is an important place in a military point of view: its fortifications command the rich valley of the River Tamega, leading straight from Spain into the heart of Portugal. It does not, however, derive its name of Chaves—"the Keys"—from this circumstance, as Murray's Handbook absurdly asserts, but because the Romans had called it " Aquæ Flaviæ," or " Flaviæ," from its hot wells; and by the not unusual change of the Latin " Fl " into the Portuguese " Ch "—as " Flamma " into "Chamma"—Flaviæ (in the accusative, Flavias) becomes Chaves. The many Roman inscriptions and milliary columns in the neighbourhood, and the fact that it was a principal station on the Roman road from Braga, and that its name is of purely Roman origin, would seem to indicate that the place was actually founded by the Romans, and not the site of a town previously established. The remains of Moorish domestic architecture in the streets show that the town was afterwards held by the Saracens, and the existence of a richly-built church of the style of the twelfth century* proves that it was in early and permanent occupation by the Christians. Thus a traveller who arrives at Chaves without even having heard of its existence before, may, by merely looking about him, construct some sort of a history of the town.

My road for the last two days had lain altogether among the peaks and precipices of the Gerez Mountains—a range presenting those abrupt changes of view, that variety of rock form and colouring, that abundance of streams, and that frequency of cascades in narrow, precipitous ravines, and above all, that wild and variously contorted sky-line, which, taken all together, go to the making-up of the finest mountain scenery. I have, indeed met nowhere in the Peninsula (except, perhaps, among the mountains of Ronda, in Andalusia) with scenery to be compared with this of the Gerez range. Amid these wild and inaccessible hills is still found one of the rarest of European quadrupeds—the Portuguese ibex, or wild goat; this range being the solitary Portuguese

---

* I have elsewhere fully described this building of good Romanesque work. The churches of this style of architecture, which would be better termed "Pre-Gothic" than "Romanesque," are very rare in Portugal. Details would probably not interest the general reader.

habitat of the species.* The wolf, the roe-deer, the Portuguese lynx *(Felis pardina)*, and, perhaps, the wild boar, are likewise to be found among these mountains; while the golden eagle is frequently to be seen perched upon the topmost needle of some precipitous cliff, or wheeling in slow flight over the narrow mountain valleys.

A traveller in Portugal has the advantage, or disadvantage, of being in a land whose fauna and flora have been less studied than those of any other country in Europe. The lofty mountain ridges which divide Portugal from Spain, and Spain from Europe, should—according to modern theories— have a tendency to separate and localize species; and apparently this has to some extent been the case in Portugal. A good, patient naturalist, of the class of Dr. Darwin or Mr. Wallace, who would be content to study the language, and then to spend three or four years in the remoter parts of Portugal, would, I have little doubt, achieve the discovery of many new species, and confer great benefits upon the science of natural history.

* This animal has been considered by naturalists to be identical with *Ægoceros Caucasica*, the ibex of the Caucasus; but the able Director of the Zoological Department of the Lisbon Museum, Senhor Barbosa, has, in my opinion, satisfactorily shown the ibex of the Gerez to be the same with *Capra Hispanica*, discovered by Schimper in 1848 in the Sierra Nevada; and this, again, is probably identical with the very rare *Ægoceros Pyrenaica*, the Tur, or wild goat, of the Pyrenees.

As a country for a mere sportsman, Portugal presents hardly any attractions. The difficulties of language would be insuperable to the ordinary sporting tourist; nor would the chance of bagging perhaps fifteen brace of red-legged partridges or quail in a day repay him for the trouble of getting to the shooting ground, or of putting up with very wretched accommodation. Woodcock visit the country in immense numbers in winter, but the pine forests over which they spread themselves are so vast, that very few, comparatively speaking, are killed. Seven brace in a day, among four or five guns, is considered a remarkably good day's sport. Snipe are abundant, but the shooting of them is an unsatisfactory sport. A bog which one day contains thousands of birds, may, the next, not hold a dozen. The great bustard is to be found on the plains of Alemtejo and Estremadura, but not in great numbers; the little bustard appears to be a half-migratory species, and, in some years, is tolerably abundant in the southern provinces; so, also, is that pretty African migrant, the sand grouse. The pheasant has been introduced in some of the royal preserves, and the fallow deer reintroduced. The red deer is supposed, by some enthusiastic naturalists, to be still found in the mountains of the Estrella range.

In the way of fishing, there is very little to be done. The Douro is the southernmost limit, in

Europe, of the migration of the salmon; one or two fish only are caught in the year. In the Lima, the next large river to the north, salmon and salmon-trout are more frequently taken; and in the Minho, on the Spanish frontier, both are netted in considerable numbers: but I never heard of any one having caught a salmon in Portugal with rod and line. In all the mountain streams, trout are abundant; and in a few they run to some size. The streams which I had crossed or ridden by, within the last three days, were full of trout; but a singular difficulty in the way of angling is presented in Portugal by the growth of the vine. Almost every river is bordered by pollarded oaks or chestnuts, on which are trained vines which grow in festoons from one tree to the other, so that an angler is greatly hindered in the casting of his line.

Although a sportsman who cared for nothing but sport would find Portugal a dull country, a person who has paid any attention to the natural history of his own land would find it full of interest. Very many quadrupeds, birds, and plants scarce or unknown in Great Britain are here common.

The hoopoe is one of the rarest visitors to the British Isles: here its thrice-repeated call, like the cuckoo's, but less resonant, is as commonly heard in the woods in summer as the cuckoo's in England; but, unlike that bird, it is not shy and retiring.

Another very interesting bird, the black wheatear (*Saxicola leucura*), a bird nearly the size of a blackbird, with a white patch on the back, is very conspicuous from its familiarity and lively motions. A bird of similar habits and appearance, but with red markings, has been described to me by the natives: it is, probably, a new species. Another curious bird is the large Calandra lark, whose song, harsh and discordant as it is, the Portuguese seem to prefer to that of every other singing bird. Their taste in cage birds is certainly strange; those most frequently seen in captivity being this bird, called by the Portuguese *cuchicho*, an onomatopoetic name—the quail and the partridge! A large proportion of the common house-martins winter in the North of Portugal, but the chimney-swallows—those with the forked tails—all disappear from the northern provinces, so far as I have observed; though a few stay over the winter in the warmer parts of Southern Portugal. The swifts entirely leave the country in autumn. If my observation is correct, this would correspond with the apparent susceptibility to cold of these three species in Great Britain. At home the martins come first and go last, the swallows next, and the swifts arrive last and make the shortest stay of any.

Of quadrupeds, the wolf and the fox of Portugal are different animals from the common wolf and fox of Europe, the wolf being a large and powerful brown variety of *Canis lycaon*. The fox is not *Canis vulpes*, our English fox, but *Canis melanogaster;* and, while rather smaller than the fox of England, has a larger head, and the throat and under part of the body black. It likewise differs from our fox in having the pads distinctly smaller, while the brush is much more bushy. The civet, the wild cat, and a species of lynx are all common in the remoter hills and woods.

Of reptiles, the great green lizard (*Lacerta ocellata*) is the most interesting. This animal is common everywhere, and, in the brilliancy of its green, yellow, and blue scales, rivals the beauty of the tropical reptiles. The esculent frog and the tree-frog, both unknown at home, are common. Very common, also, is the so-called "singing toad" (*Alytes obstetricans*), which, unlike the toad of Great Britain, lives in dry places, and whose note is heard all through the warm nights of summer like the tinkle of a small glass bell.

To an entomologist, Portugal should be a paradise. I have counted eleven different species of butterfly on one hedge of lavender,* and this fact

---

* Mostly of species common in Great Britain: *P. Macaon*, our English Swallow-tailed butterfly; *C. Edusa*, the Clouded Saffron; our two common English white butterflies; *L. Megæra*, the Wall butterfly; *C. Cardui*, the Painted Lady; two kinds of *Fritillary*; two species of the genus *Polyommatus*, the blue butterflies; and the Red Admiral, *V. Atalanta*.

will no doubt stand me in stead of further description.

Of all departments of natural history, that of the freshwater fishes has been the most neglected in Portugal. The species that are commonly known do not exceed half-a-dozen, and include the trout, the eel, the barbel, the burbolt, the gudgeon, a species of dace and another of roach, neither of the two being identical with the British species. Besides these there are the migratory fishes—the sturgeon, lamprey, shad, salmon, etc. There can be little doubt that at least thirty or forty unknown or unrecognized species are awaiting the labours of some future Crouch or Frank Buckland.

Travelling on by a good road, six miles of gradual ascent brought me to Monforte—as its name implies, a stronghold on a hill. Such places, perched on the summits of precipitous cliffs, were not inaptly christened *Aguiares*—eyries, or eagles' nests; and there is a curious legend attached to this very castle, so characteristic of the wild times of the early years of the monarchy, that it is well worth transcribing it from the monkish chronicler who relates it.

A certain Dom Gonçalvo de Souza, one of the most noble and powerful knights of the reign of King Affonzo Henriquez, was, in the words of the writer of the life of Saint Senhorina, "taking his pleasure one day on his own estate, when messengers came with word that the enemy had invaded his lands, towns, and strong places, and were then laying siege to his castle of Aguair. Whereupon Dom Gonçalvo forthwith sounded the alarm, and summoned his people, and hastened with them to relieve the said castle. When they came to where the body of Saint Senhorina lies buried, Dom Gonçalvo forgot, in his hurry, to beg for her grace and intercession, and, as they passed before the holy spot, the mule on which the Cabalheiro rode remained fixed to the ground, and neither blows nor the spur would make her stir a step. Then Dom Gonçalvo, recollecting that he was passing the shrine without having prayed to the saint, turned his mule, who willingly made towards the chapel, where the Cabalheiro performed his orisons, commending himself to the protection of the saint. After which he continued his journey, raised the siege of Aguiar, pursued the enemy, and routed them. Ever after this, Dom Gonçalvo recommended all good Christians to do proper homage to Saint Senhorina."

The enemies who thus attempted to surprise this nobleman were either the Moors or the men of Leon and Castile. Though no date is fixed by the chronicler, we learn incidentally from the Charter of the Cathedral of Braga, dated 1151, that Dom Gonçalvo de Souza, the knight in question, was then Governor of Monforte, above Chaves—"Domnus Gonsalvus de Souza tenens Montem fortem supra Flavias."

The site of this miracle is still holy ground, and a square of earth is marked out with stone crosses on a hillside, where the body of Saint Senhorina is supposed to be lying. These assemblages of four, six, or eight stone crosses, disposed in an oblong square, are exceedingly numerous in this province and in that of the Minho. They mark the site of a miracle or supernatural event in the life of some local saint, whose memory is kept green by the annual exhortations of the priest of the parish. From time to time the pious of the neighbourhood frequent the place; they kneel in front of each cross in turn, repeating so many *aves* and *paternosters*. The more zealous go the round of the crosses on their knees, but I have not observed that even this mortification of the flesh (on the generally stony ground) is any promoter of gravity, for they laugh and talk freely between the stations. Such religious exercises are, at most, little more than play, and this sort of *pious crôquet* is frequently imposed as a mild penance.

The "Romarias," or annual pilgrimages to holy places, are more serious affairs, and occupy a large place in the social life of the peasantry and lower classes. The Romaria to the church of Mathosinhos, near Oporto, which contains a miraculous image, and that to the *Bom Jesus* at Braga, last three or four days, and are the most important in the kingdom. They are attended by persons of all classes from every part of Portugal, sometimes to the number of from twenty to thirty thousand. Pilgrimages to less celebrated shrines, many of them on solitary mountains, are also very numerous. They are chiefly resorted to by the peasants, and often by as many as two or three thousand, who live *al fresco* during the few days that the Romaria lasts. Bread is baked and food cooked for this multitude daily in huge stone ovens, which, when the assemblages are over, are the only marks left of them; and these ovens to the number of twenty or thirty in a row, on a solitary hillside, might puzzle a traveller who had not learnt their use.

At these gatherings there are sermons to be heard, religious exercises to be performed, and—as the occasion has some of the characteristics of a country fair—there is an immense deal of laughing, gossiping, dancing, and singing; very much, indeed, what takes place at our own open-air Revival meetings, with some of their worst features left out.

Although a stranger might think, at first sight, that their religion sits loosely on the Portuguese, he would be much mistaken. They are not a bigoted people, but they are deeply imbued with an earnest spirit of religion.

CHAPTER V.

The Castle of Braganza—Hebrew Type of Face in Braganza—Important Part Played by Jews in Portuguese History—Conversation with a Jewish Traveller—His Story of Spinosa—Mirandella—Monotonous Cuisine of Well-to-do People in Portugal—Legend of the Bruxas—Villa Real; its Architecture—Return of Enriched Adventurers from India and Brazil—Dull Life in Portuguese Country Towns—Curious System of Courtship—Anecdote—Description of Port Wine Country—Sketch of the History of Port Wine—Has a Literature of its Own—The Pass over the Marão Mountains.

THE reader who has followed me hitherto in my ride in Portugal has been taken along the northern and eastern frontier line, through the fine scenery of the Gerez Mountains; past the numerous strongholds which were erected, during the early years of the monarchy, to guard the Portuguese line from Castilian and Leonese incursions, and past the old Roman station of Aquæ Flaviæ, and the hill stronghold of Monforte. From thence I proceeded, across the table-land of Traz-os-Montes, to the once famous city of Braganza, whence the reigning dynasty of Portugal derives its title, and which is still the most important city along the whole frontier between Spain and Portugal, though its prosperity has greatly declined of late years.

The town is neither clean nor picturesque; the cathedral is essentially mean, and has not even the merit of antiquity; but what is worth coming from far to see is the magnificent castle on the hill above the city—the most perfect remaining stronghold in Portugal, with the exception of the Castle of Villa da Feira, near Oporto. The Braganza Castle was rebuilt by the second king of Portugal on the foundations of a fort erected probably by Affonzo Henriquez himself, and made a place of great strength. The works were evidently not neglected, as time went on, for it contains remains of all the improvements and refinements in the art of defence made in the pre-artillery period.

Besides the castle, the one point of interest which struck me at Braganza was the marked Hebrew type of face in the inhabitants. The strong immixture of Jewish blood in the Portuguese race is a fact that Portuguese writers are not fond of dwelling upon. The former large population of Jews in Portugal is usually stated to have emigrated in consequence of the persecutions of the fifteenth and sixteenth centuries; but there is little doubt that the writers who have treated of this great exodus of the Jewish race from the Peninsula have very much overrated the extent of the emigration, so far at least as Portugal is concerned. Immense numbers were driven out of Spain by the cruel bigotry of Ferdinand and Isabella.

They left Spain by various issues, and embarked for Italy, Turkey, Morocco, and the Levant. Very many, perhaps the majority, made their way across the border into Portugal, where numerous communities of Portuguese Jews already existed, and had come to be treated with comparative fairness. In Portugal they had long been allowed to appoint judges of their own tribe, and were otherwise favoured. They had attained a high degree of culture: they studied medicine, science, and letters. Among a rude people of warriors and husbandmen, the Jews succeeded, to some extent, to the place left vacant by the Moors. They were the authors, the merchants, and the physicians of the nation: they founded a famous academy in Lisbon, which produced several eminent mathematicians, grammarians, poets, theologians, botanists and geographers. The first book printed in Portugal was printed by a Jew.

When the last of the Moors had been banished from Andalusia by the conquest of Granada, King Ferdinand and Queen Isabella turned the edge of their intolerance against the Jews; who were in such numbers and of such social and commercial importance that, in the opinion of a Jewish historian of these events, the Israelites of Spain, if they had not kept their eyes constantly fixed upon Palestine as their own destined country, would have been strong enough to overthrow the Spanish Government! According to the Jewish writer, Da Costa, no less than eight hundred thousand of the richest, most industrious, and most intelligent subjects of Spain were driven from her shores by the edict of her Most Catholic Sovereigns. It is not too much to say that the moral and material decadence of Spain dates from that day; for, from that time forward, the triumph of religious bigotry progressed till it reached the stupid fanaticism of Philip II., and the virtual extinction, under his reign, of all individual thought and movement.

The Spanish Jews who crossed into Portugal hoped for a good reception from the King, John II.; but they were received upon hard conditions, a poll tax was at once exacted from them, and they were only permitted to remain eight months in the country, under penalty of being sold as slaves. When the eight months had expired, many of them who were unable to leave the country were enslaved, their children were baptised and taken from them.

The death of King John, and the accession to the throne of King Emmanuel, did little to improve their lot. He released the Jews enslaved by his predecessor, but his own "piety" and the Spanish influences exerted upon him through his projected marriage with the daughter of Queen Isabella, led him in 1496 to issue a decree ordering the immediate conversion of all Moors and Jews, under pain of banishment. King Emmanuel was, however, one degree more prudent than the Spanish sovereign; fearing to lessen the population of his small kingdom by so large an emigration, he commanded that all children under fourteen should be detained and converted to Christianity. There can be no doubt that this cruel but politic order induced many Jews to embrace Christianity. The Jewish histories dwell on the complete national exodus, both from Spain and Portugal, and they paint in strong colours the heroic adherence to their religious convictions both of Spanish and Portuguese, and the terrible sufferings they underwent in consequence; nevertheless, the evidence of physiognomy and of family tradition are all against this alleged universality of the movement, and, if a change of name had not been made compulsory in the days of persecution, so also undoubtedly would be the evidence of names. There are, unquestionably, innumerable families of Jewish lineage in Portugal, and Israelitish blood flows in the veins of many noble Portuguese families. It is related that when that foolish bigot, King Joseph, proposed to his minister Pombal that all Jews in his kingdom should be compelled to wear white hats as a distinctive badge, that sagacious minister made no objection, but when next he appeared in Council it was with two white hats,—" One for his Majesty and one for himself," explained

Pombal, and the King said no more about his proposal.

That great numbers of Portuguese Jews left the country is, however, notorious enough; and it is evidence of the high culture attained by the race in the Peninsula that, upon their settling in Holland, where many Jews from Germany and other parts of Europe were already gathered, the Jews of Spain and Portugal were looked upon as the aristocracy of the race.* The Peninsular Jews in Holland preserved the tradition of their origin so long and so steadfastly that the Spanish and Portuguese languages were used by them, as well as Dutch, not only in the formal services of the synagogue, but in daily life, even until the commencement of the present century.

The type of face in Braganza is, as I have said, remarkably Jewish. I was struck by it at every turn in the street. A girl in the kitchen of the inn was in features so strongly Israelitish, that I think the least observant physiognomist would have noticed it. The reason of the attraction of the Jewish race to

---

* A liberal in politics and religion may reflect with satisfaction that the cause of Protestantism and Liberal government against the bigotry of an arbitrary King of England, was furthered by a Jew whose ancestors had been driven into exile by an intolerant and arbitrary King of Portugal. It is an historical fact that William III. received considerable pecuniary advances, on the eve of his departure for England, from the Baron de Suasso, a Portuguese Jew of Amsterdam.

Braganza was, no doubt, its importance as a trading centre. A large contraband trade—a kind of commerce peculiarly suited to the subtle and energetic Israelite—was for many years carried on between Portugal and Spain. The velveteens so much worn by the Spanish peasantry are manufactured at Braganza, and, until a recent change in the Spanish tariff, were chiefly made to be smuggled across the border.

There was a gentleman in the inn at Braganza who was a traveller on horseback like myself. He lived, he told me, at Evora, but had friends and relations in Bragança. He was about to journey to Oporto, and, as our routes were to be the same for two days, I proposed to him that we should travel together. Although he had by no means the characteristic features of his race, he was, as he informed me, of Jewish extraction: This gentleman was one of the very few travelled Portuguese with whom I have met. He had visited most of the great cities of Portugal and Spain, and had been in France, Belgium, and Holland. He was full of information about his own people, and was, generally, a well-read, well-informed man. On my asking him if the rich Portuguese Jews of Amsterdam maintained any kind of relations with the members of their tribe in Portugal, he said they did; that a Portuguese or Spanish Jew going to Holland would be recognized as a sort of distant relative by families of his own name; that all Peninsular Jews and Christians of Jewish lineage retained the knowledge of their Jewish names, though they had mostly abandoned them; that ancestors of his own had settled at Amstel, in Holland, and had subsequently either established or helped to establish the celebrated porcelain manufacture of that town; that the workers at Amstel had been, almost to a man, Jews from Saxony and Portugal. He told me that many Jewish families, long after the persecution which accompanied the great exodus, and, after their seeming adhesion to the Christian religion, had emigrated to Holland when the Jews in that country obtained civil rights, and had resumed the exercise of their own religion. This, he thought, a good deal accounted for their long retention of the Portuguese tongue. He had himself met with Dutch Jews who understood Portuguese, and spoke it, but not very fluently.

I ventured to ask him if it was true, as was sometimes alleged, that many Jewish families in Portugal, professing Christianity in public, performed their own rites in private. He smiled, and said many thousands of his countrymen had been imprisoned, and tortured, and burned at the stake by the Inquisition for doing this very thing; and though his people were very clever, they were not clever enough to fight against such an instrument of persecution as the Holy Office, which considered a bare suspicion of guilt, authenticated by a single informer, to be evidence enough to send a man to the stake. I reminded him that the Inquisition had virtually long ceased to exist. He said it had, but that a sort of Inquisition still existed, and was enough to maintain a perfect uniformity of religion. The officers of the modern Inquisition, he said, were spying servants, officious neighbours, and meddling priests. "But," I suggested, "they have no tribunal to refer to now." "Indeed they have," he answered, "the tribunal of public opinion, and I would not be the man in a Portuguese town who was suspected by his neighbours of secretly practising the rites of Judaism!"

My acquaintance was evidently proud of his Jewish lineage, but it was not, it seemed to me, the common pride of high birth. There was none of that natural, if unreasoning, pleasure in tracing one's genealogy through a line of noble or illustrious ancestors, nor, what might be supposed to take the place of such a feeling in the case of a Jew, pride in being descended from a stock the most ancient and most unmixed in the world; but he seemed to be proud of belonging to a nation who, wherever their lines have fallen, have at once taken the lead over their neighbours not only in mere worldly cleverness and the art of acquiring riches, but also in every department in which they chose to exert their talents. My Jew companion told me that many of the most successful merchants in Portugal were Jews from Braganza, and he instanced several names in Lisbon and elsewhere.

He asked me if I knew what was the most difficult and best-paid trade in the world. I confessed I did not know. "Diamond-cutting," he replied, "without a question. It is an art invented by a Jew, and to this day none but Jews can work at it. If a man in New York or in Calcutta wants a diamond cut, he can have it done but in one place, and that place is Amsterdam, and all the workmen are Jews. The jewellers of London and Paris have never yet succeeded in establishing this trade in their cities; and they never will, though there is no secret in it—only cleverness."

Then he reminded me of all the great and learned Jews of Portuguese birth, whose names are possibly better known to my readers than to myself. He gave me so much information that was quite new to me, that I came to the conclusion that he was himself either a Talmudist or a learned Rabbin. He told me of David Jachia, the poet and theologian; of Isaac Avuhaf, whose *Menoraas Hammor* ("The Lamp of Light") he seemed to suppose I must be quite familiar with; and of the great Moses Ben Thaliba, whose work on Grammar, entitled *Arcenoam*, is, of course, so well known to us all. Then he asked me if I was aware that Spinosa himself, the great philosopher of Amsterdam, was born in Holland of a father and mother who were themselves of Portuguese birth? I said I was not. Thereupon he startled me considerably by demanding to know what my opinion might be upon Spinosa's system of philosophy. I question whether a harmless tourist was ever asked so searching a question before by a chance acquaintance. It has been my fortune to have submitted myself for *vivâ voce* examination in the "schools" of a certain English University; and, later in life, to have been subjected to a still more terrible public examination; but on neither of these occasions do I remember to have been so taken aback as when called upon for an impromptu opinion upon the Pantheism of Spinosa by this grave Portuguese gentleman riding by my side on the remote mountains of Traz-os-Montes. I modestly replied that I was afraid I had not given the subject so much attention as it deserved: that the system was, no doubt, an ingenious one, but that I personally did not much hold with it.

"Nor do I," said my interlocutor, eagerly; "neither do our people. Though Spinosa is, perhaps, the greatest man our race has produced, we of the house of Israel hold him in no honour. He was a recusant and an apostate from our religion.

In his lifetime he heard the execration of his own people, and the curses uttered against him in the synagogue have clung to his memory."

"To what do you allude?" I asked.

"We have a custom," he said, "that when a Jew falls away from the faith of his forefathers, and openly reviles their sacred rites and customs, he is solemnly excommunicated in the synagogue. It is a thing seldom done, because it is very horrible, and because it is seldom required; but it was done in the case of Spinosa. He was brought into the synagogue, which was hung with black: lighted tapers of black wax were held in the hands of the assembled people: the Chief Rabbi pronounced a discourse recounting Spinosa's crimes against his faith. Then all present approached the centre of the synagogue, and held their tapers sideways over a large cauldron filled with blood; and, while the candles slowly dripped their wax into the blood, a chant was sung in low, harsh tones, reciting the curses of men against the infidel, and calling down upon him the vengeance of the Most High. When the chant came to an end, the tapers were suddenly extinguished in the blood, and the synagogue was filled with darkness, and there reigned the silence of the grave."

It is satisfactory to reflect that Spinosa recovered some amount of cheerfulness after the performance of this horrible ceremony. Almost the only fact connected with his life that I can recollect is that, in late life, he used to derive amusement from making spiders fight together in a box; whereat, it is reported, he would laugh till the tears ran down his cheeks. Although personally I entertain no sympathy with the philosopher's merriment, and could look at fighting spiders by the hour without a laugh, it is pleasant to know that Spinosa was not one of those eminent characters who, after some great tragical event in their lives, "never," as our School Histories say, "were seen to smile again."

Devising of these and kindred topics, we passed through the somewhat dreary district which leads to Mirandella—a country of upland rye-fields, vines, chestnuts, and cork-trees, but showing much bare, reddish-yellow soil—a district neither fertile nor picturesque. Of Mirandella there is not more to be said than that it has a pretty name, and a pretty situation on a hill-side, with the River Tua flowing below. The inn is clean, the landlady attentive. She regaled us with "*carneiro de forno*"—so she called it—baked mutton, which is an uncommon meat in Portugal, except in the highlands. In Lisbon, Oporto and other large cities, nothing is so rare and nothing so bad as the mutton; and of the natives of all classes in these cities, probably not one in a hundred has ever tasted this meat.

The Portuguese is remarkably conservative and

little various in his dinner arrangements, and it would be safe to predicate of a thousand Portuguese of the upper and middle classes, that the dinner of nine hundred and ninety-nine of them, on any day except Friday, would consist of " *Carne com arroz,*" stewed beef and rice; not forgetting the famous " *Caldo,*" the beef broth, with cabbages, bacon, haricot beans, etc. On Friday, it would be, " *Bacalhao e batatas,*" dried cod-fish and potatoes.

My Jewish friend had some business in Mirandella the next morning, and I could not wait for him, having a long ride to Villa Real, so I started alone. I rested two hours in the heat of the day, at a farmer's house by the way. He hospitably gave my horse a feed of corn, and for my benefit he opened a bottle of very old wine, a fine strong liquor which would pass for port, setting before me with it an excellent preserve, made of pumpkins, and some wheaten bread. We are here but a league or two from the strip of land on each side of the Douro in which port wine is made, and the wine already partakes of the character of that which is made in this famous district.

My host accompanied me on his pony for a mile or two, and, the conversation having turned upon ghostly legends, he told me in the most matter-of-fact manner of one of the superstitions current among these hills; which, without being particularly interesting, is more unnaturally horrible than any belief of the kind I ever heard of. The people, he told me, believe that if a child dies before the first communion, without receiving extreme unction, the witches ("*Bruxas*") have the power of digging it up at night-time from its grave with their nails, and that having done so they carry the body into the hills and there feast upon it; and if on the way they pass a sleeping shepherd lying amidst his flock, they will drag the dead child by the hair over his body and over those of the sheep, and every living thing that this happens to dies before the morning.

Villa Real is a singular place, high up on the crest of a steep mountain, and surrounded on two sides by ancient walls, which crown a sheer precipice of several hundred feet in height, below which flows the River Corgo, full of cascades and broken water. A broad and fertile valley separates the hill on which stands Villa Real from the fine range of the Marão, which is clearly visible, from its highest peaks to its foot, from the ramparts of Villa Real. The town has a charter from King Diniz, *que fez quanto quiz*—as the popular saying of him runs—*who did what he chose;* clearly an imputation of arbitrariness suggested by the obvious rhyme, for King Dennis was, on the whole, the best and wisest sovereign the Portuguese ever had. An old church with grotesque corbel-table, in the west corner of the town, and its surrounding poor looking, granite-built houses of immense solidity, are, I have no doubt, buildings of the time of this monarch; *i.e.*, the end of the thirteenth century. The church itself is poor, and not interesting, having been repaired and restored at a much later date. Another church, off the main street, and standing detached, is more interesting. The western window is of good early fourteenth century work. The roof, in the Italian style of the early part of the seventeenth century, is curious, the whole waggon roof being divided into panels, each surrounded by a heavy gilt frame, and containing a fairly executed oil picture. As works of art they are of no value, but the effect is singularly rich.

Villa Real, though an out-of-the-way place, with a detestable climate,—" *com nove mezes de inverno e tres de inferno,*" the local proverb says :—with a long winter and a very hot summer—could never have been an agreeable place of residence, and yet, like many of the small towns in North Portugal, it seems to have been in former days the chosen home of three or four wealthy families. One fine mansion, almost a palace in size, occupies half the side of the principal "*praça,*" or square, and looks singularly out of place in so small a town.

The existence of so many magnificent private

houses in these remote country towns is in many cases due to the immense wealth brought home from India and from Brazil during the seventeenth and eighteenth centuries. Many noble families declining into poverty and insignificance, suddenly found themselves possessed of splendid fortunes; but the captains and successful adventurers in these distant lands were not always noble, and many obscure citizens of the smaller towns, whose existence had, no doubt, been forgotten for years, returned to their fellow-townsmen loaded with foreign gold. It is these latter men chiefly who built the gorgeous palaces in remote parts of Portugal; choosing rather to dazzle the inhabitants of their native towns than to live in the capital among wealthier and more courtly men than themselves.

There is nothing that would strike a traveller fresh from England, Germany, or France more than the great rarity of real country houses in Portugal. It is entirely against the genius of the people to live a country life. The Portuguese is too sociable to endure to be surrounded only by woods and fields, and mountains. He has many of our northern tastes; he likes field sports in moderation; he rides, in his own style, better than any nation in Europe except ourselves; he has a sincere delight in country life and country scenery, but he cannot long support the utter solitude of the country. A Portuguese nobleman, if he be rich enough, lives in Lisbon or Oporto, and if he has a country house will visit it for a month or two in the autumn; even then he will often rather endure the misery of a seaside lodging among a crowd than go inland. The larger of the country towns have streets full of gentlemen's houses; and here vegetate, from year to year, families who are just rich enough to live upon their incomes without working. To live, indeed, as the Portuguese do in such towns, need cost but little. A large house, with a plot of cabbages—a *kale yard* —behind it; with whitewashed walls, floors uncarpeted, a dozen wooden chairs, one or two deal tables; no fireplace, not even a stove, either in sitting-room or bed-room; no curtains to the windows, no covers to the tables; no pictures on the walls; no mirrors; no table pleasantly strewn with books, magazines, newspapers, and ladies' work; no such thing visible as a pot of cut flowers; no rare china, no clocks, no bronzes—none of the hundred trifles and curiosities with which, in our houses, we show our taste, or our want of it, but which either way give such an individual character and charm to our English homes. All these negatives describe the utterly dreary habitations of the middle-class Portuguese.

For occupations, the women do needlework, gossip, go to mass daily, and look out of window by the hour. Except the one short walk to church at eight o'clock in the morning, a Portuguese lady hardly ever appears in the streets. As for the men, they lounge about among the shops, they smoke innumerable paper cigarettes, they take a " siesta " in the heat of the day. If there is sunshine, they stand in groups at the street corner, with umbrellas over their heads; in winter, they wear a shawl over their shoulders, folded and put on three-cornerwise, as a French or English woman's shawl is worn: for this is a fashion in Portugal, and the Spaniards laugh a good deal at their neighbours on the score of their being a nation who invert the due order of things, and whose women wear cloaks and the men shawls. In these towns there is never any news, and if two men are seen in eager discussion of some matter of apparently immense importance, and if one happens to pass near enough to overhear the subject of conversation, be sure that one of them is plunged in despair or kindling with enthusiasm at a fall or rise of a halfpenny in the price of a pound of tobacco. An American gentleman of my acquaintance told me that he had never passed two Portuguese in conversation without hearing one of two words spoken, " *testão* " or " *rapariga*," finance or love!

There are not even fashions for them to think about; young men and old men dress alike, but the younger ones wear exceedingly tight boots, and "when they take their walks abroad" it is obvious that they do so in considerable discomfort. The young men, however, have one occupation more important even than wearing tight boots, and which almost, in fact, goes with it—that of making the very mildest form of love known amongst men. The process, indeed, is carried on in so Platonic a manner, and with so much proper feeling, that I doubt if even the strictest English governess would find anything in it to object to. The young gentlemen pay their addresses by simply standing in front of the house occupied by the object of their affections, while the young person in question looks down approvingly from an upper window, and there the matter ends. They are not within speaking distance, and have to content themselves with expressive glances and dumb show; for it would be thought highly unbecoming for the young lady to allow a *billet doux* to flutter down into the street, while the laws of gravitation stand in the way of the upward flight of such a document—unweighted, at least, with a stone, and this, of course, might risk giving the young lady a black eye, or breaking her father's window panes. So the lovers there remain, often for hours, feeling no doubt very happy, but looking unutterably foolish. These silent courtships sometimes continue for very long periods, before the lover can ask the fatal question, or the lady return the final answer. I heard a story of one such protracted courtship which an ingenious novelist might easily work into a pretty romance.

About forty or fifty years ago, before the suppression of convents in Portugal, a young lady was engaged to be married. For some reason or other, the marriage did not come off, and the girl was placed in a Benedictine nunnery at Oporto. Soon after came the abolition of convents; but while the monasteries were absolutely dissolved, and the monks scattered, the nuns who were already inmates of religious houses were suffered there to remain. The young lady, accordingly, on the suppression occurring did not leave the Benedictine convent. It is to be presumed, however, that the rules of this particular establishment were somewhat relaxed, for the young gentleman who had been engaged to this nun was observed to take his constant stand before the barred window of his former mistress's cell, while she would become visible behind the grating. Here the romance I have imagined would perhaps rather lack incident, and, except in a master's hand, might grow monotonous, for this hopeless courtship lasted no fewer than four-and-thirty years, till a bowed and middle-aged man paced the pavement, and looked up to a grey-haired mistress. It only ended with the death of the lady, a few years ago. Many persons have assured me that they had often been eye-witnesses of what I have described, and I found that the fact was quite notorious in Oporto. It will, of course, be understood that the stagnating life I have described, with its narrow circle of interests and its little meannesses of household detail, is confined to the half-educated, middle class inhabitants of small country towns. The higher native society of Lisbon, with its courtly influences, and that of Oporto—which holds the same relative position to Lisbon that Edinburgh did to London before the days of steam—can compare with that of any capital of Europe. The men are high-bred, courteous, and intelligent, and the ladies have a charm of manner and talents for society which all foreigners admit.

Leaving Villa Real for the banks of the Douro, my road lay through a broad fertile valley; but soon, as I ascended the ridge of mountains which separates the valley of Villa Real from the port wine district, I became entangled in a network of paths, among which I should have lost my way, had I not brought a guide. Passing six or seven miles of half-cultivated land, we gradually lost the signs of cultivation as we got to the mountain ridge; we then descended slantingly the shoulder of a great mountain, and finally, as we rounded its eastern slope, still very high up, I got the first view of the Douro, and of the country where port wine is grown—a region which, in its way, has not its equal in Europe. On either side of the river Douro lies a district, about twenty-seven miles in length and six or seven in breadth, of steep hills, with narrow, ravine-like valleys; the soil a naked, yellow-brown slaty schist; the configuration of the land like that of the South Downs at Lewes, but loftier, less rounded, and more precipitous. Looked at from where I now stood and seen in the thin atmosphere of early morning, with every detail sharp and clear as in a photograph, with hill beyond hill extending confusedly below, the appearance was that of a wilderness of utterly bare and arid peak and valley. Not a tree* and hardly a leaf was visible, for the vines, later here than in the lowlands, had as yet scarcely burst their buds. In curious contrast to this seeming barrenness are such evidences of immense human labour, as I suppose we should have to go to China or Japan to see anything to compare with. All over the sides of each acclivity, stone terraces have been built, in lines running parallel with the horizon; and in the poor, schistous soil thus kept from being washed away by

* There are plenty of olive and other trees in the wine district, but they are in the ravines and valleys, and make a scanty show in any landscape.

the rains of winter, the vines which make port wine are grown. The lines of terrace are in most places separated from each other by only a few yards; and the effect of them would be shown on paper by representing the hills first, and then drawing over their surface innumerable faint horizontal lines with a pencil. Artistically the effect is hideous; its singularity is its only attraction. A new and strange aspect is given, not to a single hill or valley, but to a whole wide range of mountains; and if Portugal were to lapse into an uninhabited wilderness to-morrow, this monument of man's accumulated handiwork would probably outlast every single work of Roman, Goth, Saracen, or Portuguese.

Soon we began to descend a very steep bridle-path—so steep, indeed, that it took in places the appearance of a stone staircase—and I was forced to lead down my horse. We reached the Douro, and I found it a bold, rapid river, running in a narrow, rocky trough. The country, though so productive, is not by any means fertile-looking, nor in the least degree picturesque.

I was now in the centre of the region of port wine production, generally spoken of as the Douro District. The flavour of the wine here produced depends upon the nature of the soil,[*] certainly not

[*] Here is a careful chemical analysis of the soil of one of the

upon its richness, for the surface of the vineyards looks like the rubbish thrown up from a stone quarry; and it depends also upon the great heat of the summer in a district shut off by lofty hills from the north and north-east. The cold of winter among these high-lying lands is, however, for Portugal, very considerable : snow falls and lies, even in the valleys, and frost often lasts for the whole twenty-four hours. This comparative cold arrests the winter growth of the vine, and gives it the rest which the plants of temperate climates require, and is probably one cause of the superiority of produce of these vines over those grown in other parts of Portugal.

The port of our forefathers was not grown in the district where the finer port wine is now produced. The little river Corgo joins the Douro a few miles below where I now found myself, and its stream divides a district of lower elevation and greater fertility from the precipitous hill country which I had but recently been contemplating. The upland vine is less productive, but makes a finer wine than that

finest vineyards in the district :—In 100 parts there are 1·30 of moisture, 3·40 of organic matter combined with water, 3·70 of sesquioxide of iron, ·80 of protoxide of iron, 6·40 of alumina, ·20 of sulphate of lime, 1·10 of magnesia, ·10 of phosphoric acid, all the above being more or less soluble in acid; and of insoluble constituents, in the same 100 parts are 2·40 of potash, 13·20 of alumina, ·40 of magnesia, ·50 of lime, and 66·50 parts of silica. This is the soil which makes the best wine in the world.

grown in the plain. "Montibus clivisque difficulter vineæ convalescunt sed firmum probumque saporem vini præbent," says Columella, and the axiom holds good still. For a long time the wines of "Embaixo do Corgo"—the land below the Corgo—alone were used in making port wine. The two bottles a day consumed by Pitt, and the four bottles of Lord Eldon were "Lower Corgo" wines. The wine is still produced, and is, in wine merchants' phrase, an "elegant" wine; but inferior in flavour and body to the wine of the "Upper Corgo." It was, no doubt, a great improvement upon the wines which were obtainable at the beginning of the eighteenth century: for instance, upon the Florentine wines, which Swift, in a letter to Stella, complains would not keep sound; and upon the red wines of Monção and the Bairrada, which upon the passing of Lord Methuen's treaty with Portugal in 1703, were imported respectively from the ports of Vianna and Figueira under the name of Portugal wine. These wines, the rougher Burgundies and, for very wealthy people, the wines of Bordeaux, were what our great-grandfathers had to choose from in the way of red wine; and it is not surprising that they came to prefer the sound, wholesome wine of the Lower Corgo, comparatively flavourless as it was, to most of its competitors; which, like the cheap claret of the present day, seem to have been, for the most part, various forms of grape vinegar made endurable with burnt sugar and gypsum.

Port wine has a literature of its own; and the controversy that a few years ago raged on the subject was almost as serious as the famous polemical dispute, in the last century, between the rival admirers of champagne and Burgundy. In the French controversy, odes, sonnets and epigrams, as well as heavy prose, were bandied from side to side: in the port wine discussion, nothing lighter than a double pamphlet or an octavo volume was discharged. A great deal of ignorant nonsense, and a great deal of interested nonsense was written on both sides; and the end of it all is that more and better wine is now made and shipped from this district than ever was known before. Lest I should be supposed, however, to wish to contribute to either of the above categories of literature, I will say no more upon the subject.

Sleeping a night at Regoa, where many of the wine merchants have houses and agents, I followed a good road on the following day to Oporto. We made a slow ascent of several leagues up the Marão Mountains, passing continuous vineyards, till Mezãofrio is reached; and the cultivated country being past, the road winds among the clefts and ravines of bluff, round-topped granite mountains, with here and there a huge boulder of stone. At the very top of the pass is the village, or rather, the solitary inn—for I saw no other house—of Quintella.

In the old times, before the road existed from Oporto to Regoa, the English wine merchants had to make the journey on horseback at the time of the vintage. On the third night they arrived at Quintella, and dined together by previous appointment—a large and friendly party. Tradition says that no small quantity of the staple of these gentlemen's business was consumed on these occasions. Mutual confidences were, no doubt, freely made; but the secresy of the grave was maintained on one point, viz., the plan each had formed for the campaign among the farmers of the wine region. Then, *cras ingens iterabimus æquor*, on the morrow each man divested himself of his sociability and rode off alone, secretly, and distrustfully of all other men, to buy the new wine.

The large room, with its painted cornice and ceiling, in which these pleasant and convivial meetings used to take place, was shown me, and the numerous tiny bed-rooms near it—*conveniently* near it.

CHAPTER VI.

Luxuriance of Vegetation on Western Slopes of Marão Hills—A Large Cactus—Affair between General Loison and Portuguese Troops at Amarante—Cinque-cento Ornamentation of Church of San Gonçalo—Sketch of Progress of Christian Architecture in Portugal—Legend of Saint Gonçalo—Undeserved Ill Repute of People of Amarante—An Unlucky and Foolish Mining Company—Curious Waterproof Cloak—Portuguese Peasantry Lineal and Unchanged Descendants of Conquerors of the Saracens and Castilians—Old Charters—Breed of Horses Crossed with Arab Blood in Moorish Times—Vallongo—Its Ancient Gold Mines—A Toy Mine at Work—Mining Prospects of Portugal—Oporto—Its History—Its Famous Siege—Is the Centre of Political and Commercial Movement in Portugal—The Douro; its Dangerous Bar—An Old Roman Beacon.

QUINTELLA is the highest point of the pass across the mountains of the Marão. A descent of about twelve miles leads down to the rich valley of the river Tamega and past the town of Amarante on its banks, famous for its wine and for its peaches. The road down to Amarante winds prettily through high-placed valleys and mountain ravines, richly clothed with cork and chestnut woods, with springs and runnels leaping noisily down the hill sides, and here and there a distant view of a valley far below, with a stream of water in its centre.

These steep and lofty hills—their height is from 3000 to 4000 feet—by cutting off the cold east winds which blow from the great Spanish plateau, and leaving the land exposed to the mild, water-laden breezes from the sea, produce a climate which is quite different from that of the eastern side of the range, the region of the port wine growth before mentioned, with the fierce heat of its summers and the excessive cold of its winters. On the seaward slopes of the hills the summers are cool and damp, and the winters comparatively warm. The fine growth of the trees and the vivid green of the grass and undergrowth testify to this; and a still more marked evidence is to be seen in the development of a particular cactus plant about half-way down the mountain. I doubt if there be many larger plants of this family in Europe. It grows on the south side of a rather lofty two-storied house, and has already reached to above the eaves. I measured the stem near the ground, and found it nineteen inches in circumference, the size of a young lady's waist.* The species is, if I mistake not, *Cactus Peruvianus*. All the tribes of cactus, gardeners tell us, require a damp summer temperature of from sixty to ninety degrees of Fahrenheit, and a winter temperature

---

* Perhaps I am libelling the fair sex. I have read in a contribution to a lady's newspaper that no young lady's waist should exceed "*thirteen* inches in circumference!"

never lower than forty degrees. Such a climate is probably very nearly that of this mountain side.

The fine old bridge over the Tamega, the picturesque group of a church and old monastic buildings on the west side, and the *tête-de-pont* on the east of the river, all show the marks of French cannon-balls; and the blackened ruins and the small round holes made by the field pieces in the walls on the east side—held by General Silveira with his Portuguese troops against the French under Loison, in 1809—are as plain as if the houses had been set in flames and the guns fired yesterday.

The church of San Gonçalo at Amarante, with its elaborate "flamboyant" façade, ornamented with life-size stone figures of the *cinque-cento* period, its red-tile covered "lantern," and western tower, is interesting as an architectural study, and as an example of how the great Christian style of architecture, falling with age into over ornamentation and over attention to elaboration of detail, and neglect of keeping, was sinking, in the end of the fifteenth century, into decadence; and how a natural reaction against its exuberance grew into the chaster and tamer art of the *cinque-cento*. When these two styles again amalgamated into the so-called "plateresque" of the Peninsula; when the architect cut and almost *chased* the stone of his buildings, in rivalry with the elaborate work of the goldsmith: when his leading idea seemed to be to make a building a huge, ornamented stone casket, such as we see in many Peninsular churches—notably at Burgos and at Batalha—architecture seemed to have absolutely taken leave of its senses. A reaction was clearly required again; and it took place, only too completely, in what may be termed the *Jesuit* style of the seventeenth century, of which all travellers in Portugal meet such innumerable and such painful examples. Plain buildings, regular in outline; the tall façade, with its belfry tower having shapeless pinnacles at the corners, often ending in flames cut in stone; the hideous sky-line, with its ugly, scroll-like curves; the statues in their niches, in affected attitudes, and clothed in half-classical drapery floating to the winds; the *Rococo* style of ornament, with all its false taste, and without any of the freedom and richness of the true *Rococo*. This style took root in about 1650, and, to the shame of Portuguese taste, it still prevails.

I have thus briefly sketched the later development of church architecture, as we see it in Portugal. Its earlier progress is peculiar, as might be expected from the isolation of the kingdom, but is in more or less harmony with the great movement in the Christian building art throughout Northern and Western Europe. The ruthless destruction of fine old Gothic churches in the seventeenth and eighteenth centuries, under the influence of the Jesuits, and their replacement by the tasteless buildings of the order, have gone a long way to make Portugal a barren country for the ecclesiologist; but, in the poorer and more out-of-the-way districts, many interesting remains of Gothic architecture are still to be found.

The first true Christian architecture in Portugal is a rude early Romanesque; then the finer massive Romanesque contemporaneous with our own so-called Norman architecture, but extending to a later date; following upon that, the various successive developments of the pointed Gothic, borrowing a little in lightness and in ornamentation from the Saracen architecture; afterwards, the well-marked, elaborate Flamboyant, coincident with our own Perpendicular, mingling, as I have shown, in its decadence with the renaissance style imported from Italy in the sixteenth century, and growing into the mad luxuriance of the "Plateresque," which the ignorant and tasteless love, and the true artist himself can hardly forbear from lingering over half-admiringly. Then the death of all true art-feeling under the cankering influence of the gloomy Jesuits—an influence curiously coincident, in time and degree, with Puritanical influences in our own country.

San Gonçalo, the patron saint of Amarante,

was a very respectable saint in the thirteenth century; and is so far connected with Amarante and its river, that he is reputed to have charmed the fish out of the Tamega, to serve as food for the crowds of workmen whom he had assembled to build the bridge at Amarante. This excellent and benevolent saint is credited with being the patron of a certain class of persons of bad repute, natives of Amarante, who are said to resort to Oporto and other large towns, and there assume a more or less public character. I am happy to be able to believe that both town and saint are libelled in this accusation.

From Amarante over a barren country to the solitary wayside inn, at Casaes, where it is better to pass the night than to go further and fare worse; from there the road brings the traveller to Penafiel, celebrated for its horse fair, and the abode of many families of gentle birth; thence through a broad, well-wooded valley, to the hills of Baltar; cutting, in one place, through a lode of copper ore, with which the road was actually metalled for nearly a hundred yards. A passing Englishman, struck by the green colour of the stones, picked up one, and found it heavy and ore-bearing. Straightway the Oporto Mining Company was formed; and some English and some Portuguese shareholders may remember that the company sank many shafts and much money in trying to come upon the vein of ore. It never *was* found, however, and the company is now wound up. I got down to look at the remains of the works; the abandoned shafts are in an orchard close to the road on the north side, and enough of very unmetalliferous looking granite has been "brought to turf" to build a church. It seems incredible that the simple expedient of following the lode by an adit on the other side of the road, where it is still visible in a low bank, never appears to have occurred to any one. They dived for it, in fact, at great expense in a place where it might have been, but was not; but they never thought of burrowing for it, and following it in a place where it actually lay before their eyes. What a sermon might a moralist not inflict on us upon this text!

There was a fair or market going on somewhere on the road, and I overtook several parties of sturdy farmers on horseback. Many of them carried long ox-goads in their hands; and as the day was rainy, they wore the curious waterproof cloak, made of rushes, which is peculiar to this province of the Minho—a waterproof which has many advantages over the very best mackintosh coat; being, in the the first place, much lighter; in the second place it does not make the wearer hot or give him a headache, nor smell of tar; in the third place, a good one costs less than a shilling. Its appearance, however, is rather against it, and the wearer looks exactly as if he were thatched with straw from head to foot. These "*palhoças*" are extensively used by all conditions of persons, and enable labouring men to do field work on the rainiest days, when the water descends in tropical torrents, and when without some such protection, no out of door labour could be done. Like many other customs and institutions in this province, where the Roman colonists have left such numerous traces of their presence, the "*palhoça*" may perhaps be an inheritance from Roman times, and may be the representative of the *Toga viminalis* of the Romans—the toga made of twigs.

It is difficult to look at these homely-looking men with this singular thatch upon them, bestriding their miserable little ponies, and to believe that both men and ponies are lineal descendants of the cavaliers and war horses who rode down the Saracens at Ourique, and the Spaniards on the field of Aljubarrota; yet neither men nor ponies can be much changed since those days. The ponies have probably degenerated and dwindled to some extent; but I see no reason why the men should have done so at all. The Christian cavalry who rode with King Alfonzo and King John were, for the most part, farmers and tillers of their own lands; and so they have continued to this time. In the early days of the monarchy, a man—that is, a warrior, for the nation was composed of fighting men—who could keep a horse at his own cost; who, without being of noble birth, was yet above the quality of the *peões*, or rank and file of the infantry, enjoyed certain privileges. The heavy "*jugada*" tax was remitted in his case; the tax that is levied on every man who could keep a yoke or "*jugo*" of oxen. If in addition to all this, he were deemed worthy, by his prowess or proved fidelity to receive the "*conthia*" or "*maravedis*"—the Royal Bounty —he was entitled *Cavalheiro de Espora dorada*, a Knight of the Golden Spur; and, we may presume, was privileged to wear a pair of them when he liked. The possession of the horse, however, was the main point; and if the animal was not forthcoming at the periodical inquisition at harvest or vintage time, the "*jugada*" was levied.*

* The morals, manners, and customs of these ancient times are so admirably and impartially exhibited in the old charters, without any of the pious exaggerations of the monkish chroniclers, or the rhetorical embellishments and political bias of later historians, that I make no apology for here and there citing a passage from them. There is certainly no pedantry in quoting dog-Latin, which a school girl could read as easily as French. The *jugada* above mentioned was less a tax than a quit rent paid for the land; and tracts of country, as often as they were conquered from the Moors, were divided not among the great captains only, but parcelled out among the more prominent of the rank and file of the army. Those who so took land were to pay the king's tax on each yoke of oxen they kept, and were to be ready to "ride by the king's hand" in his yearly

As to the horses, it is to be noticed that though they are small, seldom exceeding thirteen hands, they are moderately strong and active; and it may be doubted if any Peninsular cavalry in the old time was ever horsed upon anything larger than a Galloway of fourteen hands. The indigenous horse of every unsettled country is undersized; and the large cart-horses of England, and the heavy Flanders races are only the result of careful breeding during many generations, and rearing on abundant pasturage. The horse brought by the Saracens was the Arab; and the Arab is itself but a pony. It might have been supposed that the taller, though less active horse of Barbary would have been imported, by a race of invaders coming from the very coast where the Barb is bred; but this is certainly not the case. The high withers and other peculiarities in the shape of the Barb are traceable in his most

---

forays. They were called "*jugarios.*" The whole circumstances are set forth in a Royal Charter of 1123, and show with admirable clearness and brevity how the waste land about Viseu was to be peopled with Christian warriors, and how a new and more stringent rule was made as to the non-remission of the tax, if the horse were not duly kept. "Completo anno si cavallum non habuerit, det sua jugada. Et illos jugarios qui venerint in meam terram veniant ad forum de jugada nova." "If the knight keeps no horse during the whole year, he must pay the jugada, and those jugarios who shall settle in my lands must come in on the new jugada tenure." It is noticeable how, in this twelfth-century Latin, cases are disregarded; the language, indeed, gradually sliding into modern Portuguese.

remote descendants. The Godolphin Arabian imported into England in the time of Charles II., was, in truth, not an Arabian but a Barbary horse; and a close observer can, to this day, detect the Barb lineage in the quarters, back and withers of his descendants now upon the English turf. I have never seen the slightest trace of such descent in the horses of Portugal. So we may conclude that the Moors and Arabs brought nothing but the true Arab horse with them; and with the greater confidence as it is all but certain that the Barbary horse was the product, in later times, of an intermixture between the true Arab and an indigenous horse of the Barbary coast.

It is probable that, to the Christian possessors of the poor little hill ponies of Portugal, the advent of the Arab horse was a perfect revelation in the way of equine perfection. That warrior was a happy one who could slay a Saracen and steal his horse. Such an animal was a gift "to set before a king." How much such a present was sometimes valued is shown by a Royal grant, in 1110, to one Bernardo Franco, of certain houses in a town, curiously named Villa Boa de Satan, near Viseu, which declares that the property shall be free of all Royal dues whatever: "quia de te unum bonum cavallum accepimus quem "adduxisti de terra Maurorum,"—"because you "gave me a fine horse which you brought out of the "land of the Moors." The horse of Portugal, undersized as he is, still shows unmistakable traces of Arab lineage.*

Coming on towards Oporto, we get among the hills of Vallongo, a metal-bearing land whose mineral wealth was extracted in ancient times, either by the Phœnicians, the Romans, or the Moors, for it is not settled which. The old shafts, galleries and drifts are found in great numbers among these mountains; but it does not seem to be well established what ore was got at Vallongo. It is generally said to have been silver, which, however, the formation of the rock makes unlikely. Pieces of quartz with gold veins running through them, are sometimes picked up by the shepherds on these mountains and brought in for sale to the goldsmiths in Oporto; and a brook in the neighbourhood contains, as I myself ascertained, minute particles of gold in its sands. The rock is precisely of that character where gold may be expected to be found in its original position; *i.e.*, in quartzose veins crossing altered palæozoic slates, in the vicinity of eruptive rocks. It is probable therefore, that gold was the metal sought in the

---

* The modern Portuguese, who know nothing of a horse but how to ride him on smooth ground, are beginning very injudiciously to use the Barb—attracted by his size and substance, to breed from; the cross between this horse and the native mare is, as might be supposed, an ugly "weed," fit for nothing but the "manège." He can neither trot, gallop, jump, nor *last*.

mines on these hills; and as gold mining could not be profitably undertaken without very cheap labour, and as no nation but the Romans had a strong enough hold on the country to compel the use either of "*corvée*" or slave labour, it is probable that the mines were Roman mines, perhaps continued by the Moors.

The only mine that was being worked at Vallongo when I passed, was an antimony mine in the hill side, close behind the church of Vallongo. I went to look at it, and found it a curiosity in its way. It is quite a toy mine. The lode runs into the hill at a spot where there is a pretty wooded dell, with a little cascade tumbling down its side. The miners were three in number—a man and two boys. A small adit, or tunnel, had been made "upon the lode;" that is, following its course into the hill. A man with a pickaxe, at the further end of this tunnel, dug out a little ore, and loaded a cart on four wheels, of the size and appearance of a child's go cart, which, when full, ran on wooden rails down the inclined plane of the tunnel till it reached the works outside, and then the boys unloaded it; and while one of them dressed the ore, the other dragged the empty cart back to the miner inside. Every now and then, the man in the tunnel got tired of his work, and came out to sit down on the heap of ore and smoke a cigarette. It was an innocent little mine, and I hardly suppose there is another conducted on such simple principles, in the whole world.

There is no doubt that much profitable mining is still to be done in Portugal, though little has yet been accomplished. It is a curious fact that metal-seekers would seem hitherto to have done nothing but follow in the footsteps of the Romans. A mining engineer has informed me that he knew of no existing Portuguese mine which had not, at one time, been worked by the Romans. That people, having no powerful pumping engines, were obliged to abandon mines, however remunerative they might be proving, where the water could gain access to the works in any quantity. This gentleman told me that in a mine which he was superintending, the workmen broke into an old flooded gallery; and when the water had been pumped out, the ancient timber supports were found to be still sound, and the men picked up tool handles of obsolete forms, and Roman lamps made of pottery.

Nine miles, through a picturesque, hilly and highly cultivated country, brings the traveller to Oporto. On his way he is pretty sure to encounter long strings of mules, bearing flour to Vallongo; the same animals having carried, in the morning, the city's daily supply of wheaten bread. Almost all the bread used in Oporto is baked at Vallongo, and brought in every day on mule-back. This singular and, at first sight, uneconomical proceeding has prevailed at least since the days of King Emmanuel, in 1500, and probably long before then; and the explanation of the fact, that bread can be profitably made nine miles from where it is eaten, is that the ovens at Vallongo can be cheaply heated with the brushwood which grows abundantly on the wooded hills round that town.

Oporto is a granite-built town of over a hundred thousand inhabitants. It should be entered from the south, or by the river; for then its picturesque situation on precipitous cliffs, rising from the river's edge, can be seen to most advantage. It is a city of many fountains, and many green and flourishing gardens; but, considering its size, importance and great antiquity, it has little in it to attract the traveller. It need scarcely be remarked that the right name of the city is "Porto," the port or harbour, "O" being nothing but the definite article prefixed. We are, I believe, the only European nation who do not call the town "Porto." It lies on the north side of the river; on the south is the suburb of Gaya, which is even more ancient than Oporto. A strong castle called Calla or Cale, stood in ancient days on the chief height of Gaya, and Gaya may boast of bestowing its name upon all Portugal—*Portus Cale*, the Port of

Cale, was the name first given to the surrounding district, and in time to the whole kingdom.

Oporto somewhat forgetfully calls itself *Invicta Civitas*, the unconquered city, but it has been taken more than once. It was captured in a very memorable manner, in 1809; and it may safely be asserted that neither Goth, Moor, nor Spaniard did the city so much harm, or caused so terrible a carnage of inoffensive inhabitants as did Marshal Soult and his French troops on that occasion. The Portuguese have rather a short historical memory—I have seen the Peninsular War alluded to in an inscription on a public monument in Lisbon, as the occasion on which *the Portuguese (with their allies) drove the French out of Portugal!*—but I doubt if the nation will ever forget the awful massacre of their ancestors by the French soldiery, in the streets of Oporto.

It proved itself, however, an *Invicta Civitas* to Dom Miguel, in 1832, suffering on that occasion a siege of eleven months' duration—a siege which may almost be said to have been conducted on peace principles, so small was the effusion of blood, and so apparently slight the desire of either side to injure the other. Perhaps all past history does not afford the record of so long a siege conducted with so little energy or enterprise on either side, where so little military science was displayed, or where the crowded inhabitants of a large town were subjected to so few privations. The true explanation of this is, of course, to be sought in political causes, not in any degree in the character of the combatants. Dom Pedro was a brave man, and his brother, Dom Miguel, brave to the verge of imprudence. The contending armies were almost entirely composed of Portuguese; and no finer soldiers exist. At the siege of Oporto, both parties were playing a waiting game. However, the fate of arbitrary rule resting on priestly influences was decided by the event; and the government of the Liberals established by the energetic Dom Pedro has lasted to this day, and it is to be hoped, and indeed to be expected, that it will endure.

The Liberal Government which now happily prevails in Portugal works, on the whole, marvellously well, considering the long generations of corrupt and iniquitous rule which had preceded it. Notwithstanding the good sense of the Portuguese people, which has taught them to appreciate a representative Government and free institutions, the Liberal party and Liberal proposals were at first by no means welcomed in Portugal. The present constitutional Government of Portugal, was, in fact, established by a species of "*coup d'état*;" though Liberals here or elsewhere would probably be slow to admit it. Liberalism was, for a time, the cause of town against country—Lisbon and Oporto against the whole kingdom; indeed, for a time, it was Oporto alone against all Portugal, and Lisbon neutral. A vast majority of the people, all the priests' party, all the peasantry, and most of the smaller towns, were in favour of Dom Miguel. When Dom Pedro landed with ten thousand raw troops, to fight for his daughter's succession and the cause of freedom, his occupation of Oporto, and his proposed defence of the city against the forces of his brother, seemed, to all who did not know the imbecility of Dom Miguel and his captains, to be the proposal of a madman. The Pedroites won the day at last, and placed Donna Maria Segunda on the throne of Portugal; not through any special activity or wisdom of their own, but from the surprising folly of their opponents.

Oporto is, and ever has been, the focus of all revolution—the centre whence all change and movement, whether political or commercial, has extended through the kingdom. Surrounded by the most fertile provinces of Portugal—situated on a river more or less navigable, the chief port of shipment for the two most important staples of Portuguese production, port wine and cattle, and possessing inhabitants more enterprising and enlightened than those of other parts of the kingdom—Oporto has become an important commercial and political centre. Its commercial importance would be still greater but for the dangerous bar at the mouth of the Douro, over which vessels of more than five or six hundred tons cannot pass. The channel across the bar varies almost monthly, as the sands, brought down by the river, shift with changing winds and varying currents; and the bar is, or is ordered to be—for there is a difference—sounded and examined daily. It would scarcely be believed that, in a professedly civilized country, such a shifting channel as this, and so short a one (for the dangerous portion of it does not exceed two hundred yards in length), should not be marked out by buoys or beacons. The Portuguese are, in truth, no less than fourteen centuries behindhand in this matter; for an ancient Roman stone beacon was fished up not long ago, which had evidently served to mark a certain sunken rock, which still exists, and has made acquaintance with many a ship's bottom since this old Roman monument, inscribed "*Navigantium Salutis Causâ*"—fell from its place.

CHAPTER VII.

Foz, the Brighton of Oporto—Sea Bathing—Douro Boats—The Portuguese a Trafficking People, but not Commercially Adventurous—Churches of Oporto—Remarkable Historical Picture—The Douro, Passage of, in 1812—Curious Reputation of the Douro in Spain—Fish and Fishing in the River—Ethnology of Portugal—Variety of Races—Appearance of the People—Gold Ornaments of Moorish Design—Railway to Lisbon—Places on the Way—Marsh Scenery—Coimbra—Erroneous Tradition about Inez de Castro—University of Coimbra; its Connection with George Buchanan—Pombal—Marquis of Pombal the Bismarck of Portugal—His Life and Character—Alcobaça—Batalha, the Battle Abbey of Portugal—Its Plateresque Style of Architecture—" Tanias El Rey," meaning of—Objection to " Interviewing" Respectable People, and Reporting their Conversation—Conversation of Chance Acquaintances very Poor—An Instance.

THE entrance to Oporto by sea is very fine. The city, with its wharves and anchorage, lies three miles from the river's mouth, and the traveller who has crossed the bar exchanges, in a moment, the always unquiet waves of the Atlantic for the smooth water of the Douro, which here forms an estuary, in which are reflected the steep pine-covered hills beneath which it winds its course. At the mouth of the river is the little fishing village and watering-place of San João da Foz—the Brighton of Oporto—with its quaint red, green, and yellow houses, making pretty groups with the trees of the quintas, or gardens, the grey towers of its two or three churches, and the old granite-built castle, with its battlements and projecting bartizans. A road shaded by plane trees runs from the castle, between the river and the tall cliffs, to the city; and along this road, in the early morning of any summer or autumn day, may be seen crowds of men, women, and children, on horseback, mule-back, or donkey-back, in public calèches or in the tram-way carriages, going to and coming from their sea bath.

The Portuguese have great faith in sea bathing, and few persons take less than twenty or thirty baths in the year. It is thought that the earlier in the day and the later in the year a bath is taken, the more efficacious it is. The bathers, men and women, wear a fairly decent costume of blue or red serge. Hundreds of small square wooden frames, covered with canvas, are put up on the sands, in the bathing season, for dressing in; and these form a perfect little town, with streets and cross streets, in which it is quite easy to lose one's way. Often an unfortunate bather is seen coming out of the sea with dripping and clinging and waterlogged garments, his face and hands blue with cold, and looking in vain for his own dressing-house in a crowd of others exactly like it.

Soon after sunrise the bathers begin to arrive,

and before seven there is a very gay and noisy assembly on the sands. Flags of all colours flying over the canvas town, donkey boys vociferating to their customers, stout bathing men and women going about, wet from head to foot, and with the radiant expression peculiar to their tribe, young ladies in pretty and fantastic bathing dresses, with their black hair flying to the winds, children in red and blue hoods, bands playing, and the shouting, talking, laughing, and splashing of water, going on all at once, make up a lively and amusing scene.

We come back to Oporto along the river side road to where the ships and steamers are moored, and boats of every sort dart about the river—of every sort but steam-boats, of which there are none except the ocean steamers from ports in Great Britain. There are large, broad-beamed, sea-going fishing boats, with the pious legend, "*Deus nos guarde*," "God keep us," painted in vermilion on the sides, open boats with a huge, single lateen sail, fast sailers on and off a wind, and among the finest models in the world for getting through rough water. There is the "*Caique*," in spite of its pure Arabic name, nothing but a single-sculling dingy; the *canoa*, or "dug out," made from a single tree; the "*Tolde*" boat, which is a clumsy imitation of a gondola; the *Biga* and *Saveira*, which are narrow boats, with bows and stern peaked up to a point several feet above the water, and quaintly painted in bright patterns. These last boats are only used by the river fishermen near the sea, and are unquestionably of Oriental form and origin: the people who use them are a race differing in dress, size, features, and manners from other Portuguese, and may, perhaps, be of Greek—possibly of Phœnician—origin. Then there are the flat-bottomed wine boats, carrying a cargo of from twenty to eighty pipes of port, from the port wine country, sixty miles up the river, with their enormous square sails and powerful oar-shaped rudders, thirty or forty feet long, hung on an upright pintle or pivot, and worked, in the rapids and sharp turns of the river, by three or four men. A few strokes of this great oar-rudder bring the boat completely round. Then, again, there are the passenger boats, mostly rowed by women, which carry crowds of working men from and to their homes every morning and evening. The rowing in Portugal is mostly done standing, with the face towards the bows, as in Italy and the East; and the art of rowing sitting has only been acquired at sea-ports from foreign sailors.

All this life and movement on the river is, however, the movement of social activity only; of brisk commercial activity there is very little sign. Yet there is far more trading energy and movement among the Portonians, as they of Oporto style themselves, than among any other population in

Portugal. What trade there is is divided between Great Britain and Brazil—we having the lion's share.

The Portuguese, in truth, have never been greatly successful as traders. Their magnificent foreign conquests and discoveries never resulted in prosperous commercial relations with far-off countries. They went forth, a noble band, in their great poet's words, "dilatando a fé, o imperio," to spread their religion and their dominion, but not to extend their commerce. The great wealth they undoubtedly did acquire was, I am afraid, far more often wrung painfully from a conquered people by the exactions of the tax-gatherer, derived from the forced labour of hard-driven slaves, or extorted in the shape of bribes from the pockets of the wealthy, than acquired by any sort of legitimate commerce. The Portuguese are not born traders; they are sharp enough as traffickers in a small, peddling way; they delight in bargaining and haggling; and even a prosperous man will spend hours over a bargain on which an amount of five shillings shall depend; but they wholly lack the boldness and the spirit of adventure which distinguish the merchant from the tradesman. I have heard, more than once, of negotiations between a Portuguese and an Englishman having lasted for days; the Portuguese actually wanting spirit to close, though to do so would be to his clear advantage, and hoping that some trifle more would be conceded to him, till at last the foreigner would lose patience, and break off negotiations altogether.

Oporto possesses little of artistic or antiquarian interest. The spacious Cathedral is of early pointed Gothic—that is, it would have been if it had been left alone; but it has been modernized and *improved* out of all true Christian shape and appearance. The cloisters retain most of the ancient work, but even there the "restorer" has been at his destructive task. An immense solid silver altar, of late Renaissance work, is spoken of with great admiration by the Portuguese; an admiration excited by its size, rather than by any artistic merit it possesses. The work, however, is decidedly good for the period.

Of other churches, that of San Francisco is a fine building, singularly incrusted inside with vulgar gilt wood carving of the last century, of a bad "rococo" character. This is a style of ornament which the monks themselves manufactured; and many an interesting church has every square foot of its interior hidden under the hideous mask. The Church of San Francisco is one of the few Gothic edifices in Portugal which an English ecclesiological writer has described. Judging from an experience of English or French church architecture, he is inclined to place the date of this building at about 1280; it was, however, built by King John I., in 1404, and a careful examination of details in the work will show that it is many years later than the great monastic church at Leça do Balio, and this, we know for certain, was built in 1330—36. The fact is that the progress of mediæval church architecture in Portugal did not at all keep pace with its movement elsewhere; and the most experienced ecclesiologist is sure to make such blunders on a first inspection of Portuguese buildings.

A small church near the Rua de Cedofeita is reputed to be the oldest in Portugal. It is asserted to be a building dating from the time of the Goths; a claim to antiquity not supported by a single stone in its structure. It is a plain and very ugly building, with many restorations and additions, and is misleading to an ignorant or casual inspector of it, because the original round Romanesque arches have, in several cases, been converted by the chisel of the mason into pointed arches—of course, *surbased* and unshapely. The Romanesque capitals and mouldings are evidence enough that the pointed form has been given at a later date.

There is a collection of very poor pictures, by native artists, in the Academy, and a number of still poorer works in the Town Hall. In the offices of the great Misericordia Hospital, founded by King Emmanuel in about 1510, are preserved the portraits of all the benefactors of the institution since that period, including several kings, bishops, and officers of high rank in state and army. Such an array of horrible daubs it was never before—and I hope never will be again—my fate to contemplate. This collection, which is representative of the art of painting in Portugal, should suffice to explode the utterly untenable theory of the existence, at any period, of a great Portuguese School of Painting. There are, however, two exceptions to the level badness of these execrable productions, amounting to two or three hundred in number; one, an admirable portrait of a monk, by the so-called Portuguese painter, Glamma, who died at the end of the eighteenth century,—a work of merit enough to found a reputation upon. Glamma, however, was only a Portuguese by the mother's side; his father was an Italian.

The other exception is a large panel painting of the highest value, by a Flemish artist, of the school of Van Eyck, representing the founder, King Emmanuel, with his Queen and the youthful Princes and Princesses, kneeling in adoration before a crucifix whereon our Saviour is nailed. Above, on one side, is the figure of St. John, opposite to a fine draped figure of Our Lady. The Portuguese ascribe this picture, as they ascribe almost every ancient painting, to the mythical Gran Vasco, a Portuguese painter who is believed to have flourished in the sixteenth century. In the background is a beautiful landscape, soft and tender in tone, in which sundry details and incidents are depicted which sufficiently prove the Flemish origin of the picture— a Gothic church-tower of a purely northern type of architecture—a man using the peculiar Walloon plough, with a pair of heavy, grey Flanders horses —a flock of geese feeding in a meadow; another of sheep. All this, together with the existence of a painter's monogram, and the northern type of all the faces, enables us to ascribe the work, with absolute certainty, to a Flemish artist. The picture contains some important historical portraits: besides the King himself, there is his third wife, Queen Eleanor, daughter of King Philip of Castile; Dom João, afterwards King John III., the most prosperous sovereign of Portugal, appears as a boy of sixteen; Donna Isabel, who was married to the Emperor Charles V., is here a girl of fifteen; Prince Alfonzo is represented as a boy of ten or eleven. On the floor behind the kneeling figure is his cardinal's hat; he was made a cardinal at nine years of age, and as he was born in 1509, the date of the picture is clearly indicated as being either 1519 or 1520. Next to him is Prince Henry, who was also made a cardinal, and became king in the last few months of his life, and with whom perished the famous House of Burgundy, and the greatness and independence of Portugal.

The Douro, at Oporto, breaks through a range of granite hills, and flows through the gorge thus formed in a somewhat narrowed stream, with great depth and force of current. On the highest point of the precipitous, rocky bank on the right side of the river, are the battlemented walls and towers of the Santa Clara Nunnery; and crowning a corresponding and loftier eminence across the river are the circular church and conventual buildings of the Cruzios Monks.

This lofty and precipitous hill, known as the "Serra," commands Oporto; and the city probably owed its safety, in the long siege of 1832, to the fact of these heights being held by a portion of the garrison. Here it was that the chief part of the fighting was done during that famous leaguer. The unstopped shot-holes in the walls of the church are as good a record of the fact as the very poor and scanty chronicles we have of this siege—which as a military event, was perhaps more memorable and decisive of the fate of Portugal than any event since the great battle of Alcacer Quibir, fatal to the flower of Portuguese chivalry and to the independence of the kingdom; for the successful resistance of Oporto in 1832 broke the strength of the Absolutist usurper, Miguel, and laid the foundations of the strong Constitutional Government which has ever since prevailed.

If the traveller walks some two hundred yards along the crest of the hill on which the Serra Convent stands, he will come to a rocky hillock; and ascending this, he will have, spread out like a map beneath him, the scene of one of the boldest and most skilful feats of arms that ever was accomplished in modern war. Beneath him, at the bottom of some five hundred feet of precipitous rock, rolls the Douro—at this spot a deep and turbulent stream. A similar steep and craggy bank opposite to him is crowned by a huge, square, granite building, known as the "Seminario." Up stream from where he stands, the banks cease to be rocky or precipitous, and the river flows in a broad and gentle stream through rich meadows, and by the walls of country houses and villages.

It was on this hillock that Wellington stood, on the morning of the 12th of May, 1809. Soult was in full occupation of the north bank, and of the city opposite; he had destroyed the bridge of boats across the river; his troops had scoured both banks for miles, and had seized every boat that was to be found. Having so taken these various precautions, being in great force in a strong position, with an unfordable river between himself and the enemy, Soult considered—and according to all the rules of war, justly considered—his position to be unassailable.

The problem for Wellington was, with raw troops of which he had just taken command, to cross the river and to dispossess Soult. "Alexander the Great himself," says Napier, "might have turned from the undertaking without shame."

Wellington, having taken command of the British army but eighteen days before arriving at Oporto, had halted at Coimbra, several days' march to the south of the Douro; and dividing his troops, operated against the French by two roads—one over the mountains towards the river, on the north bank of which the French were in force; and the other by the sea, in the direct line to Oporto. Of this latter small army of 14,000 men, Wellington himself took command. The French had been encountered, and had made a stand among the woods near the ancient Monastery of Grijó, nine miles south of Oporto; but they were driven into the city, and, after crossing by it, they destroyed the bridge of boats.

Wellington arrived on the south side of the river at eight o'clock on the morning of the 12th. From the hillock I have mentioned he took in the whole position; he saw that if he could once get a few resolute men into the "Seminario," on the opposite bank, it could be held until his troops had crossed. He sent General Murray three miles up the river with the German Brigade and some squadrons of the 19th Dragoons, to search for boats; and he meanwhile caused twenty pieces of artillery to be dragged up the steep sides of the Serra. The troops were still concealed by this hill from the French garrison. In the meantime, a solitary boat had been obtained; for a poor barber of Oporto had in the night run the gauntlet of the French patrols, and come over the water in a small skiff. In this, one or two English officers and a Portuguese priest embarked, and crossing the river, returned unperceived with three or four barges. The British troops had crept up to the river's brink; and as the first boat touched the shore, an officer and twenty-five soldiers of the Buffs crowded into it, and in ten minutes were on the French side of the Douro. Others followed; the "Seminario," was gained. Then, suddenly, the alarm was sounded in the French quarters, the drums beat to arms, and masses of the enemy hurried up from all sides, and poured furiously upon the "Seminario." The citizens were seen at the windows of their houses, gesticulating and making signals to their coming deliverers.

The attack upon the small party of British was fierce, and the defence stubborn. The English leader was shot down. The French artillery began to play upon the building; but the British guns upon the Serra commanded the position, and their fire swept one approach to it. The French, however, could double their numbers every minute: they threatened to overpower the holders of the building.. Murray, with his Germans, moreover, failed to come up, though he had already crossed the river. The moment was critical. Wellington himself would have crossed, but for the entreaties of those about him, and his confidence in the troops engaged. Some of the townsmen now pushed across the river in several great boats, and part of General Sherbrook's division was able to get over and to enter the city itself. The French began their retreat. Their columns, travelling towards the east, had to pass by the enclosure of the "Seminario," and our men poured a destructive musketry fire as they passed. Volleys from Sherbrook's people reached the retreating columns; guns were abandoned, and hundreds of Frenchmen fell. The passage was won; the town was taken; the French were in full retreat; and had Murray, with his Germans, but struck a single blow, the discomfiture of Soult's army would have been complete. Placed on the road of the retreating French army with the object of intercepting them, he let column after column pass him. "It was an opportunity," says Napier, forcibly, "that would have tempted a blind man to strike."

The Douro is a mighty river—rich in the crowded warehouses along its quays, rich in merchantmen which float on its waters, rich in brave deeds done on its banks, and, what perhaps is more to the purpose of the dwellers along its shores, rich in all manner of fish for food. The very water of the Douro is said by Spaniards to be fattening: "agua de Douro, caldo de pollas," *as strong as chicken broth*, say the people of Leon, where the river takes its rise. This high opinion of it does not reach so low down as Oporto. The Douro water, as it flows through Portugal, is, except in flood time, as clear as crystal; yet there would seem to be some foundation for the belief in its virtue, for nowhere have I seen such draughts of fishes as are brought ashore in the drag-nets of the fishermen. It is certainly, as a monkish author says of it, "*flumen piscosum*,"—a fish-abounding stream. The sturgeon runs up from the sea, but is seldom caught or even seen, except in the upper and shallower part of the river. The lamprey migrates from the sea in great numbers, and, creeping up eel-like by the dead waters near the banks, is caught in fixed nets wherever there is an eddy or backwater, formed by a projection of rock from the bank. The Allis shad, which the English at Oporto call the white salmon, enters the Douro, and is caught in trammels and in pocket nets—*donkey nets* they are called in Wales. Rights to the exclusive fishing of certain spots in the river favoured by these two fish have been established, probably from the time of the Visigoths. In 1255, the King of Portugal possessed " *vargas*," or fish-traps made of reeds and willows, at a place called Furada, opposite Oporto, and also at Areïnho, a little above the city; and he conceded to the people of the burgh of Gaya the privilege of taking shads and lampreys from these royal fish-traps.* Both Furada and Areïnho, are still noted resorts of these fish.

If a traveller wishes to satisfy himself how far the reputation which some writers have conferred upon the Portuguese, of being the plainest and most homely-featured people in Europe, is justified by facts, let him, on any Tuesday or Saturday morning (market days), rise before eight o'clock and mix with the crowds of peasant men and women from the neighbourhood which, on these days, fill the streets from sunrise. He will find well-featured, stalwart men, and smartly dressed women, in their various local costumes; almost all the women wearing the white shirt and tight bodice which is so universal in the female dress of the dark-complexioned races of the south of Europe. Nearly every woman wears more or fewer of the beautiful filagree gold

* " Item mando quod pescatores de meâ villâ de Gaya pesquent in meis varguis de Furada et de Areinio."

ornaments, still made upon the old Moorish patterns. The traveller will almost immediately arrive at the conclusion that these northern Portuguese, at least, have no claim to superiority of ugliness. Fine, deep-chested women with magnificent eyes, often showing the almond shape, and possessing the straight level eyebrow of the Moorish race, white and regular teeth, thick hair growing low down on the brow, the *frons tenuis* of Horace, a complexion generally transparent, with rich tones of colour; women with a good upright carriage of the body; acquired perhaps from the habit of carrying burdens on the head; firm and graceful in their walk, like women all over the Peninsula. Altogether a very high type of human being, more like the peasant women of Albano, whence the Roman artists get their best models, than those of any country I know; and, like them, it is noteworthy that the men, though fairly good looking, are not, either in features, in form, or in stature, proportionate to the women. The complexion of the northern Portuguese is mostly dark, and the hair black; but every now and then, among the peasants, one sees a man or a woman with hair and skin so light, that their owner would pass for a fair person in Germany or in England. These fair-haired individuals will generally be found to come from some of the mountain villages.

The truth is, that the reports of travellers as to Portuguese good looks are made, as a rule, from Lisbon; and of the middle and lower classes of Lisbon and its neighbourhood, little can be said in praise. Sallow and muddy complexions, sinister expressions, irregular features, ill-knit frames, and no approach to smartness in dress, make the people of southern and central Portugal appear to belong to a different race from those of the north.

The question as to the races of men which go to make up the Portuguese nation is an interesting one. Those who assert, as, I believe, it is commonly asserted, that the race has now become a perfectly homogeneous one—that is, a number of elements blended into a single nation, more or less identical throughout the country—assert that which is at complete variance with my own observation. The original constituents of Portuguese nationality are more numerous than those even of our own country. If the reader will allow me to steer clear of controversial points, and spare me a reference to authorities, I will state, in a few sentences, what is held by the more rational of Portuguese ethnologists on the subject.

It is generally supposed that the aboriginal inhabitants were of Celtic race; that the country was overrun by the Iberi, who probably came from the banks of the Rhone; and that a more or less complete immixture of these two peoples had taken place, resulting in a race known as the Celtiberians, at the time that the Romans first conquered and then colonized the country; that the Visigoths in their turn invaded Portugal and overthrowing Roman institutions, substituted their own laws and some of their customs. The Visigoths were themselves overmastered and their institutions subverted by the Arab races in the eighth century; and these Eastern conquerors spread over nearly the whole face of the land, and imposed their customs, their laws, their civilization, and everything but their religion, upon a people whom they ruled for four centuries; that finally the hybrid Gothic and Celtiberian races from the inaccessible mountain ranges of the Asturias, who had never been utterly subjugated by the Saracens, poured down from their mountain holds, and slowly retook the whole land from the Mussulmans.

The enthusiastic ethnologist may believe as much more than this as he chooses; but the most sceptical must admit so much. He must accept the Celts, the Iberians, the Romans, the Visigoths, and the Saracens, as denominators in the compound fraction which makes up the Portuguese nation; and besides these, he must take account of Greek colonies, of which we have absolute indications, if no proof; of Carthaginian conquests, of Phœnician immigration, for which, likewise, there is something to allege: of Frenchmen brought over in the train of Count Henry, the first prince of the royal line of Portugal; of Jews, who have long settled in the country. That all these elements combine, in greater or smaller proportions, to constitute the nation, is more or less demonstrable.

I have spared the reader much in not developing the views which the ingenuity of native ethnologists has brought to bear upon the origin of their countrymen. One industrious author will positively have it that Nebuchadnezzar in person visited Portugal, and left many of his countrymen behind him: his folio volume, however, is not sufficient to bring the matter home to the belief of unlearned readers. I have likewise spared him an enumeration of the various races, from the Arab of Yemen to the Berber of Mount Atlas, which were rolled together by the tide of Mahometan conquest, and which go to make up the so-called Moors of the Peninsula.

Now of course the question is, in what proportion these constituents of the nation are combined—how much of a Roman or a Goth, of a Moor or a Celt, goes to make a modern Portuguese? It is clear that neither science nor history can help us much here, for all that we find in all the historians put together are scattered notices, which, if collected, would not fill two of these pages. Common sense and common observation may lead us a little way.

My own impression is, that the history of an ancient race is often better written on their faces than in the pages of any book. If I find myself in a village of fishermen whose stature is lower than that of their neighbours; whose features have an entirely different cast from those of ordinary Portuguese; whose intonation is peculiar; who do not intermarry with their neighbours; whose boats are of different build—a build still found in the Levant; whose dress—the short kilt-like linen trousers of Eastern nations, the coloured waist-belt, and the long, brown cloth gaberdine—is a costume wholly dissimilar to anything in the country;—if I find these men at several places on the coast, notably at Oporto and Aveiro, where there are broad rivers or estuaries, if I find them always preserving their identity, always devoting themselves to the fishing of rivers, creeks, and tideways, and leaving the open sea fishing to the hardier Portuguese, I come guardedly to the conclusion that these men are the descendants of some very ancient colony of Eastern origin; and my belief fits in very comfortably with the established theory of a Phœnician immigration.

Again, if the whole population of a hill village turn out, as I ride into it, and I see that nine out of ten are brown haired and grey eyed, and some of the children and girls positively flaxen haired, I refuse to believe but that this village has some stronger infusion of Northern blood than the people dwelling on the plains. If I find other communities of purely dark haired, gipsy-looking people, with the slim figures, rounded features, long eyes, full lips, and soft olive complexion of the African Moor, I believe they have more African blood than any other. Again, there are whole towns where the people have faces so Jewish in type, that a man had need to be an ethnologist with an original theory to endeavour to prove it anything else.

Thus a man may go through the country harmlessly theorizing, and probably, if his observation be moderately acute, and his enthusiasm not too great, he will form juster ideas of the nationality of the Portuguese than if he had read many heavy folios on the subject.

I have already mentioned the profusion of gold filagree ornaments worn by the Portuguese peasant women. They are manufactured almost exclusively at Oporto; and one street, or rather one side of one street, is occupied by the goldsmiths who sell them. The actual workers are men in whose families the trade has been handed down from father to son—perhaps from the time of the Moors, for the designs on the ornaments are hardly changed since their time; and it is interesting to see the crescent and the star of Islam traced upon an ornament in the shape of the Christian cross of Malta. These same shops sometimes contain silver plate of the rare Portuguese *repoussé* work of the sixteenth century; and, still oftener, gems which are to be obtained for far less than their price in London or Paris. The Brazilian topaz is cut by Portuguese lapidaries, and is to be found often of good size. Amethysts were, I am told, procurable in Oporto, some time ago, of fabulous size and moderate price; but their growing value in the London and Paris markets in time reached this outskirt of civilization, and the day of bargains is gone by.

I have seen in these goldsmiths' shops several of the beautiful so-called *Bishop rings*, set generally with a single amethyst, chrysolite, or opal; and as such rings are intended to be worn on the forefinger, the stone set in them is usually large. The true opal, I am told, bore in Oporto, a few years ago, little more value than the common milk opal or the amethyst; and a stone the size of a man's thumb-nail might have been bought for a few pounds. Such a stone, if a good one, would, it is needless to say, be worth more than a hundred pounds. The absolute ignorance which, in these former happy days, seems to have prevailed on the subject, may be gauged by a fact that was related to me: A goldsmith had one to sell, and found an intending purchaser, who, however, did not conclude the bargain, because he feared, *from the play and fire in the stone*, that it was a fictitious one! The story will seem rather pointless to the general reader, but for the lapidary or mineralogist it will, I am certain, possess an exquisite humour; the point of it being that the opal is absolutely inimitable—the only gem indeed that is so, and therefore the one of all others that the German, Lessing, should have abstained from choosing for the apologue in his "*Nathan the Wise*," which turns upon the imitation of an opal.

To go from Oporto to Lisbon by railway takes twelve hours. The journey should not occupy more than half the time, but even this rate of speed is an improvement upon old times. A certain Richard Twiss, an English traveller in Portugal, exactly a hundred years ago, having arrived at Lisbon, says: "I hired a chase drawn by a pair of mules, and agreed with the driver that he should drag me to Oporto in nine days."

The railroad, on leaving Oporto, skirts the seashore and passes Granja, the resort of a few sea-side visitors in summer. The Portuguese have a singular taste in the matter of sea-bathing, and prefer a crowd and a good, shelving, sandy beach, to everything else in their sea-side health resorts. They neglect the quiet village of Granja, with its shaded walks through pine forests sweet with a profuse undergrowth of myrtles, for Espinho, a little further on—a place surrounded by shifting sands where no tree or shrub grows, and where the town is crowded with a fishing population; for Espinho is the centre of the sardine fishery, and the sardine is to the Portuguese all that the herring is to the Hollander, the pilchard to the Cornishman, or the haddock to the Scotchman. Espinho with its glare, its fishy breezes, and its many abominations, is yet a paradise to the Oporto tradesman. Sanitary science does not flourish in Portugal, and therefore the death rate of Espinho is neither known nor guessed. It must be terrible in the summer months.

The line passes by several interesting towns, and by some cities memorable in Portuguese history. This is true tourist ground; an easily accessible region where the traveller may comfortably wander about, guide book in hand, sleep in fairly well ordered inns, and eat tolerable meals. I have already mentioned that it is my purpose not to take the reader over beaten ground, and describe again what has been better told by others; but rather to show him the byeways of the country, and to tell him something of the everyday life and habits of the people. I shall have very little to say, therefore, about the "show places" of Portugal—about Coimbra, with its university — Thomar, with its fine conventual church—Alcobaça, with the remains of its magnificent Cistercian monastery and its abbey, which holds the tombs of the sovereigns of Portugal—Batalha, with its inimitable architecture, inimitable not always in a complimentary sense —Mafra, with its huge eighteenth-century palace and convent—and Cintra, with its shaded groves and Moorish castle. All these beautiful, famous, or magnificent things are to be easily reached and seen from different stations on the railway between Lisbon and Oporto; and upon every one of them the guidebooks have descanted, with more or less of copiousness and with more or less of correctness.

The railway passes the marsh-girt towns of Ovar, Estarreja, and Aveiro, through a country of canals, dykes, and level meadows; a country where the farmers are half fishermen and the fishermen half farmers; where men are for ever engaged in their high-prowed, canoe-like boats, fishing up the weed which grows in the stagnant lagoons to serve for manure to the land, and where earth and water are so intermingled that barges in full sail seem to be passing through the midst of corn-fields. The whole country is a series of Dutch pictures; but there are features which go to make up the landscape here, which the painter never sees in the Low Countries. There are cattle, of a shape and rich tawny colour such as Snyders or Potter never beheld; there is the graceful, waving rice plant, the luxuriant growth of huge feathery reeds and bulrushes, such as no Northern painter could find the models of in his native marshes and moorlands; and there are the picturesque, red-sashed boatmen, and their high-prowed, gaily painted skiffs, in place of the burly Dutch boor and his clumsy *trek-shuyt;* and, above all, there are such glories of bright Southern light and warm shadow, such sunsets and sunrises, with their golden haze and accumulated splendours of colouring, as even Cuyp or Both never dreamt of.

Next comes Coimbra; a city dear to every educated Portuguese, for at Coimbra is the university at which almost every Portuguese who has attained distinction in letters or in law has been taught. The town lies upon a hill side, looking down upon the river Mondego, whose gently flowing stream and pleasant banks have been sung in the verses of nearly all the poets of Portugal, who had learnt to love them while they were *alumni* at Coimbra.

I leave it to the guide-books to describe the scene of the assassination of the beautiful Inez de Castro, and to go into the necessary raptures over an unfortunate young lady, whose romantic frailty and dramatic death have done as much as the poets to make her the national heroine of the sentimental Portuguese. But I must protest against "Murray's" recording the very obvious misrepresentation inscribed upon a tree in the Quinta das Lagrimas, where

Inez lived,—"*Eu dei sombra á Inez formosa*" (*I gave shade to the lovely Inez*). It is very simple and pretty, and deserves to be true; nevertheless, it is false at first glance, for the simple reason that the tree is a so-called Goa cedar, and the species could only have been introduced into Portugal about two hundred years after the death of Inez de Castro. So are guide-books written!

The university system at Coimbra is professorial, as in Germany and Scotland; not tutorial, as at our two great universites. There is a small literary fact connected with one of its professors, in the sixteenth century, which may interest our men of letters at home. The celebrated George Buchanan was for some years a professor at Coimbra.* There is every probability of his having been the friend and instructor—for he was twenty-two years his elder—of the great Portuguese poet, Ferreira, the precursor of Camoens, who polished, refined, and classicized the Portuguese language almost to the same extent that Pope and Dryden did our own tongue. That the essentially classical Ferreira should have availed himself of the instructions of a man like Buchanan —the most brilliant scholar of his century, and the best writer of Latin prose and verse perhaps since

* Bayle makes Buchanan's residence in Portugal last six years. Unfortunately for his influence upon Portuguese literature, most of these years were spent in the prisons of the Inquisition.

the age of Statius and the Younger Pliny—is so probable as to be akin to a certainty.

Leaving Coimbra, the line goes due south to Pombal, whence the Marquis of Pombal, the Bismarck of Portugal, derived his title, and where he spent his last years in banishment. Pombal was a man whose history is so bound up with that of his country that the travel writer who passes his name by without a word or two is not doing his duty by his reader.

The patriotism of Portuguese writers, or their preconceptions, either liberal or ultramontane, have hitherto stood in the way of their fair appreciation of the state of things in Portugal which Pombal was enabled to reform. An impartial and fair account of the Portuguese court and its king, the government and the people, would at the present juncture of European affairs constitute an exceedingly salutary bit of reading.

John V., whom history has named the "Magnanimous," dying in 1750, had left the kingdom in a very pitiable condition, after having misruled and ruined his country during forty-two years. He had tried to combine the magnificence and the piety of Louis XIV. with the debauchery of Louis XV. He copied Versailles at Mafra, and set up a "*Parc-aux-Cerfs*" in the convent of Odivellas. He encouraged neither learning, science, the arts, commerce, manufactures, nor agriculture. He squandered the vast treasures of his country without doing anything to further its prosperity. His inconceivable folly and extravagant superstition were almost an excuse for the indecent rapacity of churchmen during his whole reign. Confessors and panders, fiddlers, singers, dancers, and courtezans streamed in from Spain, France and Italy, and devoured what they believed to be the inexhaustible treasures of the Brazilian dependencies.

Portugal endured this monstrous rule for forty-two years, and when the king died, in 1750, the country was several millions sterling in debt. Literature only existed in the worthless and lying lives of the saints; the arts were represented by daubs depicting their histories. The navy had forgotten its old glories, and the great race of navigators and discoverers had died out. The army was completely disorganized: officers wearing the uniform of their king took service in the houses of the nobles and waited upon them at table: sentries on duty in the streets of Lisbon openly begged alms from the passers-by.

Nothing but this melancholy condition of the country could have justified the rule of Pombal. The imbecility of the king had brought about a government which may be described as ecclesiastical rule, tempered by feudalism and corruption. The obvious result of this would have been the relapse of Portugal under the dominion of Spain, from which she had now been free more than a hundred years. The character of the new king was feeble in the extreme, and nothing but the energy of Pombal saved the people their independence and the king his crown.

The great minister began life in the unpromising character of a roysterer and blackguard. Towards the end of the reign of the before-mentioned king John, the streets of Lisbon were overrun at night by bands of well-born ruffians who emulated the rowdyism of the London Mohawks. Conspicuous among these scamps was Sebastian de Carvalho, afterwards Marquis of Pombal, who in time sobered down into the statesman who was the saviour of Portugal, and who ruled the king, his master, for twenty-seven years.

Few ministers have been so completely and for so long masters of the situation. He did good work, which certainly would not have been done but for him; he checked the growing pride of churchmen and of the great nobles at a moment when they were threatening immense mischief to the State. He persecuted and banished the Jesuits. He was not a scrupulous man; he imposed his will without stopping to inquire whether he did so on any constitutional principle. Neither was he an economic philosopher of advanced views, and he forced upon the ignorant community ideas of political economy which would have made Adam Smith groan.* He set up monopolies in all directions, but as he at the same time established a reign of law and order, and afforded comparative security to property, and a prospect of continuance to commercial adventure, and as a bad system well administered is better than a good one not administered at all, it came to be that his ideas took root and throve. Commerce revived, the country grew rich; and bribery, extortion and corruption ceased, while he governed, to be absolutely rampant and in the ascendant.

Pombal was a man of extraordinary energy, courage and resources. When the city of Lisbon was thrown into a tumult of fear and despair by the great earthquake of 1755, when half the city was in ruins, and the flames were gaining on the remainder, when thousands of corpses lay unburied in the streets and in the shattered houses, when bands of desperadoes roamed through the city to rob, destroy and murder, Pombal alone seems to have kept his senses. The king is said to have asked him, in

---

* "*Trade in order to be prosperous should not be free.*" This, according to Sir Philip Francis (reputed author of "Junius," and who was attached to Lord Kinnoul's mission to Lisbon), was a favourite maxim of Pombal.

an agony of abject despondency, what was to be done, and he to have answered, "Bury the dead, and feed the living!"* It is related that for a fortnight he spent the greater part of each day and night in his carriage, seeing to the execution of his instruction; he restored order, and in time composed the minds of men. It was certainly owing to him that the court of Portugal was not transferred to Rio de Janeiro; so shaken was the confidence of king and courtiers in any sort of stability in the very order of things in Portugal, and so utterly terrified were they by this great convulsion of nature, that this measure had actually been resolved upon.

It is singular with what respect his own countrymen still regard the memory of Pombal. "Never," one of them has neatly said, "had so small a kingdom so great a minister." Though he died but ninety years ago, he is often spoken of by half-educated Portuguese almost as a hero of antiquity, whose appearance divides civilization from barbarism, a being on the confines of history and fable. To the question, "When did such and such a thing happen?" the answer will often be, "Oh,

---

* It is alleged that this memorable saying was not Pombal's, but uttered by the Marquis Alorna. It matters little who made the speech. It was Pombal who did the thing, and Portugal is a country where wise sayings are commoner than wise acts. There has never been a scarcity of epigrams in Portugal.

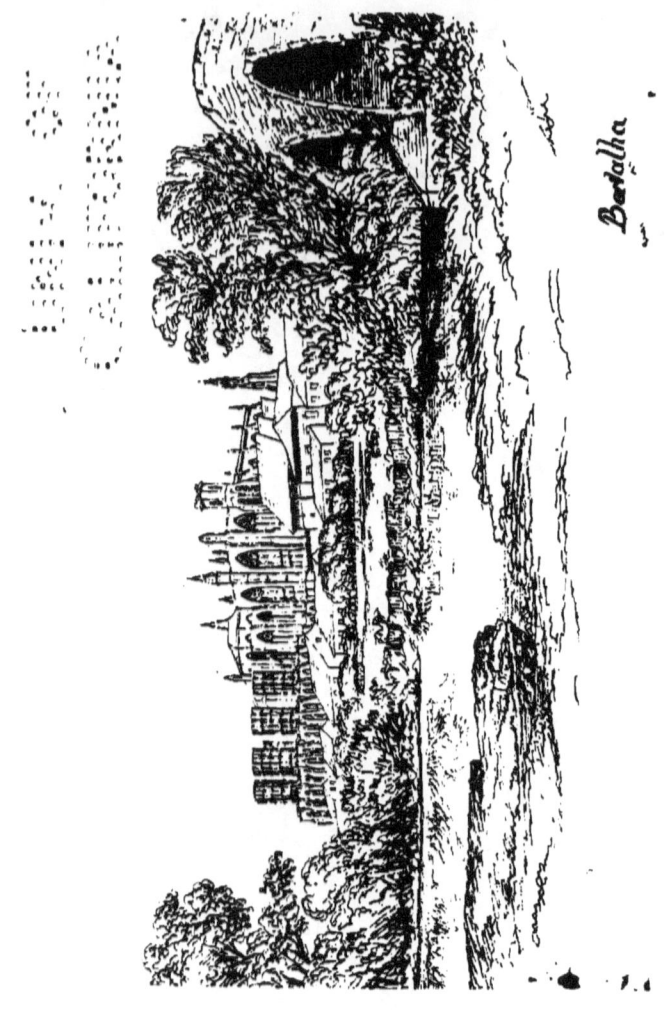

hundreds of years ago—*antes do tempo de Pombal* —before Pombal's time!"

Of course it is easy to get up a certain enthusiasm for such a man as this; but it is easier to admire this type when it has the surroundings of a Bismarck than those of a Pombal. Both, great statesmen, at once ambitious and patriotic rulers, and on the whole, benefactors of man; but while we can unreservedly admire the character of a Bismarck, because we see in it the noblest and highest development which is possible in a nation of bureaucrats and martinets who have never tasted any form of freedom, it is melancholy to see a people who had, in ancient times, carved out for themselves their independence and a noble liberty, it is melancholy to see the Portuguese bow down before a type of minister who must perforce make slaves of his fellow-men before he can either rule them, or benefit them.

Nobody who cares to look at a fine old church will pass by the abbey of Alcobaça. Of Batalha, not far from Alcobaça, it may perhaps be said that no architecture in the world ever got so many enthusiastic admirers among those who looked upon it. There is true beauty enough in the earlier work to satisfy the soundest artistic taste, and enough of tawdry superfluity of detail and of marvellously executed ornamentation to make the vulgar stare, and, to judge by the printed ecstasies on the subject, be beside themselves with admiration. The conventual buildings stand on or near the site of the great battle of Aljubarrota, which decided the independence of Portugal. It need hardly be said that the name "Batalha" has the same meaning and derivation as our own "Battle," and "Battle Abbey." Three years after the date of the battle with the Castilians, which was fought in 1385, the building was begun; and the works continued till 1515. The earlier executed portions of the church and convent are exquisite, but much of the later work is simply abominable. The whole building has been excellently criticised in the "Ecclesiologist," and a very good summary of the article will be found in "Murray."

Although a severe architectural taste must condemn much of the work of the celebrated *"Capella Imperfeita"*—the unfinished chapel, built by the great King Emmanuel—even a critical judgment is carried off its balance by the magnificence of design and the astonishing elaboration of detail in this building—the work of a genius utterly despising the common rules of architecture. A fitting monument of the king who, through the discoveries of Vasco da Gama in the eastern regions of the world, and his conquests in South America, was raised to a pitch of wealth hitherto unknown among European sovereigns. I quote from "Murray" part of his description borrowed and abridged from the "Ecclesiologist:"

> "The glory of this chapel is its western arch, surpassing in richness anything even in the cloisters. The west side of the arch has seven orders of the most elaborate foliation, springing from hollow sockets; amongst knots, flowers, and foliage, the words TANIAS EL REY have been repeated over and over again. The meaning of the words has been much disputed. The tradition of the spot is that *El Rey*, The King, is of course King Emmanuel, and that *Tanias* was his favourite chronicler. The only objection to this is, that there never was such a person as *Tanias*. Other equally inadmissible derivations have been proposed by the antiquaries."

It is certainly not a little characteristic of Portuguese archæologists that they should have occupied themselves for more than three centuries in puzzling over this curious inscription, without arriving at any conclusion. A book might be filled with the ingenious extravagances of the native antiquaries, who, with their eyes fixed on the clouds, are apt to disregard what lies at their feet. *Tanias el Rey* is, I have no doubt, only an anagram of *Arte e Linyas*. The puzzle is a good one, though not quite fair, for the *El Rey* is very misleading, and the use of the Latinized Portuguese of the period has clearly thrown the antiquaries off the scent. In Latin it would of course be *Arte et lineis*, and in modern Portuguese *Por arte e linhas*.*

* Latino-Portuguese and Latino-Spanish were not uncommon in

The motto has no very thoughtful or profound significance, but neither was the pious, prosperous, art-loving King Emmanuel a very profound or a very thoughtful person; and certainly this exquisite chapel is a signal instance of the marvellous result that a man may bring about, *arte e linyas*, by applying his artistic skill, and multiplying the traces of his hand, by stroke upon stroke, and line upon line.

I hold it to be no slight misdemeanour in a traveller to make public the ways of life and the conversations of those who have hospitably entreated him in a foreign country. Even to publish nothing but what is good of our hosts is, surely, a dire offence against good taste: but to hold up the good and the bad together, to make literary capital out of the amiable eccentricities of those who open their doors to us; to desecrate the hearth of a kindly host, that we may stimulate the curiosity of our readers; to act the part of a literary free lance, and, getting free quarters and a welcome, to cram our wallet with all we can lay hands upon that we may, in our turn, furnish forth a feast

inscriptions, epitaphs, mottoes, and other writings in which point and succinctness were sought after. The well-known legend on the sword-hilt of Isabella the Catholic, will occur to many readers, " *Deseo siempre onera: nunc caveo, pax com migo.*"

—this is surely a grave offence against the laws of hospitality, and may, if it continues, go far to destroy that noble virtue altogether. I trust I may never (in the lack of "copy") ask the public to listen while I "interview" a distinguished native, nor take my reader inside a house where I have been made a welcome guest. The reader may suffer—the reviewer may complain—but the writer, secure in his virtue, is inexorable.

There can however, of course, be nothing objectionable in any publicity given to the talk of chance acquaintance—wayfarers by coach, train, or steamer. If anything is to be gained by it, let their conversations reach a discerning public. For my own part, I have seldom been instructed or amused by the utterances of the many chance friends I have been thrown against. Men on their travels are taking in ideas, not discharging them; and the process is not interesting to their neighbours. It is notorious to all travellers by sea, how dull their shipmates become after a day or two. Dana, the American, acutely remarks that it is the having to go without their daily dose of newspaper reading which makes ocean-going travellers so little entertaining as companions; and the fact is sadly suggestive of a general poverty of ideas.

Dana is speaking of American or English travellers; foreigners, who seldom read newspapers, have not this excuse for their dulness on board ship. It is a fact, however, that a man will learn very little of, let us say, the inner life and modes of thought of his fellow-passengers, even in a long voyage. I once travelled by a large steamer, the captain of which had spent half a lifetime in conveying passengers of various nationalities, chiefly Brazilians and Portuguese. It was the first time I had encountered individuals of either nation, and I was curious.

"What sort of people do you find them?" I asked the captain one day, as we paced the quarter-deck together.

"Well, sir," he answered, "they're a queer lot, and that's the truth of it!"

"How so?"

"For one thing," said the captain, "they all of them, man, woman and child, squeeze their feet into boots that it gives a man the cramp to look at."

"And what besides?"

The captain turned short upon me, as if the second development of nationality was really almost beyond his patience.

"*When they eat roast beef, sir, they won't take a bit of mustard with it. Now, that's a fact!*"

When four or five Portuguese, of the shopkeeper or small merchant class, enter a railway carriage or a diligence where I am sitting, and talk to each other at the top of their voices for several hours at a stretch, I consider myself under no delicacy as to reporting what they say, but, if I may be believed, the report would be a dull one. The Portuguese shopkeeper in his own shop is polite, sleepy, listless, thoroughly inefficient, and apparently quite indifferent as to whether he sells his goods or keeps them. He would always rather gossip than deal, and seems to be in fear that if he diminishes his stock, he will have to be at the trouble of renewing it. He yawns across the counter at his customer, and makes a foreigner laugh at the incongruity of a man keeping things for sale, and not caring to sell them. The same man, out of his shop, is a different being—a talkative, pushing, rather noisy, and not over well-mannered person.

I have often listened to the talk of such people, and have marvelled at the deplorable vacuity of their minds. The conversation of working men and peasants is infinitely more intelligent and entertaining. They would seem to care for none of those things which stir the minds of the thinking world. I have never heard a Portuguese of this class talk rationally, with any breadth of view, or with anything but parrot-like repetition of set phrases, about politics, religion, commerce, literature or art. We know how, in our own country, there are circles in which such topics are never cared for nor spoken of, and how, among such sections of society, men and women are apt to be voluble for all time upon how A was connected with the Bs of C, and married a D, whereby he had come to be a relation by marriage of all the Es; and how each of the letters of the alphabet will, in its turn, suggest some new genealogical complication to each of the persons present.

This manner of talk is painfully prevalent among the Portuguese, and is, I think, more unendurable than at home; for, while their family histories are as long, each individual will often have as many as five Christian names, to forget one of which is an unpardonable offence.

CHAPTER VIII.

Lisbon—Cintra Overpraised—Monserrat, and the Author of Vathek—
*Moorish Palace Fort at Cintra—Pariah Dogs of Lisbon have
Ceased to Exist—Dog Hunts—Humanity of the Portuguese—Mild
Bull Fighting Practised in Portugal—Singular Tameness of
Domestic Animals—Native Newspapers—Their Timidity and
Scanty News—Curious System of Avowedly Paid Literary Criticism—Modern Art Progress in Portugal disappointing—Repoussé Work—Point Lace—Ancient Furniture—Caldas Faience—
Paintings Deplorable—The Academy Exhibition—Gran Vasco and
his supposed School.*

THERE are few more beautiful cities in the world than Lisbon. Without any particularly imposing buildings, with few churches, no parks, and only one or two good-sized squares, the first aspect of Lisbon is very striking; rising from the water's edge on its many hills, with its regular rows of tall, stately houses built of a peculiar greyish-yellow limestone, which has nearly the appearance of marble, and with everything looking bright and clean in the clear southern atmosphere.

So large a proportion of travellers to various countries touch at Lisbon, and make this city the subject of a chapter in their books—so much printed expatiation has been made upon its noble river approach, its terrible earthquake, its architecture, its squares, the exquisite beauty of Cintra, and so forth, that, following the rule I have set myself, to avoid the repetition of what has been often and well said before, and to write only of what previous observers have not cared to touch upon, I shall say nothing more of Lisbon, than that the beauties of its neighbour, Cintra, have been in my opinion greatly overpraised ever since the days of Byron and of Beckford; that its scenery owes much of the charm it possesses—and it does possess considerable charm—to the fact of the nineteen miles of road (the journey is now performed by rail) through a treeless, dusty and sun-baked country which intervene between it and the capital, and afford to Cintra, with its hills and greenery, all the charm derived from a strong contrast.

Cintra has almost as undeserved a reputation as that once enjoyed by the eccentric and conceited sensualist Beckford, who built a cockney palace in its midst. When the history of defunct reputations comes to be written, a chapter will no doubt be given to show how it was that a whole generation persuaded themselves that there was real literary mastery in the stilted periods of *Vathek*, and real architectural genius in such monstrous erections as Fonthill, in Wiltshire, and Monserrat at Cintra. This latter outrage upon architecture is now owned by a London gentleman, who has filled it with *Art Treasures* from Wardour Street—fit contents of a building which can be compared to nothing in Europe but the Pavilion at Brighton, which it somewhat resembles in general appearance, as well as in bad taste, poverty of conception, and pretentiousness. The gardens at Monserrat, however, with their rare shrubs, tree ferns, and palms, are quite lovely. They are liberally thrown open to the somewhat cockney public which frequents Cintra.

A few hundred yards from Monserrat, and near enough to form a striking contrast with it—the contrast of true with false art—is the ancient Moorish fortified Palace of Cintra. The Portuguese are fond of speaking of this building as the Alhambra of Portugal, and the phrase has been unguardedly caught up by two or three English writers of travel, of whom it may in consequence be asserted that they have not seen either one or the other of these buildings—perhaps neither. Both are ancient Moorish buildings, but Cintra is about as like the Alhambra as Kenilworth Castle is like Westminster Abbey. Moreover, the Moorish portion at Cintra is nearly quite overlaid with Christian architecture.

Old travellers used to make a great point of the dirt of Lisbon, and no doubt with perfect justice. Another stock subject with them used to be the packs of half-wild dogs which prowled over the city, and even made its streets dangerous at night-time; but these charges can no longer be made. Lisbon is now as cleanly as any large city of Southern Europe, that is, in its best parts, and in those likely to be frequented by foreigners; in its slums and crowded courts evil smells exist that might be photographed, but I have experienced as yet nothing quite so unsavoury as the atmosphere of Monmouth Street or Dudley Street, in London, and the English tourist may here again complacently point to the superiority of his native country.

As to the bands of half-wild pariah dogs, which in old days made Lisbon like an Oriental city, a great reform has been effected, and human scavengers now do the work of canine ones. The reform was not easily accomplished, for it was found difficult to diminish the numbers of the self-constituted scavengers by poison, seeing that the spectacle of dead and dying dogs in the streets aroused the susceptibilities and indignation of the inhabitants, although the animals had become a real pest. Their ever-increasing numbers are now checked by periodical hunts, which are effected at night and offend no one. A net is drawn, on a dark night, across a leading street, and the dogs of a whole neighbourhood driven towards the spot; as they become entangled in its meshes, a man kills them with a blow on the head, and throws their bodies into a cart. This method is at once more effectual and more merciful than poison; and by its employment the homeless dogs of Lisbon have come to be no more numerous than those of Paris or London.

Humanity—innate and instinctive mercifulness, as distinguished from the noisy humanitarianism of which we hear so much in these days—is very characteristic of the Portuguese people. Many evidences of such true humanity are to be met with. The bullfights of the Portuguese are singular exhibitions of imbecility on the part of all concerned, but there is no spice of cruelty in their imitation of the bloody Spanish sport, of which it may safely be alleged that no more demoralizing and brutalizing spectacles have been shown to the people since the gladiatorial combats of Imperial Rome.* In the Portuguese bullfight the bull is teased, but while neither horse nor bull is ever seriously injured, the danger to the men is positively greater than in the Spanish exhibitions of cruelty and cowardice.

* Among the various causes which have contributed to convert the most chivalrous into the least chivalrous nation of Europe, these detestable exhibitions probably hold a chief place. The loyalty and fidelity of such men as Pescara and Alva, the tone of the sixteenth century Spanish drama, the chivalrous loyalty breathed by the old Castilian romances, and, if further proof were wanting, the spirit of "Don Quixote" itself, are evidence enough of the intense loyalty of Spaniards in old times. Things are very different in the Spain of to-day, where the people seem to be incapable of loyalty either to their rulers or to their principles.

The tameness in Portugal of all domestic animals —cattle, sheep, pigs, and poultry—resulting from habitual kind treatment, is striking to a foreigner. The especial favourite of the Portuguese is the dog; and the nation differs in this respect, so far as my observation goes, from every other people of Southern Europe, among whom the dog holds a low place, compared, at least, with his estimation by the Teutonic races.

The natives of Portugal, though from motives of whimsical delicacy, they hesitate to pronounce the word *dog*,* treat the canine race with extraordinary kindness, and care for their dogs as much as we do ourselves, the traditional Moorish antipathy to the animal extending only to his name. A fanatical Mussulman has been heard to wonder at the Christian's affection for an animal which his own religion holds so low. To love one's dog is, indeed, a purely Christian virtue. The Mahometan and Brahmin despise him, and the Buddhist ranks him with swine, and sometimes eats him; it is only the Christian who has learnt to appreciate this type of attachment and fidelity. The Catholic Portuguese and the Protestant of Northern Europe can here meet on common

---

* Even in print they slide over the objectionable word with an initial and two stars, as we designate a "wicked word" in our police reports. I have seen the name of a well-known place in Lisbon, *Fonte do olho do Cão*, the fountain of the Dog's eye, printed *Fonte do olho do C***. Can a delicate susceptibility be carried further?

ground; and if the one can cite St. Francis and St. Hubert, the other can quote the authentic legend of Martin Luther to support his attachment to dogs. "Don't growl, Hans," the great reformer is known to have said to his dog, "and when the resurrection comes, I promise that you shall have a golden tail!"

An Englishman, or an American, who should expect to get much knowledge of Portuguese ways from native newspapers, would be disappointed. The newspaper fills but a small part of the life either of Spaniards or Portuguese. Religious, literary, scientific, legal and social life in Portugal are hardly reflected at all in the journals; and if it were not for the political news they contain, newspapers would probably not find readers at all. Portuguese ladies rarely take up a newspaper, and men only look to them for their politics. The speeches of the Portuguese Parliament are scantily reproduced; the most important arguments in their own law courts are seldom reported at all, and deliberate discussion on questions of home politics is hardly ever introduced into the columns of newspapers.

Their own domestic concerns, indeed, hardly seem to trouble the newspaper writers, and they visibly shrink from all strong expression of opinion on vital quests. oniI happened to be in Portugal when the so-called Iberian Question, the question of a union with Spain, was stirring the minds of all classes. Mass meetings were being held, and indignant protests were being made against the proposition, yet the newspapers, with hardly an exception, gave no echo of the strong feeling that animated public opinion. Reports of interviews between the Russian and German emperors, vague speculations on the policy of the great powers, reported conversations of Prince Bismarck or M. Thiers—all the unsubstantial rumours that fill the columns of European journals, all the *canards* started on the Boulevards of Paris, or in the clubs of London—these are what the politicians of Portugal care to read about, far more than to know and watch the doings of their own statesmen.

A modern Portuguese newspaper, on its tiny sheet, brings home to us very vividly the days of *News Letters* and *Flying Mercuries* in our own country. There is the same scantiness of domestic intelligence, the same triviality in the incidents related, the same preponderance of foreign over domestic news, and the same absence of all serious debate and argument.

Not many years ago, Mr. Bright publicly deplored the discussion of political questions by journalists, and seriously suggested that the newspaper press of Great Britain should be confined to the imparting of news alone, unaccompanied by remarks thereon. This eminent politician, departing not a little from the sound common sense which so often characterizes his political judgments, deprecated the criticism of public men and of political events by anonymous writers, and conceived that for such criticism should be substituted the utterances of politicians at public meetings. He would, in fact, prefer oral appeals to the feelings and the impulses of noisy assemblies, to calmer ones to the reason of individual readers. Under such a proposed *régime*, the Lisbon and Oporto journals would form admirable models for our "Times," "Standard," "Daily News" and "Pall Mall Gazette." Our weekly journals, dealing with political matters, our "Saturday Reviews" and "Spectators," would, of course, cease altogether to exist.

Although regular Law Reports are seldom given, the incidents which our newspapers bring together under the heading *Accidents and Offences*, are the staple of home news. The French mode of recounting the event is adopted; it is told as a story or anecdote, with as much literary artifice as the journalist can employ; and often the story is well told, and with a little dash of fun. The following description of the accumulated misfortunes of a pleasure party is in a vein of grave humour which it seems the Portuguese much appreciate:—

"On Sunday, a serious accident happened. Five individuals were on their way in a hired carriage to ——, taking with them four dozen rockets. One of the party amused himself by firing a rocket on the way, and, in doing so, unfortunately ignited the whole bundle, which began to explode in all directions, some darting out of the windows, some out of the door, and others doing no inconsiderable hurt to the persons inside. The horses took fright at the repeated explosions, and bolted through the village of ——, the unfortunate passengers adding to the terror and speed of the animals by putting their heads out of the carriage windows and screaming loudly for help. Finally, the coachman lost all command of the reins, and the horses bolted from the road and plunged into the river, where the depth of water and mud finally arrested the further progress of the vehicle. The discharge of rockets, and the cries of the half-drowning passengers still continuing, a large crowd collected on the banks, and after exertions, which lasted for several hours, the passengers (who are all seriously burnt) were drawn with ropes out of the carriage through the water and on to the shore, whence they were immediately lodged in prison, charged with breaking the public peace."

Here is a police case reported with the same somewhat grim humour :—

"An individual, calling himself Jeremy da Silva, twenty-five years of age, was charged with purchasing a water-melon without manifesting any disposition to pay for the same. The weather is at present very hot, and the water melon is a singularly agreeable remedy for the thirst occasioned thereby; but is this a reason why Jeremy da Silva should be oblivious of one of the first principles of political economy? To buy without giving an equivalent in specie is, if we may tell him so, only another name for stealing. This, also, was the opinion of the worthy magistrate. Mr. da Silva is now in prison."

This solemn banter soon gets very fatiguing to a foreigner, but it seems to have a great charm for native readers, if one may judge from its frequent occurrence.

The weather, in the dearth of more stirring topics, is a fertile theme. There happened to be a day or two of rather stormy weather, and this is how *copy* was made out of the fact:—

"THE WEATHER.—For the last two days we have undergone the unchained fury of the most rigorous winter. Wind, rain, lightning and hail, have combined to make the most astounding atmospheric disturbance. . . . ." and so on for half a column, ringing the changes upon the very tallest adjectives, and only telling the reader what he knew very well by the report of his own senses.

Perhaps the most singular of the contents of the Portuguese newspapers are the obituary notices. Written in a style so exquisitely pompous and stilted as to make the foreign reader incline at first to think them ironical, these long eulogies on the dead are paid for as advertisements, and are generally signed with the name of one of the relatives of the deceased person. A few extracts will suffice to show how false emotion and a false style can desecrate feelings which it is only commonly decent to hold back from observation:

"It is now seventy-two hours since the pious Mr. A. B. ceased to exist!

"It is now seventy-two hours since the most severe affliction has stricken the hearts of his bereaved relations in their most tender fibres!

"It is now seventy-two hours since he died, in the summer of his life, as also in the height and summer of his virtues!

"It is now seventy-two hours since this great man, great in his intelligence and in his practice of all the Christian virtues . . . .;" and so on, through a long list of paragraphs, beginning with the same minute chronological calculation, and all full of the same rhetorical foolishness. The deceased gentleman, if I recollect rightly, had kept a cigar shop in Lisbon.

Another similar and very curious development of Portuguese journalism is the insertion of paid eulogies of literary productions. I use the expression "curious" only because the payment is avowed and open, being honestly signed with the name of the friendly critic, and placed in a column set apart for advertisements. It is impossible altogether to disapprove of this practice. It is odd that it has not yet occurred to Portuguese critics to enhance the value of their approval by occasional dispraise. I have never seen an unfriendly literary critique in a Portuguese journal.

The traveller in Portugal, with any curiosity as to the development of modern art, is likely to be disappointed. Architecture is at a standstill, painting is at a low ebb, sculpture, to my knowledge, hardly exists as a Portuguese art; and the Portuguese for the last two hundred years have made no figure whatever in the arts of design; though the beautiful Portuguese *repoussé* work of the fifteenth and sixteenth centuries, the old Portuguese pointlace, the marvellously fine and massive carved black wood furniture of two hundred years ago, testify to latent faculties in this direction of a high order.

Some attempts have recently been made to establish art potteries. Imitations of majolica are produced in or near Lisbon, of a very poor sort. At Caldas da Rainha, to the north of the capital, a *faience* has been made of a very high art value—groups and figures of birds and animals, modelled with singular correctness and spirit, are covered with a thin stanniferous glaze, wonderfully rich and brilliant. I know nothing of the sort in the country which can compare with this Caldas pottery.

Painting is, as I have said, at a low ebb. In the last Paris International Exhibition, there were, as every one knows, several departments devoted to the works of modern painters belonging to each separate nation. The world looked with some astonishment at the art work of Portugal; and was inclined at first to suspect that some huge practical joke underlay the exhibition of Portuguese pictures. The serious art critic was taken aback. Immense framed canvasses were hung on the walls, on which kings and generals, regardless of perspective, bestrode horses even more remarkable in colouring and proportion than themselves. The colouring was so conscientious, the uniforms so uncompromisingly red and blue, the horses so vivid in hue, the high boots of the riders were so intensely black, the hair and whiskers of the noble personages who bestrode them so precisely corresponded in colour with their boots, that the spectators who found their way into the room were delighted: their eyes, wearied with the uniform mediocrity of the other exhibitions, rested with a sense of relief on these novel works, and shouts of laughter were to be heard all day long in the Portuguese department.

These wretched daubs were, however, not quite representative of Portuguese art. It is a small country, and not a rich one; there is little educated art criticism, and no demand for pictures of a high class; and, until recently, no state or public patronage of painters. Moreover, the Portuguese neither are, nor ever were a people with strong art sympathies like the Italians, the Flemings, or even the Dutch. Yet under all these unfavourable circumstances, this small people has produced several fairly good painters, and, if tradition may be trusted, at least one excellent artist.

There are two living Portuguese painters who would be distinguished anywhere. Senhor Resende of Oporto is a pupil of the French artist Yvon, and has done work not unworthy of his teaching. Antonio Pereira of Viseu has learnt his art from, and founded his style upon, the works of the unknown artists of the school, apparently, of the Van Eycks, whose pictures enrich the walls of the cathedral of that city. Senhor Pereira's most important work is a large altar-piece in the cathedral; pure in conception and true in design, the colouring is a little conventional, and the whole treatment somewhat "academical;" the picture is nevertheless a noticeable one. A more original work and, in my opinion, one of far higher value, is his portrait of the bishop of Viseu—lately prime minister of Portugal—a striking portrait of a fine and expressive head.

A good general notion of the art capabilities of ancient and modern Portugal can be got by a visit to the *Academia das Bellas Artes* in Lisbon. There are many pictures with good foreign names attached to them in the catalogue; but of genuine works by the great masters, I have seen no gallery in Europe with so much "canvas spread" of so little value. It is not quite proper to reduce works of high art to a money standard; but if I desired to bring the value of the collection home to the comprehension of a connoisseur or collector of paintings at home, I should do so most readily by saying that not a dozen pictures in it would bring fifty pounds at Christie's auction rooms in London, or at the Hôtel Drouot in Paris; and that the vast majority of the works would fetch less than five pounds at either of these establishments. Mediocrity and positive rubbish are the words which best describe the National Gallery of Portugal.

It would indeed be little to the credit of a small country with a by no means flourishing exchequer, had it chosen to treat itself to a really valuable national picture gallery. There has, however, been no sort of improper generosity, and the grants or government have been exceedingly scanty. With one exception the Lisbon gallery, like our own in Trafalgar Square, owes a great deal to the liberality of individuals—chief among them of Dom Ferdinand, the king's father, who in three years presented from his private income no less than £14,000 for the use of the gallery. To this munificence, and to this prince's great art knowledge and judgment, and to the zeal and taste of the Marquis de Souza Holstein, the gallery owes its existence.

It was formed in 1836, and the foundation was the stock of pictures found in the various convents suppressed in 1833. Of these pictures, five hundred and forty of the best were selected by a Government commission appointed for the purpose, and again the best of these were hung on the walls of the gallery. They are now contained in a single room, and can be studied as a whole with convenience.

These paintings, some years ago, would have been set down by almost any Portuguese as the works of Gran Vasco—the great Vasco—a renowned but mythical Portuguese painter of the sixteenth century; but they are now more cautiously ascribed, in the gallery catalogue and elsewhere, to the "ancient Portuguese school of painters." The theory adopted is that the Van Eyck style of painting was adopted by the Portuguese in about the year 1500, that they maintained its curious mannerism unchanged for no less than a hundred and fifty years. If the works in this room are representative of this singular native school, as according to this view they should be, the sooner Portuguese critics abandon a theory so little creditable to Portuguese originality and so suggestive of an almost Chinese subservience to precedent, and a quite grovelling instinct for conventionality, the better for the fame of Portuguese art.

Looking to the fact that the great poet of Portugal, keenly alive to everything that could contribute to the glory of his country, distinctly deplores the circumstance that at the very time when the painters of these canvases would have been at work, there were no Portuguese artists in Portugal, for the reason that native artists could win neither fame nor profit in their own country; looking to the fact that Flanders was at that time the Birmingham of art, and that, while Flemish studios produced some of the grandest masterpieces of the period, they sent forth an immense quantity of cheap, second-rate work in every department of art; looking to the recorded fact that when these pictures were being painted, many Flemish artists were actually in Portugal and Spain, working for the convents and churches of the Peninsula—I am absolutely convinced that the majority of these pictures are the work of Flemish painters.* Some of them were doubtless exported from the cities of Flanders, some the work of foreigners too poor in skill to hold their own in their native country; some of the very worst are perhaps too bad to have been the work of any foreign painter, and may have been accomplished by an ambitious Portuguese colour-grinder, or an idle monk with a little talent for imitation.

There is not a spark of true artistic genius, there is no sign in the best picture in the collection of anything more than a decent workman's execution. There are a sameness, a respectable mediocrity, and an evident appearance of being manufactured to order about the pictures, that make one certain of their origin; and if any picture in the collection were claimed as a gem of early Portuguese art,

* The Marquis de Souza Holstein, in his excellent introductory notice prefixed to the catalogue, has, I am sorry to say, adopted the position of the Portuguese origin of these works. He lays some stress upon representations in a few of them of Portuguese coins, architecture, and church vestments; but that this should occasionally be the case proves nothing. A foreign painter working in Portugal would, of course, imitate native objects, so far as his conventionality allowed him; but the attempt at such imitation generally breaks down. As one instance among many, let the drawing of a Portuguese cart in the picture of the "Body of St. James drawn by oxen," be examined, and it will be conceded that the construction of the common country cart—naturally familiar to every native Portuguese—was not understood by the painter.

one might be tempted to exclaim with Captain Bobadil,—

"*A Fleming! by the foot of Pharaoh! I'll buy them for a guilder apiece, an' I would have a thousand of them!*"

CHAPTER IX.

From Lisbon to Evora—Lost Fertility of Great South Tagus Plain—Fine Roman Remains at Evora—Abundance and Triviality of Roman Inscriptions—Elvas—Wrong Choice of a Guide—His Blunders, his Ghost Stories, and General Imbecility—Legend of the Seven Whistlers—The Guide's Terror—Benighted in a Forest—Recovery of Horses and Guide.

IN travelling by railway due east from Lisbon on to Evora, and thence by road towards the Spanish frontier, we are once more on ground described over and over again. We get hurried glimpses of a dismal country through the windows of the railway carriage; for a long way a dreary plain, here and there a collection of pine trees, wind-tormented and stunted, then a long reach of sand, then a canal-like stream, too sluggish for irrigation; then great sea-like prairies of heath and cistus, with scarcely a sign of human habitation or cultivation. Few inhabitants are visible anywhere, and those seen are listless, sallow and gaunt-featured, as if from breathing all their lives the ague-laden air of this inhospitable region.

A French traveller who had reached Lisbon by this route from Spain, had spoken to me but a few days before of the marvellous fertility of the country. He had talked of the great droves of pigs, of cornlands and vineyards, and of olive groves so numerous and productive that, as he picturesquely observed, the ground " seemed to be actually oozing with oil." It was not till I reached Evora and the comparatively rich country between it and the border, that I began to understand the cause of the discrepancy between the French traveller's observation and my own. He had come from Madrid by Badajoz over the interminable yellow sandy tracts which make up five-sixths of the central table-land of Spain. On reaching the Portuguese frontier he had seen well cultivated land, much chestnut wood, and many olive trees. Travelling by diligence through Elvas, he would pass through the most fertile district of the province of Alemtejo, and taking the train again at Evora, it was clear enough that my acquaintance had paid little attention to—had probably *slept through*—the melancholy tract of country which had made so strong an impression upon me.

It is something of a puzzle why this great plain to the south of the Tagus should be thus barren; the soil is deep and rich, the climate good, and it is only here and there that fevers are prevalent. An explorer coming upon such a stretch of country might well think he had found a land which should turn into an El Dorado of corn-lands, a typical wheat-producing earth, where he might match the American's thousand-acre fields, plough a straight furrow for miles in any direction, and find water conveyance for his corn to a central market; and so far as the actual capabilities of land and climate go, his expectations would be well founded. This province of the Alemtejo was once famous for its great wheat crops. The Romans called it the Sicily of the Peninsula, and the Moors made it the granary of Southern Spain and Portugal. It was a garden when the great founder of the Portuguese monarchy overthrew the Saracens, winning his decisive victory upon them at Ourique, in its midst, and laying waste this fertile province of his enemies, which has never since recovered its ancient fertility.

Political economists may settle it how they will, and may ascribe the present barrenness of Alemtejo to what and to whom they like, to want of capital or want of energy in the population. The history of Alemtejo is the history of the once fertile Roman provinces of Asia, of the great corn-producing plain of the Campania, and of Sicily itself.

At Evora there are Roman remains of great interest. Evora was at one time the Roman capital of that considerable part of modern Portugal which the Romans called Lusitania. This city, Braga in the north, and Santarem in the west, formed the triangle of Roman centres corresponding to the similar triangle in Roman England of York, Chester, and Exeter.

Here are the remains of a fine aqueduct, and the ruins of a temple to Diana, and of a tower, or, technically, a *castellum*—the reservoir for the water of the aqueduct. Both these buildings are set down to so early a period as that of Quintus Sertorius, the Roman general; that is, about seventy or eighty years B.C. These ruins, which have been perhaps not unjustly described as the finest Roman remains out of Italy, are interesting to the student of architecture, apart from their archæological value which I do not profess to assess. The well-marked Christian Romanesque of Portugal, and the long lingering of this pre-Gothic style in the country, are facts intelligible enough to one who looks upon such admirable work as this aqueduct, this temple, and this tower.

The traveller in Portugal, unless he have long before imbibed the tastes of an antiquarian, is apt to get his appetite more than satisfied with the vestiges of Roman dominion. I doubt if the monumental inscriptions in all Great Britain, all the English-Roman mosaics, baths, coins, milliary columns, put together in a single county, would lie so thickly on the ground as they do in the small district round

Evora, Elvas, and Beja. The traveller finds these remains at every step. In a house at Mertola, on the Guadiana, is a handsome square bas-relief with an inscription wanting but a letter or two. Such a monument as would make the pride of any provincial museum in France or England has only been preserved at Mertola because it made a convenient lintel to the door of a cow-house. Near Ponte de Lima, by the roadside, lies a milliary column half imbedded in the earth, with a mouldering inscription, from which a good antiquary could no doubt fix the exact position of the ancient Forum Limicorum. On the bank of the Douro, near its embouchure, and close to its very dangerous sea bar, I found lying uncared for, as I have already mentioned, the curious inscribed beacon formerly set on a rock in the main channel; but antiquarians are rare in Portugal, and to the non-antiquarian mind such inscriptions are often singularly poor in interest. The old Romans seem to have been possessed of the mania to hand down to posterity the most trifling occurrences; the proceedings of Caius and Balbus, as related by Mr. Thomas Kerchever Arnold, are eventful and important as compared with the facts I found recorded on most of these ancient stones.

Arrived at Elvas, famous for its military lines, its aqueduct, its cathedral, and its plums—all of which the optimist inhabitants fully believe to be the best and finest of known plums, cathedrals, aqueducts, and fortifications—I bought the best horse I could find, hired a guide, and started with the intention of riding through the wild country on either side of the Guadiana to the sea at its embouchure in the ancient kingdom of Algarve.

I had travelled but a little way before I made two unpleasant discoveries—one, that I had got a horse so lazy that after the first league he was continually coming to a dead stop; the other that my guide was as great a fool as he looked, which I had thought impossible. Finding that he had failed to pack up one or two of my own things, I made him turn out the contents of his own saddle-bags, and found even greater deficiencies than in my own. His forgetfulness brought home to him, he exhibited such excess of astonishment, and talked such nonsense on the subject, that I felt that the question of fool or knave must be settled forthwith.

"Francisco," I said, "either you are a greater donkey than it is permissible for a human being to be, or else you are a rogue. In either case, we must go back to Elvas," and I turned my horse's head round.

Francisco's innocence and his stupidity were triumphantly established when we reached the inn, the clothes and rugs he had forgotten being still in the room I had occupied; and the poor fellow showed so much delight at being reinstated in my good opinion that I could not find it in my heart to get rid of him. I looked well at the man to try to take some measure of the troubles I could foresee he would bring upon me. He was a well set-up young man, strong-looking, but with a shambling walk that betrayed his lack of fibre, a good-humoured face, a constant smile, a perpetual flow of conversation, and that universal sign of simplicity—a hat set on the back of his head. I determined to run my chance, on the good principle that an amiable fool is always a better companion than a sulky knave; but I made a great mistake in this instance, and I was not to get through the first day's travel without very serious cause to regret my choice of a guide.

We rode on together in a south-westerly direction, through a well cultivated, hilly country, well wooded and well watered. Towards evening our road lay over a cistus and heath covered moor, where the aromatic shrubs of various kinds reached in places to the horses' girths; a slight drizzle of rain began to set in, and the night promised to be wet and disagreeable.

"We shall reach Juromenha at about eight o'clock," said my guide, who assured me he knew every inch of the road, and could find his way blindfold.

"I am glad to hear it," I said, "for in an hour it will be quite dark."

We journeyed on in silence. The night was cloudy, and it was pitch dark, that is, as dark as it ever is where there are no trees or buildings to obscure the little light that almost always remains in the heavens. We had been moving across the level plain for some half hour. A low-lying, black cloud, dimly seen in the obscurity, got blacker and more distinct as we neared it, but not till we were almost in its shadow did I make out that it was a thick forest.

"I wonder if there are any wolves in this part of the country?" said my foolish guide in a tone of assumed indifference.

"Quite certain to be," I said; "but I thought, Francisco, you knew every inch of the country."

"So I do by daylight; but I think we should have kept the high road to the south," he said, and I went on not reassured.

"It is lucky there are no brigands, at any rate," said Francisco presently, "or else I should think twice before I entered a wood like this by night."

"They could shoot you better in the day-time," I observed.

"Ha! ha!" he laughed; "they would never be able to see us in a wood like this, would they?"

"No; but the ghosts would."

He had been plaguing me all day with very silly ghost stories.

"There are no such things," he said bravely.

I made no reply.

"Your Excellency does not really believe in ghosts?"

"I never saw one. What sort of ghosts do you mean?"

"I mean," said my guide, drawing his horse close up to mine and dropping his voice, "I mean the spirits of the dead released from purgatory and compelled to wander about the earth with witches and warlocks. They say that if they can catch a man alone on a dark night like this, coming up behind him and pouncing on him before he has time to say an 'Ave' or a 'Pater,' he is a lost man."

"But no doubt, Francisco, you carry some blessed relic or other about you, and then, you know, no ghost can do you any harm."

"No, your Excellency, worse luck! I carry no such thing. I left a little picture behind me at Elvas that was blessed by the Beata of Arifana.* I would

---

* The *Beata*, or Holy Woman, of Arifana, a small town in Northern Portugal, is a poor, bedridden old creature, who has, for I know not how many years, abstained, or all but abstained, from meat and drink, and who is miraculously elevated about a yard above her bed whenever she takes the sacrament—that is, about once a give three cruzados to have it in my pocket at this moment!"

"Never mind," I said, "I am a heretic, and the ghosts will seize me first, if they are true orthodox ghosts. Then, Francisco, do you put spurs to your horse's sides, and gallop away for your dear soul. I only hope, for your sake, the evil one was not at hand just now, when you valued it at three cruzados. If he were to take you at your word, it would be the worst bargain you ever made in your life!"

"I see your Excellency laughs at the ghosts, and, to be sure, I, myself, when I am in the wine-shop with my friends, have laughed too at these old women's stories; but if these are lies, there is no lie about the Seven Whistlers, for many a man besides me has heard them."

"And who are the Seven Whistlers?"

"Yes, to be sure, who are they? If we knew that, the priests could exorcise them so that they should not frighten honest folk at dusk on winter's nights."

"You have seen them yourself?"

"Not seen, thank heaven, or I should not be alive to tell your Excellency the story, but I have

week. Her reputation throughout Portugal has greatly extended within the last three or four years. I had the pleasure and privilege of paying this future saint a visit.

heard them plenty of times—heard them whistling and screaming in the air close over my head. Some say they are the ghosts of children unbaptized, who are to know no rest till the Judgment Day. Once, last winter, the night before the New Year, I was going with three donkeys and a mule, laden with flour, to Caia; the road passes by the bank of the river nearly all the way, and I stopped to tighten the *mulo's* girth. Just at that moment—Holy Virgin! I shook all over like a milho leaf—I say just at that moment I heard the accursed Whistlers coming down the wind along the river. I buried my head under the *mulo's* belly, and never moved it until the danger was over; but they must have passed very near, for I heard the flap and rustle of their wings as clear as I hear the tread of our horses' feet on the ground at this moment."

" And what *was* the danger?"

" The danger? Only that if a man once looks up at them, and sees them, heaven only knows what will not happen to him—death and damnation at the very least."

" When I think," said I, " that I have seen them scores of times!"

Francisco clearly did not believe me.

" And what did your Excellency do?" he asked, after a pause.

" I shot them, or tried to."

"Holy Mother of God! you English are an awful people. My father and mother have stories about your nation that I never believed till now. You shot at the Seven Whistlers?"

"Yes; we call them *marecos* (teal or widgeon), in our country, and shoot them whenever we can. They are better to eat than wild ducks."

Francisco said nothing to this. I believe he crossed himself at this revelation of irreverence, but the darkness would not let me see; I know he was terribly frightened, and presently I had good cause to wish I had dealt more patiently with his folly.

We had been going for some time through the forest, and had Francisco been the best guide in the world, he would have been out of his reckoning in a dark wood, where the cattle paths crossed and recrossed each other in every direction. I had been endeavouring to steer some sort of a course through the wilderness of trees by making from one to another opening in their tops. At last I became uncertain and puzzled, and pulled up to strike a light and consult my compass. I knew that Juromenha, which we were making for, lay on the right bank of the Guadiana, which here forms the boundary between Portugal and Spain, and at a spot where the river is joined by an affluent from the north, and therefore I felt no doubt that we should reach our destination in course of time, seeing that by keeping either south or west till we came to either river, and following its course, we must, in time, come to Juromenha. It was to be my fate, however, to pass neither that night, nor any subsequent night, within the fortified walls of Juromenha.

I pulled my horse up, and got off him to strike a match. It was a perfectly still night, with a continual drizzle of rain. I had got out my compass, and I was searching in the dark for the match-box, when a noise, quite close to us, broke upon the silence of the night, and caused my guide to start and make a pious exclamation.

"What was that?" he asked in a voice trembling with terror.

"Only a branch cracking. Don't be a fool, Francisco."

I struck three or four of the wax matches at once to make a strong light, the better to see the face of the compass. The explosion and the sudden glare startled my horse, whose rein had been dropped by the guide in his own terror, and the loose horse set off at a hand gallop through the wood, pursued by Francisco. In a few minutes they were out of hearing. Then presently I heard the returning sound of horses' hoofs coming towards me. I shouted out loudly several times, but man and horses went on unheeding, clattering through the wood like the wild huntsman and his attendant demons. The ground was uneven, and I listened anxiously, fully expecting the chase to be brought to a sudden conclusion by the precipitation of the whole party into one of the many ravines that crossed the wood; but fortune favoured them, and, finally, the sound grew less as they got further, and I heard nothing more.

It was a singularly unpromising situation. I did not know within two or three leagues where I was. During the two hours since we had been passing through the wood, we had not once seen the light of a cottage. I did not even know whether the track I was in led anywhere, or was a path used by pigs or cattle. Even should Francisco recover the horse and his senses, he would be unable to find me, for he would have lost his bearings and all knowledge of my whereabouts when the horse had doubled back, probably from having arrived at a wall or impassable ravine. So I sat down under the shelter of a chestnut-tree, struck a light, and discovered from my compass that the guide and horses had disappeared in a due northerly direction. This could certainly not lead to Juromenha, and it was useless to follow them. It was a warm, still night; the rain did not reach me through the leaves of the tree. I fortunately held in my hand, when the horse bolted, the smaller of the two pair of saddle-bags that my horse carried, and these contained what experience had taught me never to travel without, a store of bread and a skin of wine.

A man in a heavy cloak, long riding-boots, and carrying a pair of saddle-bags, is not in the condition to take a long walk in the dark, but he has all that he wants for a bivouac, and there is that—or, more correctly, there are those—about Portuguese beds and bedrooms which make the prospect of a night spent *al fresco* not altogether disagreeable. I took off my spurs, I wrapped my cloak round me, I ate some bread and wine, I leant back against the tree, and in a few minutes was fast asleep; and I must admit that I have spent many a worse night than this short summer's one that I passed in a rainstorm in a Portuguese wood, with my back against a chestnut tree.

I awoke very early, dreaming that I was at a concert whereat a solo performer on the violin drew so exquisitely plaintive and prolonged a note from his instrument, as filled me with admiration and woke me up. The musical sound was in my ears as I opened my eyes, and so distinctly, as to make me think for a moment that I was listening to the notes of a real instrument. It was a sound well enough known to every traveller in Portugal—the rubbing of the revolving wooden axletree of a cart in its groove—a noise which, heard close by, is by far the most ear-rending that I am acquainted with—a deafening sound, compounded of a shriek and a groan. The carters get accustomed to it, and the oxen are said to like it; moreover, it is sovereign against ghosts, and frightens off wolves; on which accounts, though a drop of oil would stop it, and though the friction must wear the cart and increase the labour of the oxen, the noise is endured, and even aggravated by rubbing the parts with lemon juice. But this hideous noise is much softened by distance, and heard from a mile or two off, it has a positively musical tone, not unlike the long-drawn *legato* notes of a violin.

This was the sound that woke me in the early dawn. I walked towards the cart, not a little astonishing the driver by my sudden apparition. He had heard nothing of my guide and the horses, but he advised me to enquire at the neighbouring village, and to speak to the priest, as the person most likely to know; and thither I took my way.

The village of Cruados lies six or seven miles north of Juromenha—so far had my guide led me astray. The people were already about, and the first thing I saw was the prints of the horses' hoofs in front of the priest's house; but the padre himself, apparently an important person in these parts, whose hospitable stable was no doubt well known to my runaway steed—the padre himself was from home. An old woman answered my knock with an

"Ah, Jesus!" from an upper window, then let me in, and began to explain, with horrible volubility, how the guide had come in in the middle of the night. *Coitado!*—poor fellow!—he was nearer dead than alive—he was frightened out of his senses. I had been spirited away; he could see nothing; he had heard awful sounds, and had fled for his life and his soul—and so forth.

I strode towards the stables, filled with an immense anger against my faithless guide. He was comfortably wrapped up in my rugs, lying in the wide manger—the groom's bed in a Portuguese inn —between the noses of the feeding horses. An unfriendly hand on his collar and a good shake woke him up.

"Now," I said, "you insupportable idiot, what do you mean by leaving me last night in the middle of the wood?"

"Is that really your Excellency," the man said, "alive and well?"

I gave him half-a-dozen sufficient proofs of my existence in the shape of additional shakes by the collar.

"Why did you not answer when I called to you, you rascal?"

"Was that really and truly yourself that called?"

"And what or who did you think it was."

"Who did I think it was, your Excellency?"

"Yes; who could you suppose it was but me?"

"I thought," said my foolish guide, "I really thought it must be an *alma do outro mundo*—a soul from the land of ghosts!"

This is, I am obliged to confess, the only adventure that ever occurred to me in my travels through Portugal—an admission which, I trust, the reader will accept as an apology for making so long a story of so small a matter. Portugal is a safe country; there are no brigands; the only thieves keep inns, and the only formidable wild beasts live in them.

CHAPTER X.

Hostess at Monsaras a Shrew—Her Volubility and Use of Proverbs—Spanish Frontier—Line of Demarcation Distinct between Spanish and Portuguese Character—The Portuguese Language—Affectation of the Brazilians—Portuguese Share in " Pigeon English "—Portuguese a Living and Growing Language—An Instance; Origin of Word, Fajardismo—An Intelligent Swindle—Olivença, once Portuguese, now Spanish—Radical and Important Difference between Spanish and Portuguese National Character and Institutions.

I HAD always held the people of Northern Portugal to be the greatest talkers in the country, exceeding in loquacity the people of the province of Beira, who are yet not a silent race, and greater talkers than those of the Alemtejo, who seemed to me for the most part a down-spirited and listless people; but in inexhaustible conversation the Portuguese of this south-eastern corner of the kingdom bear the palm. My guide was a great talker, the padre's housekeeper was a greater, and in the hostess of the inn at Monsaras, where we put up on the following night, I encountered a woman who was decidedly the superior of both. She was also a terrible shrew. Like Mr. Nichol's heroine, she

"Made a golden tumult in the house,"

and began very early indeed in the day. Her tongue was the last thing I heard at night, and it woke me prematurely next morning. Having heard the story of our misadventure of the previous day, she took upon herself, I know not why, to rate the guide soundly for his stupidity, telling him that he talked too much—an odd reproach from her! She bid him remember that silence was golden; that *pela bocca morreu o peixe*—his mouth was the fish's death; that *na bocca cerrada não entra moscarda*—if his lips were shut, hornets could not fly down his throat. She advised him to *fallar pouco e fallar bem, ou ter-te hão por ninguem*—to talk little and talk well, or be counted as nobody.

Proverbs are not common in Portuguese mouths, and I never heard any one who made such a trade in this second-hand species of wit as this hostess of Monsaras. Perhaps it is the close neighbourhood of Spain, and of that province of it where proverbs most abound, which influences the people of this corner of the kingdom. Andalusia is only half-a-dozen leagues from us at Monsaras, and lower down, only the Guadiana separates Portuguese and Andalusians.

There is a brisk contraband trade across the river, though it is a broad, rapid, and treacherous stream; the mountainous nature of the country on both sides, the vicinity of important trading seaports on the Spanish and the Portuguese sides of the Guadiana, make smuggling a tempting as well as a profitable speculation, so long as the two countries continue the stupidity of separate tariffs.

Notwithstanding this degree of intercourse, the line of demarcation is nearly as sharp here as I had already observed it to be on the northern frontier river of Spain and Portugal. There is that inherent antipathy between the two races which has so marvellously kept them apart, with but one short and violently-effected union, for so many long centuries —a circumstance by no means to be deplored in the interests of Portugal. "Spain and Portugal," a Portuguese gentleman once said to me, "though in such close contact at so many points, can never naturally coalesce; *they are like two men sitting back to back to each other who will never turn their heads.*"

I expected to find Spanish words and a Spanish accent in the Portuguese of this district, but I found no trace of either. The language, to be sure, is different from that of the north, and this again differs from that of Lisbon and its neighbourhood; but the difference is in no case so marked as between the English of Yorkshire and of Cornwall. In the northern provinces it is broad, in the south sharp in sound, and it is in the north that confessedly the purest idiom and purest accent are to be found. The sub-province of Beira Baixa is the Tuscany of

Portugal, and the university town of Coimbra, set in its midst, is to Portuguese what Hanover is to Germans, or Blois and Orleans to Frenchmen. The language spoken at Lisbon is by no means so pure, being a decidedly cockney Portuguese, marked by a lisping drawl, and some amount of affectation.

The Brazilians claim to speak better Portuguese than the Portuguese themselves, just as our former colonists in North America claim to have taken with them the language of Shakespeare, as well as our whole available stock of virtue and intelligence. The claim can only be admitted in either case by allowing the claimants to set up their own standards, and to judge by them. The European Portuguese affect great purism in language, and their claims to exclusive correctness are quite as ridiculous as our own and those of our American cousins. "The Brazilians talk a wretched Portuguese." A gentleman once remarked to me; "they say *Bĕlleza* instead of *Bēlleza*, as of course they ought to pronounce it. Now," he said, "what can be more thoroughly ridiculous than that?"

There is commonly repeated the error that Spanish and Portuguese are dialects of the same language, and that Portuguese is but a broken down Spanish. No one, of course, who had even a smattering of both languages—still less any one who had instructed himself ever so slightly in the early history of the Peninsula, but would know that this was a mistake. Both tongues, it is true, are constructed from the ruins of the same great ancient language—like two fine buildings both built of stones hewn from the same quarry—but the result is strikingly dissimilar. The Portuguese is, next to English, perhaps the most flexible and adaptable language in Europe. For conversational purposes it is admittedly better suited than the more formal Castilian; and if there happens to be not a single tolerable comedy in Portuguese and a hundred good ones in Spanish, it is only that the genius of Portuguese literature has not lain in that direction. The earliest and one of the best of novels in the partly romantic and partly analytical style was written, more than three centuries ago, in Portuguese. Antonio Vieyra's famous satirical *Arte de Furtar*, the *Art of Thieving*, is a masterpiece in its own picaresque style, and the same language which is so suitable to these humbler themes is the vehicle of one of the four great epics that have appeared since the new birth of letters. As a historical medium, Barros and Herculano have shown that it is nearly perfect. For travels it is admirably suited, admitting easily of every variation of narrative. The most singular recognition of the versatility of the Portuguese language is the remark I once heard from a dignitary of the Church—that it is the pleasantest of all languages to preach a sermon in.

Of all the tongues of the Peninsula, though the Galician and the Catalan seemed at one time to promise well, only the Castilian and the Portuguese have crystallized themselves into true national languages, possessing real literatures of their own and distinct characteristics; and not one whit a less true and living language than the grand speech of Spain is that spoken by the smaller nation who, though numerically but a fourth of their neighbours, have spread their race and their language* far the more widely of the two over the face of the world.

* The Portuguese must share with ourselves the responsibility for that most barbarous and ridiculous of all *lingua francas*, the "pigeon-English" of China. "Joss house," a temple, and "Joss," a god, are from the Portuguese *Dios*. The model word upon which the dialect seems to have been formed is the Portuguese *sabe*, he knows, or, do you know? It no doubt got to be a constantly repeated expletive and interrogation with those who were bungling on in the attempt to make themselves intelligible, and has become the "savey" of the modern pigeon-English. "Piccey," another indispensable word, is not from the English "piece," as is generally asserted, but from the Portuguese "peça," a much commoner and more serviceable word. It comes simply to express unity, and the "one" of the dialect is not the English "one," but obviously the indefinite article "um" in Portuguese. "One sheep" in pigeon-English is equivalent to a sheep; "one piecey sheep," a single or individual sheep. Even such reduplicated words as *chow-chow* and *chop-chop*, which give pigeon-English such a ludicrous and idiotic sound, are probably a trick of Portuguese speech. *Vai logo* is in Portuguese "go now;" *vai logo logo*, "go at once." Writers on the etymology of pigeon-English do not admit its full indebtedness to Portuguese, and oddly enough the word they do invariably trace

Portuguese, like all true languages, is a living and growing one, lending to and borrowing from its neighbours, and even coining words afresh as it needs them. It has as curious a philological history as our own, and only requires a Trench or a Max Müller, or, may we say, a Gladstone, to make this history a most interesting one.

As evidence of the readiness of the Portuguese to coin words, I will record one curious instance which has come to my own knowledge. There lives in Portugal an individual who has during several years been acquiring a certain fame of an unenviable kind. I could not do this gentleman a greater disservice than to refrain from stating that his name is Fajardo. Senhor Fajardo lives by his wits, and is not often restrained by any excessive scrupulosity from allowing full scope to his genius. As a *preux chevalier d'industrie*, he is perhaps without a rival anywhere. A tall, thin man, with a peculiar, cynical, but not disagreeable smile on his face—a face singularly like the prints of Talleyrand—he is well known in the streets of nearly every large town in Portugal. He is also not unacquainted with the interior of some of the gaols, but Fajardo has too many friends and too

---

to that language is Mandarin from the Portuguese *mandar*, to send or order—one in command. It is however certainly an imported Indian word, *mantrin*, signifying a counsellor.

much influence, and too lofty a genius, to be long restrained by iron bars. There is an element of humour about Fajardo's misdemeanors that quite redeems them from the doings of inferior criminals. A hundred stories circulate about the cleverness of this rogue. Some no doubt are the deeds of less notorious scoundrels than himself, but one particular anecdote has Fajardo for its acknowledged hero.

At Lisbon it appears that it is the custom for farmers who have for sale fields of those large and valuable onions which are exported to foreign countries to wait upon the merchants or shippers for the purpose of disposing of their crop. One year, when onions were scarce and the price particularly high, a farmer waited upon a principal merchant, and offered a small field for sale. The merchant, who had often before dealt with the farmer, offered him rather less than he asked, and the farmer went off. Next day came a person who represented himself to be the farmer's son. He brought a letter from the farmer, in which the merchant's offer was not accepted, but met half way. The merchant prepared to pay the usual earnest money, but the son, a stupid country fellow, refused to charge himself with the receipt of any money. As he was leaving, the merchant perceived a couple of large onions in his hand.

"What are those?" he asked.

"Never mind what they are," said the countryman, boorishly; "that is my affair."

But the merchant, seeing his way to another bargain, finally drew from the man that these particularly fine onions were samples of another much larger field belonging to his father, and that he was about to exhibit them to another dealer. The merchant insisted on being shown this field, and with some trouble persuaded the man to take him to a field five or six times as large as the one already bought, and filled with superlatively fine onions, he sitting on the wall of it while the merchant walked through and examined the crop.

"I offer you a hundred pounds," said the merchant, astutely naming half the true price.

"No," said the countryman, "I have been losing my time with you; my father said Mr. So-and-so would give me one hundred and fifty pounds, and that I was to have a hundred pounds of it down as earnest."

"Very well, come to my office. The field is rather bigger than I thought, and your father and I are old customers. He shall have his own price."

The countryman put the earnest-money in his bag. "Now I shall go to Mr.——, and offer him the first field; you can't want both."

"Stop!" said the merchant, "a bargain is a bargain! you have already sold it to me."

"No I have not!" cried the farmer's son, losing his temper, and shouting at the top of his voice, "you gave me no earnest. I shall go and offer it to Mr.——," and he went to the door.

"Come, come, my good fellow," said the merchant, drawing him back into the office, "business is business—an honest man has but one word. Here, take the earnest, make your mark on this receipt and go your way."

Grumbling, and half unwilling, and complaining of the badness of the bargain, the countryman suffered the coins to be counted into his hand.

It was only when the merchant sent labourers to take up his crop, and found a rival doing the same thing; it was only when he learnt that the farmer never had a son; it was only when some friend whispered the word *Fajardo* in his ear, that the merchant discovered that he, too, had fallen a victim to the terrible Fajardo.

As a story, this has little point; as an illustration of Portuguese finesse, it is particularly instructive. Fajardo's swindles have all the complexity and ingenuity of a Hindoo or Chinese intrigue. Let the mystification be examined step by step, and the completeness and long pre-arrangement necessary to bring it about, the knowledge of all the circumstances, the time and trouble necessary to inform himself of the particulars of the dealings of the merchant, the caution and the foresight, as of a skilful chess-player; his assumption of the character of a simple countryman, his skilful reticence when the money is offered, his final triumphant sweeping of the whole stakes from the table. It is, the French say, *tout un drame*, a little comedy of itself, with careful plot, brilliant dialogue, costume in character, and skilful *dénouement*—wanting indeed a moral and a "tag;" for the next thing that is heard of Fajardo is, that he is telling the story to a circle of admirers in a town a hundred miles away, and the victim, who had hoped to keep his simplicity a secret, finds the story related in detail in every newspaper he takes up.

It is this man who has the honour of having his name enshrined in his country's language. *Fajardismo*, in the sense of an ingenious swindle, is intelligible in the remotest corner of Portugal and Brazil. In ten years it will be in every Portuguese dictionary; in a hundred, probably a puzzle to philologists, and a subject for correspondence in the "Athenæum" and "Notes and Queries." I have, therefore, thought well to place on record my own personal knowledge of the origin of the word, not, indeed, anticipating that my Travels will be read a hundred years hence, but in the full confidence that some literary Fajardo will steal the story from me unacknowledged; that some one else will do as much by him, and that thus the history of the word may be handed down, by a succession of philological pilferers, to posterity. The somewhat similar origin of the French word *Bismarquer* (with a not dissimilar signification), is so connected with notorious historical occurrences, that it is never likely to be forgotten; but Fajardo's performances are known to a smaller circle.

Like the French language, Portuguese has been in peril of being *academized*, and, like the French, it has escaped from the pedants with very little hurt. Ever since the beginning of the seventeenth century, there have been attempts made by certain literary cliques to Latinize its structure, and to do away with all the character and richness it had acquired during the vicissitudes of its long growth. A certain Duarte de Leão, somewhere about the year 1600, had the wisdom to enunciate that the learned alone have the right to decide as to the currency of a word, and he protests solemnly against such barbarisms as *espirito* and *esperar;* they should, he asserts, being taken from Latin, be *spirito* and *sperar*. He would have put down all those curious phrases that the people have acquired from their contact with so many various nationalities—such Hebraisms as *riquezas e mais riquezas, loucura das loucuras,* and so forth; such quaint terms of speech as they picked up from the Arabic, like *Oxalá*, would to Allah; such words as they have got from Indian sources, as *Zumbada*, an act of reverence; *Chatim*, a merchant, and *Lascar*, which they have handed on to ourselves. Wherever the Portuguese have gone, they have brought back riches for their language, as well as wealth for themselves. Even the barbarous dialects of South America have yielded rich prize, and I have heard it said that a good Portuguese dictionary should contain at least two thousand words of Brazilian origin. A very few of them, however, are current in daily speech.

Then, as I have said, the Portuguese have lent as well as borrowed, a curious instance of which is connected with the well-known history of the old English word Aumbrey, or Almery—the receptacle for vessels from the altar. This had been most ingeniously and learnedly derived from *almary*, a word signifying cupboard in some Indian languages. Every sound philologist of course knows that this is nonsense, and that Almery comes from the good classic *armarium;* but it is not, perhaps, so generally known that the *Indian* "almary" is the Portuguese *Almario*, a cupboard, with of course the same derivation as our English Aumbrey.

I am afraid the classicists of Leão's time did succeed in banishing some good Arabic words—the Arabic *Chafariz*, a fountain, for instance, once in universal use, is now hardly more than a provincialism, having been replaced in polite circles by the Latin *fonte*. On two or three occasions, I have thought I had stumbled in remote districts upon a true Arabic word lost to common speech, and once I was able to make sure I was right. It was in the mountains of Beira, near the famous cathedral city of Viseu, a wild, roadless country, heath-covered and with long hill ridges extending to the horizon's edge. Not a roof, not a green field nor a tree was visible for miles together; and every now and then a covey of partridges, as large as grouse, starting with noisy wings from the horse's feet, made the resemblance to a Scotch moor still more perfect. It was in this wilderness, whose contact with the outer world must be very slight and very rare, that, having lost my road, I accosted a brown-cloaked shepherd tending a flock of goats and sheep, and holding up a new crown in my hand, offered it to him, if he would guide me to Viseu.

"Is it *kasmil?*" said the man, looking suspiciously at the coin.

"Is it what?" I asked; for the word is not Dictionary Portuguese.

"Is it kasmil? Is it good?"

"Take it and try," I said, putting the money into his hand. "Show me the way to Viseu and you shall have another piece as soon as I see the houses."

He girded up his loins in the most literal sense, having but one garment, a long brown cloak, reaching to the ankles, and piloted me safely to my destination, proving himself a very competent guide and an agreeable companion.

It was not till long afterwards that I found the word *kasmil* mentioned and truly explained in an old Spanish author. The word signifies *pure* or *current*, and comes from the Arabic *kadim*, ancient. *Soldos kadzimis* or *kazmis*, are silver pieces of pure metal, and the phrase often occurs in ancient Peninsular deeds and charters. The word perhaps fell into disuse when the tamperings of the Kings of Portugal with the currency of the realm did away with the propriety of its application to coin issuing from the Royal Mint.

To the question often asked, Is Portuguese a difficult language? I should be inclined to answer that it is the most difficult to an Englishman of all the languages of Southern Europe, pronunciation and idiom alike presenting greater impediments to an individual of the Teutonic races than either Spanish or Italian. There are freaks of syntax, such as a declension of the infinitive mood. It is, the only Roman language which has retained the true Latin pluperfect of the indicative, and it retains, likewise, the use of the gerund. As to pronunciation, it is a perfect mine of difficulties; it possesses no fewer than sixteen different diphthongs, of which six are more or less nasal. There are sounds in it which cannot be matched even in Russian, and one diphthong in Portuguese exists nowhere else, it is said, except in Chinese.

It is not to be wondered at, then, that Englishmen have been known to live thirty or forty years in Portugal, and speak Portuguese very much as the Frenchman of the London stage speaks English. The natives find, of course, precisely analogous difficulties in speaking English; fluently, indeed, they often speak, but it is difficult to say how badly. It was a long time a mystery to me how an intelligent people like the Portuguese could succeed in making such a hash of a language which foreigners as a rule profess to find easy, and which Italians often speak very well. I at last found the clue to the mystery in a bookseller's shop in Lisbon, in the shape of a conversation-book, from which my Portuguese friends had, I now perceived, largely borrowed. A volume on the difference in the genius of the English and Portuguese languages would not tell so much as the few extracts which I give below from this instructive little work.*

---

* I transcribe exactly from the English preface of the "*Nova Guia.*"

"A choice of *familiar dialogues*, clean of gallicisms, and despoiled phrases, it was missing yet to studious portuguese and brazilian

To resume the story of my ride from Elvas. Leaving the priest's house, we rode towards the south, passing Juromenha, a fortified town, and I abandoned for lack of time my intention to cross the

Youth; and also to persons of other nations, that wish to know the portuguese language. We sought all we may do, to correct that want, composing and divising the present little work in two parts. The first includes a greatest vocabulary proper names by alphabetical order; and the second fourty three *Dialogues* adapted to the usual precisions of the life. For that reason we did put, with a scrupulous exactness, a great variety own expressions to english and portuguese idioms; without to attach us selves (as make some others) almost at a literal translation; translation what only will be for to accustom the portuguese pupils, or foreign, to speak very bad any of the mentioned idioms. .... We expect then, who the little book (for the care what we wrote him, and for her typgraphical correction) that may be worth the acceptation of the studious persons, and especially of the Youth, at which we dedicate him particularly."

The dialogues follow the Portuguese idiom still more closely, and are for that reason still more valuable to the foreign student—hardly so much so, perhaps, to the Portuguese. For instance, "*Dialogue* 18.—FOR TO RIDE A HORSE" is a true rendering of *Para montar á cavallo*. "*He not sall know to march, he is pursy, he is foundered,*" when spoken of the same animal is, to be sure, a slight departure from our English idiom, but still intelligible. "*Dont you are ashamed to give me a jade as like?*" "*Take care that he not give you a foot's kick.*" "*Go us more, fast.*" "*Never i was seen a so much bad beast,*" are all racy and forcible rather than common phrases in English mouths. "*Let us prick,*" recalls Spenser and the "Faerie Queen." "*Pique strongly make to march him*" is also good and new, and we have no exact equivalent for the idiom. In another dialogue on shooting, occurs the following. "*Question: There is it some game in this wood? Answer: Another time there was plenty some black beasts, and thin game, &c.*" This is puzzling; *another time* is *outra vez*—formerly; *thin game* is *caça miuda*—partridges, hares, and rabbits, but *black beasts*, meaning deer, is

Guadiana, and visit the Spanish town of Olivença, which, and the transriverain strip of country, was once, and should still be, Portuguese. Taken with the assistance of Napoleon's troops in 1801, it was most solemnly stipulated at the great National Congress of 1815 that Spain was to restore it. No Spanish Government has ever yet found the shadow of an excuse for keeping the town and territory during their sixty years of wrongful occupation. It is one among the many causes which keep alive the salutary bitterness of Portugal towards her neighbour.

It will always be a subject of regret to me that I was unable to visit Olivença, which has now for three-fourths of a century ceased to be Portuguese, and to judge for myself whether the people,

beyond my interpretation. An English laundress is to be told, of a white waistcoat, "*who that be too washed, too many soaped.*" The lively author of these dialogues, confident as he may appear, is quite aware that linguistic studies have their difficulties,—"*Do you speak French?*" occurs in one dialogue. "*Some times—though i flay it yet.*" This is surely an admirable expression. No less forcible word will do justice to the sort of English spoken by most Portuguese, and the English in Portugal no doubt do similar violence to the native idiom.

Since the first publication of these Travels, Senhor M. Lewtas, the well-known Lisbon *librairiste* and an excellent literary authority, has told me that the *Nova Guia* is a Brazilian production, and was never much circulated in Lisbon. The Portuguese he maintains to be good linguists. So far as French and Spanish are concerned they are so, but, with submission to Senhor Lewtas, I do not think they are so proficient in the Teutonic languages.

like the Alsatians, are loyal to the country of their forefathers. The Portuguese agree that this is the case. It would be a curious study; and it is one of the many deficiencies of these Travels, that I cannot enter in them the record of my observations on this pseudo-Spanish soil, but must build up my theories from the wrong side of the Guadiana.

If Olivença be governed no worse than the majority of other Spanish towns, it will probably be better governed than when it was Portuguese. Municipal government in Spain is, as is well known, the best sort of government, and has often been nearly the only government, prevailing in that country. Bad as it is—for it is not without corruption—it is better than burghers' rule in Portugal. The mad imbecility of the central Spanish Government has, as all students of Peninsular history know, always been arrested on the brink of anarchy by the comparative respectability of the provincial middle and lower classes. They have acted like the weighted keel of an over crank vessel, and steadied the ship of state as she was heeling over with too much sail on.

There is just this difference between Portuguese and Spaniards—the larger nation is capable of cohesion only of small numbers; the other, of the whole people. It is not easy to say why, but all history shows that this is the case. Like some chemical substances which crystallize in a great single mass while others form a hundred crystals each coherent and perfect in itself, Portugal has always been a nation, though a small one; Spain always virtually, even under its most despotic rulers and at its greatest, an agglomeration of municipalities. When federalism was made a "cry" by the extreme party in Spain, it by no means possessed the terrors for moderate men that might have been supposed. Spanish experience of district rule was not unfavourable. In Portugal, I am inclined to think, the very reverse would be the case, and communism in any form would probably have a peculiar horror for a people who are so intimately acquainted with the shameless and almost universal corruption, the unblushing bribery, the petty intrigue and nepotism which reign in the Town Councils in Portugal.

The little kingdom is, notwithstanding, so well governed on the whole, and so generally contented, that little fear need have been entertained for its safety and prosperity, had it not been for this foul contagion, extending through one whole important class of the community; here, too, as elsewhere, there are interested and ignorant men enough to make themselves the apostles and the party of Internationalism and Red Republicanism, and there are already signs that it is time for the nation to set its house in order while

> ——— "That two-handed engine at the door
> Stands ready to smite once and smite no more."

Spain struck down and splintered into a congeries of communes would still perhaps be—political prejudice apart—a not ill-governed country; but if such a fate should ever overtake Portugal, may Heaven save her! Anarchy would be complete.

CHAPTER XI.

Juromenha—Desolate Country—Last Stand of Moors of Portugal Made in this Region—Final Wars of Moors and Portuguese Treacherous and Bloody—Sketch of History of the Great Portuguese Home Crusade—Names of Different Sorts of Christian Marauding Expeditions Preserved in Charters to Towns and Convents—Mertola—Final and Crowning Misadventure of the Guide Francisco.

JUROMENHA lies on a cliff overlooking the Guadiana, which here narrows and runs in a rapid stream. Above the town the banks of the river are low and sandy, and the river broad, shallow and fordable in places for nearly three miles. The fortifications of Juromenha, therefore, if they be well furnished with artillery (a point as to which in Portugal it is prudent not to be curious) would command the passage in case of an attack from Spain.

Following the course of the river to the sea, through a dreary district, and crossing the river, which near Monsaras, runs through wholly Portuguese territory, to Mourão, I slept there, and reached Moura, due south of it, the following day; always passing through the same desolate country, relieved here and there by some signs of cultivation, but for the most part cistus-covered, treeless, and arid. A monotonous and tiresome ride, not made more agreeable by the overpowering heat of the weather, and by the fact of my having got a slight attack of ague at Mourão, which, though going no further than headache and a feeling of oppression, warned me to hasten to the end of my journey.

As the small and ancient town of Serpa is reached, the mountains grow more rugged, and the valleys richer in cultivation.

It was in the country which I had been passing through for the last day or two, that some of the battles took place in the long crusade which ended in the expulsion of the Moors from Portugal. It was in these fastnesses that the Infidels made their last stand; in this difficult country, with a broad and rapid river in their front, and behind them the yet unconquered Moorish districts of Andalusia and Spanish Estremadura. This trans-Guadianian district had indeed been pierced long before by the first and most enterprising of the Portuguese monarchs. Serpa itself, Mertola (a little to the south), Juromenha, and other strongholds, as far as Truxillo, in Spain, were wrested from the Moors by the great Portuguese conqueror;* but the district was regained by the Moslems, and did not become

* According to both Christian and Moorish chronicles, though they differ by ten years as to the date of this extensive raid.

Christian till the best part of a century afterwards.

The fighting that was done towards the end of the wars in these outlying corners of the monarchy, was bloody and cruel. The day of chivalry had gone by. If its influence had ever done much to mitigate the ferocity on either side, or to diminish the treachery of Moors and Christians, all which is very doubtful, that influence had ceased to prevail. Moura is supposed to owe its name to the treachery with which a Moorish maiden was slain, or driven to suicide, after the foul murder of her lover by a Portuguese soldier, who dressed himself in his habit, and so entered and took the town with his followers. The legend, notwithstanding its popularity, possesses no particular flavour of authenticity, and the derivation has obviously no sort of probability. Such legends as this, whether they be true or false, like that of the treacherous capture of Santarem by the Portuguese during a truce, and the cruel stratagem which gained Evora, faithfully reflect the altogether unchivalrous nature of the struggle, which was becoming embittered by religious hatred and bigotry on both sides.

It has been my habit in my travels in Portugal to make a point of inquiring into the existence of old charters, deeds, and other documents in the various towns. Such ancient muniments are often preserved with scrupulous care by the chapters in cathedral cities, the priests of parish churches, and the municipal bodies of the town. Some jealousy —a very natural and proper feeling—has often been exhibited; but with a little management I have almost always succeeded in getting access to the deed-box or muniment chamber.

I had hoped to find these trans-Guadianian towns peculiarly rich in ancient documents, and so they doubtless are, but my inquiries in every case were checked. Either the near neighbourhood of Spain made them suspicious of a stranger, or they had been careless keepers of their muniments, and had nothing to show. Inquire where I would, at Moura, Mourão, or Mertola, I found nothing.

The tenure of land, originally for the most part vested, as it was taken from the Infidel, in the church, or in the Militant Orders of the Templars and Knights of Jerusalem who fought in the van of the great home crusade, might certainly have been expected to be recorded more distinctly in the case of the comparatively recent endowments in these districts than elsewhere. At Mertola I was told of a transfer deed, dated 1302, and at Moura of a charter of King Sancho, who died in 1211, alluding to the original grant of a tract of land on the left bank of the Guadiana, but these documents are, with many others, hidden away in the Lisbon State Paper Office.

Cursory as has been my study of these old Portuguese charters, transfers, and royal grants, and incompetent as I am, in many ways, to speak with authority, I have seen enough of them in various parts of Portugal to perceive what a mine of historical wealth they afford—a mine, too, which has been as yet hardly at all worked. Herculano's narrative of the early years of the monarchy, admirable as it is, is founded mainly upon the chroniclers, Christian and Mahometan, neither of whom can be considered quite honest. His history is like the summing up by a good judge of the evidence of a host of untrustworthy witnesses. It is good, thoughtful history, and the author does not sin on the side of credulity; but the reader cannot accept a narration in which the historian is himself too honest to put his whole faith; and when Herculano leaves off at the end of the thirteenth century, all is doubt and confusion.

The history of mediæval Portugal is peculiarly interesting as being to a great degree complete in itself, as being less complicated with the affairs of other countries than perhaps that of any European kingdom, and yet as containing in itself all the elements of change, and all the causes of vicissitude, which have presided at the rise and fall of other states. Feudalism, or rather the germs of it, which grew into a sort of national clanship; the great faith-feud which succeeded to what was, at first, a race-feud—a struggle between two nations for domination; then the usurpations of the church, and the prudent temporizing of the rulers of the country with the Court of Rome ; their wise absorption of the Military Orders into the state; the balance of the various estates of the realm—all this would make most instructive reading, treated not, of course, as a patriotic Portuguese can only treat his country's history, but from the point of view of a scientific and impartial foreign historian.

In travelling through the parts of Portugal which I had hitherto visited—the northern and north-eastern frontier—and now through this long-contested border land of what was once the Moorish kingdom of Al Gharb, and is now shrunk in dimension to the modern province of Algarve,—in passing through this range of country, with the ruins of Moorish and Christian strongholds on every prominent height, one is singularly impressed with the obstinacy of the long fight which was maintained for centuries among the defiles, the forests, and by the river fords and mountain passes. It was like our Scotch and Welsh border fighting—a war of raids and border frays, of sieges of walled towns and strong places. Pitched battles were rare; the Saracens were superior in cavalry, but they could not withstand the shock of the Portuguese infantry, and avoided encounters in the open field.

Wherever the shifting border-line lay, it was crossed regularly year after year, when the crops were ready to be harvested, by whichever party felt itself the stronger; and the ground gained on these occasions by the Portuguese finds record in the various existing deeds, grants, and charters. For this reason, these ancient documents furnish a far more true and lively picture of the manners and history of those times than the half-romantic annals of the mediæval chroniclers.

The mere variety in the nomenclature of these marauding expeditions is, of itself, an evidence of the long continuance of the warlike mode of life in mediæval Portugal. We learn from the old documents how many different ways were adopted by the Portuguese of carrying death and destruction among their border enemies, and of saving themselves from similar incursions. In ancient charters such words *Azaria*, *Hoste*, *Appelido*, *Fronteira*, and *Anaduva*, are frequently met with, each one of which tells its own wild tale of a warlike people inured to arms, but never ceasing to till the soil. The *Azaria* was the name given to an expedition made into the enemy's lines, when the farmers yoked their oxen to their carts, and carrying axes on their shoulders, ventured into the enemy's country to cut firewood. The *Azaria* was the band who accompanied the waggoners and wood-cutters, armed with the *aza*, or woodman's axe. Land in Portugal is still held by the grant made to the captain who would lead an *Azaria* into a dangerous tract.

The *Aduana* appears to have been an expedition of working men to repair fortifications, though its apparent derivation from *adua*, a herd, would seem to imply some connection with cattle-lifting. The *Hoste* was an expeditionary force, a small army, taking the field regularly. The *Appelido*, as its name implies, was a sudden call to arms of the whole population of a town or commune. These *Appelidos* were often made necessary at a moment's notice by the sudden irruption of the enemy; and it is more than once related how the people would be roused from their beds by the fearful cry of *Mouros na terra! Moradores ás armas!* " The Moors are on us; to arms! to arms!"

These picturesque calls to arms were apparently not always justified by the actual presence of an enemy, and were, it may be presumed, sometimes made to gratify a private pique against a neighbour, or a desire for his flocks and herds; for it is stipulated in a charter given to the town of Freixo d'Espada Cinto, in 1098—one of the earliest of Portuguese documents—that the knights are to join the *Appelido, cum opus fuerit*, when necessary, *sed non transeant aquas Durii nisi cum rege*, " but they are not to cross the Douro unless the king be with them;" whereby it would seem to be implied that these persons were in the habit of taking the law into their own hands, and harrying their neighbours without provocation. Another charter, given nearly a hundred years later, lays down, evidently with the same purpose, that the people of Folgosa are not to form an *Appelido, nisi ergo super vos venerint Mauros* vel gens aliena*—" except upon an actual invasion of Moors or Spaniards."

The *Fossado* was a raid of a more actively offensive character made into the enemy's country *com mão poderosa*, "with the strong hand," to cut down and appropriate his harvest and his fruit, and to carry off his sheep and his cattle. The *Fronteira* was a marauding excursion primarily to guard the frontier line, and secondarily to rob, murder, and destroy whenever the chance offered. All these varieties of raids and expeditions were, as might be supposed, the origin of the tenure of land,—the circumstances being often fully and exactly recited in grants and charters.

At Mertola, on the right side of the Guadiana, and within a few leagues of its mouth, the river

---

* The critics must not accuse me of false syntax. In Portuguese and Spanish the nominative plural is formed from the Latin accusative, and with proper names the mediæval Latinists follow the vernacular form. *Gens aliena* are here the people of Leon.

begins to be practicable for large boats; this fine river, a deep and sluggish stream through a great part of its earlier course is interrupted in its navigability as it flows through the gorges of the Abelheira range of hills between Serpa and Mertola by a series of falls and rapids. South of Mertola, a strong place in Mediæval times, with, as usual, a Moorish castle on its tallest hill, the country is still mountainous, the hills bare-topped, but with signs of cultivation more frequent in the valleys.

I was tired of my stumbling and lazy horse, and my guide, like myself, was suffering from ague. In a country where marsh malaria prevails, even to so slight a degree as it does in Portugal, all one's trifling disorders, one's colds and headaches, are apt to hang about one in an intermittent or agueish form. One is slightly feverish and uneasy at one time of the day, listless at another, and chilly at a third. Englishmen in these times fortunately scarcely know what the old words "tertian" and "quartan" mean, and English travellers in the Peninsula are puzzled what to make of their symptoms at first, but they soon learn the virtues of quinine, and if they are wise, never go without it.

Francisco who, as I have related, was not difficult in the matter of faith, had absolutely none in the bitter powder of which I made him take large doses. He had become very sulky, and it was partly my own fault. Two days before, we had had to cross a deep and narrow stream, and disliking to get as wet as he inevitably would if he remained in the saddle, he persisted, against my strong advice, in trying to cross dry-foot at a place where a fallen and rotting tree had nearly spanned the channel. His horse followed mine through the water. When I had got safely over I watched him, fully expecting to see the tree bend with his weight and let him down into the water; but almost the reverse of this happened, for Francisco, getting upon the trunk, safely reached the middle of the stream, when his weight slowly forced down the branches which all but reached to my side of the stream, and the tree-top dipping into the stream and catching the full force of the current suddenly broke off short, and as the tree was still firmly attached to its twisted roots, their strain lifted the trunk, thus relieved of its top weight, three or four feet into the air, and with it the terrified Francisco.

He had been cautiously and very skilfully creeping along the narrow trunk on hands and knees with so knowing an expression of countenance that I made sure he would get over safely, when, as our children's books say, "Lo and behold!" he was suddenly jerked up into the air in this astonishing manner. The jerk, too, as ill luck would have it, disturbed his equilibrium, and in his scuffle to maintain it, he remained hanging across the tree trunk, suspended helplessly by the middle, like the sign of the Golden Fleece over a mercer's shop, while his hat floated gaily down the stream.

I laughed to that extent that I could not for a moment get off my horse. When I recovered I called to him to wriggle himself back to the other side, which he did very successfully, with fearful muscular exertion and contortions of face, managing to throw himself on the muddy bank and clasp it with outstretched hands and feet, and only slipping back into the water up to his knees.

His first proceeding was to pursue his hat and angle for it with a long stick from the bank; his next to beg me, with tears in his voice, to bring the horses over and let him ride across over the ford. All this being done, and Francisco on the right side of the river, I lost no time in administering to him a very stiff dose of brandy and quinine.

We rode on our way, but Francisco was in a bad humour. It was partly my having laughed at him, partly, I believe, the bitter taste of the medicine, for if I looked at him during the rest of that day, he would make a horribly wry face as if he still tasted the quinine.

"I will never touch that stuff of your Excellency's in all my life again," he said, after riding by me in silence for an hour.

"What stuff—the brandy?"

"No, those *pozes do inferno*—those devil's powders, which you put into it!"

CHAPTER XII.

Boat Journey down the Guadiana to Villa Nova—Scenery and Botany of Province of Algarve—The Locust Tree—Boatmen's Stories —The Ginet—Mr. Mason's Successful Mining at San Domingo— Embark for Lisbon in a Trading Schooner—The East Wind; its Bad Reputation—Proverbs—The "Rock" of Lisbon; Why so called—Viseu—Its Famous Pictures—Gran Vasco—Discussion as to his Authorship of Pictures ascribed to him—The Province of Beira—Its Unsophisticated Inhabitants—Their Singular Dress— Their Probable Origin—Remarks on Travel Writing—Culture and Good Manners and Nature of the People—A Theory Unsupported by Facts—A Portuguese Priest—His Stories about Wolves—Diminution of Wolves in the Country—Good and Inoffensive Character of the Priest—His Views on Sport—Through Oporto Northward—Monastic Church of Leça do Balio—Description of a Pine Forest—Barcellos—A Portuguese School Inspection—Farming—Strong Traces of Roman Farm System— "Green Wine;" its Taste and Good Effects—Recapitulation of Impressions of the Portuguese, as a People.

A SULKY guide, a lazy horse, and a slight attack of ague, all indisposed me to continue my journey on horseback along the course of the frontier river, the Guadiana, towards the southern coast of Portugal. I therefore got rid of both horse and guide at Mertola, sending back my guide and selling the horse to a farmer at the inn.

A little south of Mertola, the Guadiana, which for some sixty miles had flowed between Portuguese banks, again forms the boundary between Spain and Portugal, and continues to separate the two kingdoms, till it enters the sea at the town and harbour of Villa Real de Sant' Antonio. I hired a boat at Mertola, and was taken down the river to Villa Real, a most pleasant and luxurious expedition. I have seldom so enjoyed a boating excursion. My three boatmen were tall, slight, Moorish-looking men, very lively and communicative. The banks of the river, down which we glided with great rapidity, are in the upper part of its course exceedingly lovely, and, in places, richly cultivated. The maize and wheat fields of the north and centre of Portugal are replaced in Algarve (we enter this small province a little below Mertola) by orchards of figs and of almond trees; waste land is covered not invariably by cistus and heath, as in the central provinces, nor by gorse and broom, as in northern Portugal, but occasionally by a dense undergrowth of the dwarf palm of Portugal.

The locust-tree, in shape, size and appearance like an apple-tree, but evergreen and very ornamental, is a marked feature of the landscape in Algarve. The horn-shaped pod, with its sweetish, starchy contents, is a valuable food in southern Portugal, and is sold at fruit-stalls, as nuts and apples are with us in England, in every town and village of the kingdom. In a dry climate like this of Algarve, where if water fails, all cereals must fail too, what a boon and blessing must this tree be! It is poor food to live on, my boatmen told me, but it is abundant enough, even in very dry years, to stave off a famine. A single tree, they told me, has been known to produce twenty *arrobas*—more than 600 lbs. I ate a handful once, to try to realize the feelings of the Prodigal Son—for it is as nearly certain as can be that the "husks" of the New Testament were the fruit of the locust-tree—and I thought he was better off than he deserved. In the Levant, where these trees are common, I learnt to call them locust-trees, which is a foolish misnomer founded on the theory of their having been the *pièce de résistance* in St. John the Baptist's fare. All over the Peninsula the tree is called Algaroba, which is from the Arabic, Kharoùb, so that, after all, in our English trade name of *Carob bean* we have stumbled on something like its true name.

Lying back on a heap of palm leaves and empty sacks, with a mat stretched overhead to keep off the sun, and gliding swiftly with a following wind through the gorges of the Algarve mountains, I came to the conclusion that there is no locomotion in the world so agreeable as this boat travelling through pleasant scenery: but then in such river voyages it is absolutely necessary to have the stream with one.

My boatmen were good-tempered, companionable people, telling me all about their brothers, sisters, wives, and children, and singing songs (which I could not understand) in very dismal strains. They told me wonderful stories of huge water-snakes, which came up the river from the sea, and at night-time attacked the sleeping boatmen; and of a breed of wolves in the mountains of the interior, so large that one could kill and carry off a yearling heifer! I set down to the same category of fable a description they gave me of a cat-like creature, known as *rabo-longo*, that lived in the woods, very fierce and strong enough to kill a dog, but which, if caught young, would get tame enough to follow its master about, and would rid the house of rats and mice, and the garden of snakes and lizards. When I expressed strong doubts on this matter, they assured me it was the commonest thing in the world, and if I would wait till we arrived at a place called Alcoutim, I should have proof positive of their having told me the literal truth. What was my astonishment, on returning from a stroll through the town that afternoon, to see a girl near the landing-place, holding in her arms an animal like a huge spotted ferret. It was a genet, for which the true Portuguese name is *gineto*, but it had every claim to its local appellation, *rabo-longo*, or long-tail, as its tail was quite as long as its head and body put together. The animal was quite tame, and even playful, and being set on the ground, no more tried to escape than a dog or cat would. It allowed me to handle it, and except for its not very pleasant musky smell, seemed as pretty and desirable a pet as could be.

Villa Real, on the sandy estuary of the Guadiana, has within twenty years become of commercial importance. At San Domingo a copper mine has long been known to exist; but as it was also known to contain but a very small percentage of metallic copper, that is, less than four parts in a hundred of ore, no prudent person would meddle with it. The ore is a sulphuret of copper, and contains fifty per cent of sulphur. Herein lay the undetected richness of the ore. An English gentleman bought the mine, and the ore is largely exported to the smelters of Great Britain, who extract both copper and sulphur. It is now by far the richest mine in Portugal. The proprietor constructed a railway to Pomerão on the Guadiana, eleven miles from the mine, and there the ore is loaded. About six hundred British steamers and sailing ships annually enter and leave the port of Villa Real, where formerly a dozen coasting vessels sufficed for the whole trade in tunny, sardines, and dried figs. Mr. Mason is commonly said to derive £80,000 a year from this mine—a fair reward for his skill, energy, and intelligence; and if the Portuguese government had not made him Baron of Pomerão, the moral of his history would be complete.

Anxious to escape a longer stay in the country which had already given me an ague, I took a passage, not without difficulty and compliance with endless formalities, in a Portuguese schooner bound for Lisbon, and at daybreak on the following morning we were dropping down with the tide to cross the river bar. A fresh breeze was blowing from the north-east, and our captain, showing no fear of being embayed if the wind chopped, boldly made for Cape St. Vincent, eighty or ninety miles to the west, keeping at a distance of little more than a league from land, assuring me that if he were to steer to the south we should lose the wind.

We passed the prettily situated town of Tavira before breakfast, and in the course of the day Faro, the capital of Algarve, with its ancient castle and ruined houses, and its groves of dark green trees—oranges and carob trees, as far as I could make out with the captain's glass. Early next morning we " made "' Cape St. Vincent, and were soon out of sight of land, the wind having veered completely and blowing a pleasant breeze a little north of west, and we were making a " long board " to the westward. It was like coming into a new world, to exchange the hot east wind that had accompanied me since leaving Juromenha for the breeze charged with the fresh salt spray of the Atlantic. In every part of the Peninsula the east wind is detestable, and in none more so than in Portugal, where, in addition to its own demerits, it comes charged with the hot, unwholesome emanations of the great sandy table-lands of central Spain, where reigns a climate which, though Spanish, even Spaniards abuse. The air of Madrid (it is a type of this climate) they say,—

"Es tan subtil
Que mata a un hombre y non apaga a un candil,"

—*is so treacherous that it will kill a man and yet not put a candle out;* and the Portuguese, who favour neither Spaniards nor things Spanish, couple marriages made across the frontier and the east wind that comes from the land they hate,—*De Espanha nem bom vento nem bom casamento,*" is a proverb in Portugal—" A Spanish match and a Spanish wind are two bad things."

Two days in the Atlantic passed tediously, though my deck cabin was comfortable and even clean—for the sea, to everyone not born to it, is insufferably monotonous,—and on the third day (the fourth from Villa Real) we had sighted the " Rock of Lisbon," as our sailors call it, the tall, slender mass of granite that stands furthest seaward of the range of the

Cintra Hills, and which the Portuguese have christened "Roca," the distaff. We have called it the Rock of Lisbon for at least three hundred years, and ninety-nine people out of a hundred who hear it so called never doubt that "rock" is an ignorant translation of *Roca*, and is used in its common sense of cliff. To anyone who enters the Tagus the name must seem singularly inappropriate, seeing that five hundred other rocks, nearly as conspicuous, surround it; and it is quite possible that our early navigators, who were clever at giving appropriate names, struck by this curious distaff-shaped cliff, called it for this very reason "the rock," which three hundred years ago was the commoner English name for distaff.

Leaving the "Rock" a league or so to our north, we pass through the broad bay and smooth water of "Cascaes," so called from the village of that name, the Brighton of Lisbon; then comes the picturesque tower of Belem, standing a stone's-throw out in the river; then the long streets of the Lisbon suburbs; then the hills of the city itself, the stately houses and palaces, and the hanging gardens, and the churches, all glittering in the sun, and looking bright and clean, and new and regular, as a town might be expected to be that was in ashes a short century ago;—and all delightfully refreshing and pleasant to look upon to one who has been among the half-ruined and half-deserted towns, and along the dreary plains and the barren mountains of the southern provinces of Portugal.

Lisbon is, in some respects, the finest capital in Europe, but to the mere stranger, to the tourist without introductions, certainly the very dullest. Among the frugal Portuguese, public amusements meet with little support. No one but a native, and not the best among them, would go twice to a Portuguese bull fight,—always a very foolish and very shabby exhibition, and with just that spice of wanton cruelty which such exhibitions require to get the support of the roughs and blackguards among the population. There is almost always an opera in the two chief towns, but the company is generally only third or fourth-rate. The Portuguese are themselves born actors, as good as the Neapolitans perhaps in farce and low comedy, but they have little originality, and the vast majority of their pieces are adaptations from the French. I should doubt if there is any contemporary drama so little known or understood as that of modern Portugal. To follow Portuguese as spoken on the stage, and stuffed with colloquialisms, local allusions, and curious idioms, requires more than a mere literary acquaintance with the language, and is a task within the competence of but very few foreigners.

It is singular that the Portuguese, who, taken as a nation, are second to none in good sense and good breeding, make audiences whose silliness and rudeness are the despair of *impresarios*. A paid *claque*, in the French acceptance of the word, is not a Portuguese institution, but there is a self-constituted *claque* of rowdies in every audience, and these fellows tyrannize in the most summary manner over the rest of the house. Actors or actresses who offend this body are seldom allowed to be heard, and offence is often given, unconsciously to the actor, by some act of the management, by the personal dislike of some member of the *claque* or some quite trivial, trumpery cause. Foreign performers are particularly subjected to such attacks, and I have seen a *débutante* vocalist, a modest, well-behaved English girl (on this very ground apparently), assailed with a perfect storm of disapprobation, accompanied by gross personal insults, and pelted with missiles in keeping with the verbal assaults, by twenty or thirty young men of the shopkeeping classes, while the rest of the audience sat still, in abject patience, never dreaming even of showing any indignation at the proceeding, or at the loss of their evening's amusement.

I once had the honour of making the acquaintance, at the inn of a provincial town of Portugal, of two distinguished members of an English troupe,

—the clown and the manager of a well-known circus company, and these gentlemen gave me a most curious account of the "manners and customs" of Portuguese audiences, giving me to understand that no audiences in Europe or America, in India or the Colonies—and they had travelled professionally round the world—were so hard to please, so violent in their conduct, or so unfair in every way to performers.

The tourist or sojourner in Portugal will not have travelled far or stayed long in the country before he hears a good deal of Gran Vasco, the famous mythical painter of Portugal to whom every good and nearly every old picture in the country is ascribed, and of whose life, parentage, birthplace, and handiwork, nothing but vague rumour has survived. Tradition points, but by no means with any satisfactory degree of certainty, to the north of Portugal as the native country of Gran Vasco, and to the episcopal city of Viseu, among the remote mountains of the province of Beira, as the place where he was bred and where he worked. The Cathedral of Viseu, at any rate, contains several pictures which by general Portuguese consent are ascribed to this master.

It is not a very intelligible circumstance that Portugal, which has run her larger neighbour so close in almost everything that distinguishes a civilized nation, whose wealth was very great during the period covered by the revival and reflorescence of arts and letters, whose great nobles were patrons of culture of every kind, should be so poor in art work; it is not easy to understand how while Spain has produced so many famous painters, Portugal should have possessed absolutely none at all; none, that is, of any fame, for with the exception of the above-named Gran Vasco, I can think of but two Portuguese painters who deserve to rank with even fourth or fifth-rate names in the great European art roll.

If Gran Vasco be mythical, as some few sceptics allege, it is not difficult to see how such a myth, once getting birth, would be nourished into full growth among the most credulous and patriotic people in Europe. A great artist is wanted in the Portuguese Valhalla, and Gran Vasco is welcomed: *populus vult decipi*, and it deceives itself into the full belief that it has a Raphael of its own. To say that half-a-dozen educated Portuguese at this day entertain the smallest doubt of the existence of Gran Vasco is probably an exaggeration, so deeply and widely does the belief in him prevail.

So often had I been tempted to go out of my way to look at a masterpiece by Gran Vasco only to find some wretched daub, so often have I had to keep my countenance and restrain my impatience while I was being lectured on the beauties of some monstrous work of the Wardour Street school, that I had long ceased either to have any faith in Gran Vasco, or even to believe in the existence of a really first-rate picture in the country by a native artist. I therefore made the long and tedious pilgrimage to Viseu rather to be able to say that I had examined this painter's most famous pictures, than because I expected to find them worth seeing.

Happening to be at the time in the province of Traz os Montes, I crossed the river Douro at Regoa and proceeded to Lamego, prepared to ride thence to Viseu. Lamego is the centre of an episcopal diocese, and Viseu of another, though they are but fifteen or sixteen leagues asunder; but the country between is roadless, and includes three wild hill ranges and three fair-sized streams, and as it so happens that no single inn lies between the two cities, the traveller is in consequence compelled to ride the whole distance in a single day. In my case it happened to be a winter's day, and the journey was performed on a weak and stumbling horse hired at Lamego. Begun before daylight, the last few hours were ridden in the gloom of a winter's evening, and the last of the three rivers forded was crossed (it was in full flood and very cold) in pitch darkness, save for and by the flickering light of torches held by the family of a friendly miller. Tired, cold, and faint for want of food, bitterly did I repent the misguided æsthetic enthusiasm which had prompted me to travel to Viseu to see pictures which I was sure would be worthless, and ascribed to a painter whom I had never believed in.

Early on the following morning I went to the Cathedral. Passing under its lofty aisles and through its dingy cloisters, we reached the Sacristy, a large well-lighted chamber. What was my astonishment, when after some little fumbling with the key the door was thrown open, at finding myself in front of one of the grandest masterpieces of the art of painting! Not even before the few greatest pictures of the world, not even when standing before Raphael's Madonna at Dresden, the great pictures in the Vatican, or even the frescoes of the Sistine Chapel, have I felt so unmistakably that I was in the presence of the handiwork of a great and rare genius; and after the interval of several years I have not the slightest hesitation in recording my opinion that this great picture at Viseu ranks among the six or seven masterpieces of the world.

Count Raczynski, in his work on Portuguese art, written some thirty years ago, had indeed, spoken very handsomely of the Viseu pictures, but the Count,—a lively writer, and an industrious observer—is by no means a safe guide in the matter of art,* as I had already had reason to discover. His taste is the taste that found favour with his employers, the Academy of Fine Arts at Berlin, some thirty or forty years ago; and these somewhat Philistine and academic sympathies find little but antiquarian interest in the art of periods which he lumps together as Gothic. I had hitherto found that what Count Raczynski praised, I could not, and what he condemned I sometimes found admirable; therefore his praise of the Viseu pictures had weighed with me not at all.

There are in the Cathedral, or rather within its precincts, two quite distinct series of pictures—a set of fourteen narrow panels (about four feet by two) apparently about the date of 1500, and contained in the Chapter House, and a series of later date and far higher importance in the Sacristy, consisting of four large panels and seven smaller ones. Among this latter series is the picture which fixed my attention on entering the Sacristy. The other pictures are, in my opinion, one and all, so inferior in every way

---

* Count Raczynski's book is a very curious one, and in spite of the author's pleasant style, his diligence and research, one of the most unsatisfactory that ever was written. The work consists of a series of apparently hastily written letters on "Art in Portugal." It is without an index or table of contents, it has no sort of arrangement, and the opinions arrived at in the early letters are generally abandoned in the later ones. It is a book to be begun at the end and only half read through.

to this one, that I cannot bring myself to believe them to be by the same hand.

The masterpiece is a large work on panel, about eight feet square, in very fair preservation, and in three compartments. The central compartment represents St. Peter in rich pontifical robes, sitting on a throne of polished white marble, over-canopied by silken-fringed hangings. The throne with its draperies reaches to the top of the picture, and filling the archways formed by pilasters and rounded arches on each side are exquisitely painted landscapes, distinct but soft and tender in tone, with water, trees, bridges, castles and towns. In the one is represented St. Peter walking on the waves; in the other, the saint receiving the keys of heaven from our Lord.*

It is hardly possible to say too much for the *technique* of this magnificent picture. The drawing is masterly, the colour harmonies throughout are marvellous; again and again I turned to dwell on the exquisite passages of green and rosy pink in the narrow silken fringe of the canopy, set off by the cool grey-yellow of the marble. The picture is clearly of the early part of the sixteenth century, and shows Flemish influences very strongly. But

---

* As to the subject of this latter compartment I am not quite sure that my memory serves me right. I made, I regret to say, no notes either here or elsewhere in Portugal.

the draperies are not marked by the angular folds and narrow "pipings" which are characteristic of the earlier Flemish schools; they fall in fine, ample masses, with a truth and freedom in their drawing which forcibly bring back the broad, unconventional treatment of Andrea del Sarto—and yet the elaboration is such that no square quarter of an inch of chasuble, tiara, or stole, but is finished with the care and precision and richness of a Memling or a Matsys, the countless precious stones and threads of gold in the embroidered orphreys, glow with the light of gems and the brightness of real gold; and yet the first and most lasting impression made by the picture, is singleness of purpose and breadth of treatment.

The glory of the picture is the principal figure. The painter has represented the saint in the conventional attitude of blessing, with the two first fingers of the right hand uplifted; the left holds the key and rests on an open book. The attitude is simple and noble. The saint is a bearded man hardly past the prime of life; the eyes look directly forward and are somewhat lifted as if to take in a great crowd; the expression of the face is benign but full of boldness and energy. The impressiveness of this face is almost startling. It has something of the force and intensity of the Raphael portraits of Julius II., but the expression is infinitely more direct, more commanding, and more noble; it has something of the power of Michael Angelo's Moses, but it has none of the pagan element which some critics have found in that great statue.

Who was the painter of this grand work of art? Is this the handiwork of the great legendary painter who lives so persistently in Portuguese tradition? It would be pleasant to be able to think that it was. I tried hard to believe it, but unfortunately the probabilities are all the other way, and the great mass of negative evidence makes the belief in a real Gran Vasco wholly untenable.

A closer examination of the St. Peter leaves little doubt as to the age of the picture. The manipulation is of a particular period, and that a short one; it certainly was not painted before 1500, and it could not have been painted later than 1550; it was the work probably of about 1520. It was a period when the richer lines in drapery and more flowing curves of outline had been adopted from Italy. The painter of this picture had, I believe, looked on the works of the great Tuscan artist, but he is no imitator of Michael Angelo. The proportions of the human figure in the background are no longer the somewhat stunted proportions given by the Flemish painters of the previous generation, they are here precisely such as Raphael himself might have drawn; the architectonic details are of that marked Renaissance period, which is named in Portugal "Manoelino," after the art-loving King Emmanuel, who died in 1521.

Seeing that the *technique* of the picture is distinctly Flemish, and the somewhat free treatment such as was at this period becoming common to painters of this school, I should have no hesitation in ascribing this picture and the others in the Cathedral to a Flemish origin, I should have supposed it to be the work of one of the many Flemings who were then employed in various parts of the Peninsula, but for the fact that it is difficult to imagine a man of northern race painting a picture and leaving no trace whatever of his foreign birth and foreign training. I have shown how the fine picture at Oporto betrays its origin at once in the fair skin, light hair, and markedly northern type of the faces; in the unmistakable northern landscape background; in the characteristic Flemish plough and Flemish horses; and even in the weeds and flowers in the foreground, several of which are not commonly to be found in Portugal:—but in the Viseu pictures there is nothing of all that. The faces are distinctly southern in type, and my closest research did not reveal any northern characteristic whatever.

Here, then, is a dilemma; if this painting be the handiwork of a Peninsular artist, it is unique in possessing not the mannerism only of a certain northern school, but a degree of artistic skilfulness which only two or three masters of that school have ever attained to; again, if it be Flemish, how comes it that it bears no internal traces of its origin. There is, it seems to me, only one possible reconciliation of the alternatives. The picture may be the handiwork of a naturalized northerner. There is a familiar case in point. The well known Pedro Campana was a native of Brussels; he painted in the very generation in which this great picture at Viseu must have been painted; he lived and worked nearly all his life in Spain; and his pictures have, to my perception at least, no trace of their painter's nationality, save his manipulative dexterity. Can the painter of this Viseu picture have been some such a Peninsularized northern painter, who retained his skill and had dropped his nationality? I had for a time supposed that it might have been Campana himself who had been at work at Viseu, but having had a subsequent opportunity of again inspecting this painter's masterpiece at Seville, I satisfied myself that in spite of some resemblance in the type of the head, and a certain Michael-Angeloesque force and character common to both works, the workmanship of the pictures is essentially different.

Count Raczynski, who had, on his first inspection

of these pictures, arrived at the obvious conclusion that they were works of the early part of the sixteenth century, had this opinion quite unsettled by his discovery that the registry of a birth in the year 1552 existed at Viseu of "Vasco Fernandes, son of Francisco Fernandes, painter." Here was a discovery indeed! "*Eureka!*" cried the count, "I have solved the great mystery; these pictures are the work of Vasco Fernandes, the painter of Viseu;" and who more worthy to be called the "great Vasco" than the author of these wonderful works? The Portuguese have gladly accepted the Count's theory, and the old mystery of Gran Vasco is for them solved and explained.

Unfortunately the solution breaks down most completely. The father of the Vasco Fernandes of the register is indeed stated to have been a painter, and possibly the son may have followed his father's profession; but what proof have we that he did? Further, if the pictures were the work of the son, and he was born in 1552, they could not well have been painted before he was twenty or thirty years of age, that is, before about 1590, but it is beyond all doubt that these pictures were painted before 1550. Moreover, it is assumed that Francisco Fernandes, the father, was a painter of pictures; but the presumption is, that a man, described in the register as a painter, *pintor* (in old

Portuguese, *paintor*), was a painter indeed, but in the less elevated sense of being a "painter and glazier." Again, there is another hitch. In the register, the supposed artist is plain Francisco Fernandes. Now, the Portuguese are fonder of giving honorary titles than any people in Europe. If a man has to write to his shoemaker, he superscribes the letter—" To his most Illustrious Lordship," and even the little street-boys address one another as "Your Worship." If the painter, Francisco Fernandes, had been above the rank of a working man, he would most assuredly have been described as "Mestre," Master, the common designation at that time of an artist. That he is not so mentioned, is, in my eyes, conclusive evidence that Francisco Fernandes was no artist at all.*

My views as to the Viseu pictures were in the somewhat vague condition that I have indicated, and my mind very sceptically inclined as to Gran Vasco, when I had the advantage to meet with a descriptive account of these pictures from the able pen of Mr. J. C. Robinson, who made a journey to

* Here is a literal transcript of the entry: M^a of course stands only for *Maria*. "Aos xvij. dias do mes de Setembro de 1552 años bautisei Vasquo f⁰ de fr⁰⁰ Fez. paintor e de mª Amriques sua molher forão padrinhos e madrinhas Egas Velho e p⁰ Lopes f⁰ de A⁰ do Rego e R⁰ A⁰ madrinhas mª Lopes molher de Gaspar Vas e Cª Pays molher de Geronymo Tavares todos moradores nesta cidade e por verdade asynei aquy, "AFONSO ALVES."

Viseu in the year 1866. Mr. Robinson's opinion of the technical merits of the pictures is so valuable and so well worth recording, that I take the liberty of quoting a few sentences. "All the Viseu pictures," says Mr. Robinson, "are distinguished by a remarkable gaiety and lightsomeness of colour; . . . . a beautiful warm yellow, often in considerable mass, and frequently in contrast with varied tones of a fine purple brown or mulberry tint, is especially remarkable in the Chapter House pictures, whilst in those of the Sacristy, crimson draperies of a peculiarly vivid, clear, lightsome ruby colour, apparently produced by glazing over an under-painting of black and white, will not fail to be observed. The latter pictures are, on the whole, more lightsome in effect than those of the earlier series; and although they are overlaid by the accumulated dirt of centuries, yet, to the professional eye, accustomed to allow for such merely temporary obscuration, they still gleam forth like jewelled mosaics of rubies, emeralds, and sapphires, in a framework of silver."

Mr. Robinson knows a great deal too much of pictures not to reject Count Raczynski's theory of Vasco Fernandes—the dates are enough for him; but I was disappointed to find that Mr. Robinson so far accepts the questionable *Vasco Fernandes* as to believe that he was a painter of pictures, and even to believe that a certain triptych for sale in Viseu, whose central compartment is signed "Vasco Fernandes," is actually the work of the said Vasco!*

It was hardly to be supposed that so learned and keen an art student as Mr. Robinson should leave Viseu without enunciating a new and sufficient resolution of the Gran Vasco problem, and this he has accordingly done. In the church of Santa Cruz, at Coimbra, Mr. Robinson had seen the well-known sixteenth century panel picture representing the Pentecost. He was struck by the resemblance in the manner of this picture and that of the Sacristy series at Viseu. What if the same man had painted both? "The head of the Viseu St. Peter is repeated," says Mr. Robinson, "in a St. Peter in the Coimbra picture." Only one thing was wanting, the name of the painter; and here Mr. Robinson's good luck was really extraordinary. Where had been the eyes of all previous observers? Here, in a corner, was "a well preserved and conspicuous signature of the artist," VELASCO, L. "Here then,"

---

* More caution might have been expected of a veteran London picture dealer. The triptych is a ruined work of considerable merit; but with every desire to believe in human nature, I may say that never did I look upon a more questionable signature than this distinctly traced VASCO FES. I could elicit nothing definite of the previous history of the picture, and until such information be freely given and fully substantiated, I shall continue to believe that the signature is of a later date than Count Raczynski's discovery. One would expect Mr. Robinson to be the last person to be taken in by a doubtful signature.

continues Mr. Robinson, with almost excusable enthusiasm, "we have, as I believe, revealed the real name of the painter of the St. Peter. . . . It is, I think, evident, that M. de Raczynski's Gran Vasco in reality was this same Velasco. There is something almost painful in this discovery; but, after all, this substitution of one name for another is of little real moment; the pictures remain in evidence, and they reflect equal credit on the country of their production, although no longer enshrouded in an atmosphere of mysterious tradition."

Mr. Robinson, in short, had solved the mystery that had endured three hundred years; and if I venture to hint that the chain of evidence is incomplete, and that some hard facts remain to be got over, it is in no spirit of disrespect to Mr. Robinson, who is replete with that spirit of enthusiasm which is the first qualification of a discoverer.

First, as regards the picture at Coimbra, I must hasten to say that, to my own observation, there is no such resemblance between it and the Viseu series as would constitute a common authorship. They are not, to my thinking, even pictures of the same school, and the Coimbra work appears to me the later of the two; indeed, until reading Mr. Robinson's paper, it had never occurred to me that any such resemblance could be alleged to exist. Further, as to the name found on the Coimbra picture, would Mr. Robinson be surprised to learn that there is a well-known Spanish painter named Luis Velasco? In his later manner, he borrowed from the Italian artists brought to the country by Phillip II.; but in his earlier works much of the harder and more precise manner of the Flemish school is visible. On first seeing the picture at Coimbra, conspicuously signed *Velasco, L.*, I never doubted, and still do not doubt, that it is the work of this same Luis Velasco. To any one familiar with pictures in the Peninsula, it will not be necessary to give evidence of the Christian name being made, as in this case, to follow the surname. The *chef d'œuvre* of Velasco is at Toledo, and is well known to art tourists.

Now I have a further surprise for Mr. Robinson. What will he say if I tell him that Velasco is not a Portuguese name, and that it is Spanish for Vasco? Had Mr. Robinson known this, I suspect that he would have carried the solution one stage further. He would assuredly have said—" It is a melancholy duty that I must perform, *there is something almost painful in* having to inform the world that 'Gran Vasco' is no Portuguese at all. It clearly should be 'Gran Velasco,' and Spain must get the benefit of my discovery!"

There is one more, and, if possible, a greater difficulty to be encountered before a Portuguese

Gran Vasco can be accepted. Mr. Robinson, paying a flying visit to Portugal, could not be expected to make himself familiar with the literature or the history of the country. He is clearly not aware that the period to which he ascribes, correctly as I believe, the works of his great Portuguese painter, is precisely the most glorious and also the most busy literary period in Portuguese history. It was also the period during which art was more patronized than it ever had been before or has ever been since. Moreover, in Damien de Goes, whose chronicle embraces this whole period of literary and artistic activity, we have an annalist of a most exemplary carefulness; nothing escapes this most tedious of chroniclers, and especially nothing relating to the building, or restoration, or adornment of a convent or a church; for it was in these things that King Emmanuel, his master, chiefly delighted. Was such an important fact as the existence of so great a painter as Mr. Robinson has imagined likely to escape so keen an observer? Why, he chronicles the arrival, the departure, the board, the lodging, the daily pay and the daily progress of a dozen Flemish and Dutch painters! It is dangerous to assert a negative, but I have little hesitation in asserting that neither in Goes, nor in any contemporary writer whatever, is there even a hint of the existence of a native painter of any sort of merit or eminence; and this negative evidence in so small a kingdom is surely very strong; not conclusive, indeed, for it is not in the nature of negative testimony to be absolutely conclusive. But, curiously enough, there does happen to be evidence even stronger than this—evidence of a positive kind and of absolutely overwhelming weight. Every one who knows anything of Portugal and its history, knows that among no race has love and pride of country been so strong. Never was Portuguese patriotism so strong as in this very generation, and no poem ever breathed so intense a fervour of patriotic enthusiasm as the "Lusiad" of Camoens. Everything which could redound to the glory of his country is insisted upon again and again in this great epic. "In every heroic quality," says the poet, "our nation is pre-eminent; our men are more heroic than other men, our women fairer than other women; in all the arts of peace and war we excel, with one exception only, the art of painting; we have absolutely no painters in our country," says Camoens;* "not that our people have not in them the making of artists, but because, in Portugal, native painters meet with no encouragement. For they get," he says, "neither fame, reward, nor favour, and these are the things that nourish art." Is it credible that Camoens could have written this

---

* "Os Lusiadas," canto viii., stanza xxxix.

in the very generation in which the great Viseu picture was painted?

These are a few of the difficulties in the way of Mr. Robinson, and when he has overcome these, I can promise to find him as many more. A really ingenious hypothesis, as this one certainly is, is a thing to be thankful for, since on no other terms than a controversion of it could I have ventured so fully to develop my views on the Gran Vasco myth; and if I *have dealt somewhat severely with Mr. Robinson's views, it is with no feeling of disrespect towards that gentleman, who has rendered no small service to the history of art progress, but because the question involved is really not one that can be trifled with. No particular reproach can be addressed to Mr. Robinson for having these few fatal faults in his armour—an art-critic is hardly bound to be "well up" in the history of such an unimportant little kingdom as Portugal, or be expected to have read a difficult author like Camoens; nor perhaps can Mr. Robinson be taken to task for following Count Raczynski in his failure to appreciate the two meanings of the word "pintor;" but I think he should have hesitated before he set down Velasco as a possible Portuguese painter. His very guide, or muleteer, could have told him that Velasco and Velasquez are Spanish for Vasco and Vasquez. His blunder here is of the very sort that a man ignorant of the country he is writing about is sure to fall into unawares. That a Portuguese should paint a picture at Viseu, and sign it Velasco, is as if Mr. John Brown should paint a picture at Rochester or Ely and sign it Jean le Brun! On the whole, therefore, we must come to the conclusion that the mystery of Gran Vasco is still a mystery.

It is by no means necessary to take the tedious route followed by me, in order to reach Viseu. The city is well within reach of travellers. To get to Viseu from Lisbon, or Oporto, or Coimbra, is an easy matter. From Mealhada, a station on the Lisbon and Oporto railway, a diligence reaches Viseu in about eleven hours, and this ancient episcopal city is better off for inns than most towns of its size in Portugal.

This whole district of Portugal is probably less known than any portion of the kingdom, and the neighbourhood of Viseu is particularly interesting in respect of buildings and of scenery. The neighbouring towns all contain curious churches, and the traveller who passes on the route chosen by me will find at Tarouca a fine early Romanesque church, which I believe has never even been gazed upon by ecclesiological eyes. The great central mountain range of the Estrella is in full view and within easy distance of Viseu, and Lamego itself may be reached in two days by a carriage road trending to the eastward which passes through the flat country about Trancoso, not an interesting town or country, except as having been the site of a famous battle between the first Portuguese monarch and the Moors.

This portion of the great province of Beira is an elevated table-land; Viseu itself is 2000 feet above the level of the sea, though the traveller, approaching the town from either the north or the south, looks down upon the roofs of the houses and the turrets of the cathedral. The whole district is a moorland country of sheep flocks and shepherds; and the natives, men and women, in their hooded gaberdines of brown cloth—their only garment—without hats, with unkempt hair and with bare legs, are as wild and savage-looking a set of mountaineers as I ever saw; but they are well-mannered and well-behaved. They are a taller and more robust race than I had yet met with in Portugal, and ever since their long-continued resistance to the Romans under their shepherd leader Viriatus, to the time of the Peninsular War, when the soldierly bearing and behaviour of the Beira regiments won praise from the Duke of Wellington, the fighting qualities of these mountaineers have been famous. The finest regiments in the Portuguese army are to this day recruited in this part of Beira.

Wild as the inhabitants of this rugged region appear to be, there is a considerable degree of culture about them. Few parts of Portugal have from the earliest periods been so brought under ecclesiastical influence. Bishoprics, as I have shown, come very close together, and in my hurried journey from Lamego, I passed the remains of three different conventual buildings, which I had no time to examine or inquire about. These monastic influences are of course now replaced by the feebler influences of the parish priests; but all travellers in Catholic countries know how strong and how lasting are the good effects of monks on the manners, at least, of the surrounding peasantry.

Like mountaineers elsewhere, the Beira men are probably a race of purer blood than the dwellers in the plain. Their stature and physiognomy show no trace of any Moorish cross. They are not a very well-featured race, but have a frank and pleasant expression. Looking to this, and to the known history of the Moorish conquest and occupation and the Christian reconquest, I should be inclined to consider them more or less identical with the race which inhabited these highlands in the second century B.C., when the heroic Beira chieftain kept the whole power of Rome at bay for many years. It is not likely that the Beira races of men would suffer any considerable deterioration from the Moorish conquest, for it was never the practice of the Mahometan conquerors to depopulate an invaded territory. They would have made use of the mountaineers, and these latter would have exchanged Moorish masters for Christian landlords and employers, when the land was again won from the Moors in the early years of the monarchy. Later on, as manners softened, the Moors were made slaves,—" to work like a Moor" is still a Portuguese proverb—and victors and vanquished came in time, and under certain circumstances, to mingle their blood, and we see the result in the semi-Moorish inhabitants of the southern provinces; but the conquest of northern Portugal was not effected under such circumstances as these. The faith feud was, when that conquest was made, still bitter, and while the Moors were yet a powerful nation, clemency to the conquered was a dangerous virtue: we may therefore conclude that a very clean sweep indeed was made of the Moorish dwellers on this great Viseu table-land.

If a man could be induced to travel through such a country as Portugal, and content himself with setting down the conversation of guides and muleteers, of landlords and of chance companions; if he would avoid airing his own theories and recording his own generalizations—vicious practices!—if he would make up his mind that readers are incurious beings, who desire only to have a languid interest aroused—it would be not difficult for him to write an interesting book of travels, at least in Portugal. The Portuguese talk well; conversation is with them an art. The working classes, who have no book learning, who can seldom, indeed, read or write, study the art of conversation as the only form of culture possible to them, and they do it very well. They modulate their voices, they use incredibly long words, they gesticulate with a certain grace and propriety, they round their sentences beautifully; in short, they "talk like books." In the upper and especially in the middle classes, where the natural talent for "tall talk" is aggravated by some educational advantages, conversation is often intolerably priggish and tiresome; but among the peasantry these graces of style are more or less natural, and what they say is really often well said; so well that their talk could be transferred easily and with advantage to a printed page.

If it were not that readers in these days are somewhat exacting, a man might do well to follow the old recipe for travel-writing, and, ceasing to cater for the fancied wants of intelligent persons, give himself up unreservedly to the narrative of his own personal adventures, and record the small talk of the people he encounters. Be sure, he would make an eminently readable book, a far more readable one than the humble writer of these pages can pretend to write, whose constitutional timidity makes him fear to thrust his individuality too prominently before his reader, and who has much too high an opinion of the intellect of his readers to think they would condescend to be so easily interested.

It is because the Portuguese are so friendly and open-hearted a people, and so anxious to do their utmost to entertain those who are thrown in contact with them, that travel in Portugal, with all its drawbacks, is so pleasant. It is a melancholy fact, against all accepted theory on the subject, and a thing only to be hinted at in a whisper, that education is a terrible social disadvantage to a man. Reading and writing are, it must be confessed, great drawbacks. Monsieur Renan, who had seen much of the ignorant peasantry of Syria, notices with surprise their extraordinary culture, their social tact, their courtesy, their perfect manners. The peasantry of some parts of Portugal are equally unlearned, and their social education equally advanced. Their culture too, is not, to use something of a bull, altogether illiterate; they know not their letters and yet are men of letters—*literati illiterati*. I could pick out from a certain hamlet in the Minho province a dozen men who shall extemporize better rhyme, and better reason too, who shall know more of pause, metre, and cæsura, than any minor poet of my acquaintance. Their long sentences are perfectly grammatical. A Portuguese literary friend told me that the peasants round Coimbra talked quite as good Portuguese as he could write, using, he said, their imperfects of the subjunctive and all the refinements of the gerund and declined infinitive better than many a Master of Arts in the neighbouring University.

How is this? I thought once it must be the work of social contact, and was prepared with a theory. Unhindered by the pedantry of schools and schoolmasters, I was ready to believe they had leisure to cultivate more important things than spelling-books and the rules of arithmetic, and were not made to store their memories under pretence of sharpening their intellects; and this view of the matter might be supported by the known boorishness of the well-taught German peasantry, the education and discourtesy of the working classes in Scotland, and the absence of any sort of good manners in English common rooms and convocations: in all which cases there is social contact and a certain amount of intellectual cultivation. But this hypothesis breaks down in its turn, for let us only think of the ignorance and the manners of a village in the Black Country! Common rooms, convocations, and Scotch peasants, are as nothing to these "rude sons of toil," and learning once more assumes her empire in our estimation. Therefore I wash my hands of theories altogether, and only note the fact that people ignorant of book learning have often an education that is more softening than book learning, and that the book learned are sometimes insufferably self-sufficient prigs and pedants.

During my long day's ride from Lamego to Viseu, I should have found the way dreary enough but for the society of chance companions. A priest of a neighbouring village, hearing I was to make the journey to Viseu, joined me at day-break, and kindly guided me over the first three leagues of roadless hills. A big, ruddy-complexioned, genial man of middle age, his talk was not of "matin, laud, and compline prayer," and I doubt if his Latin carried him further than the reading of his breviary and mass book. His Reverence was, I was told at the inn, "*um grande caçador*"—a famous sportsman; and much learned talk passed between us on his favourite pastime. He told of waiting for woodcock at nightfall by the edge of damp meadows, and killing them by a pot shot on the ground. He told me of great shooting parties of a more legitimate kind, in autumn, on these heath-covered hills, where twenty or thirty or more sportsmen would walk in a line, interspersed with beaters and dogs, and get excellent sport with hares and the red-legged partridges; great, strong coveys of which birds rose now and then at our horses' feet as if to corroborate his account; and the priest told me how sometimes an outlying she-wolf with her cubs would get up before the line, and then men and dogs would go wild with excitement, and every gun far and near would be fired off, and every cur start in pursuit; and in the enthusiasm of his description the jovial priest favoured me with a Portuguese equivalent of our national "Yoicks!" that rang again in the morning air.

"And the wolf," I asked, "do you ever shoot it?"

"Never!" he said, with great positiveness.

I remembered how Portuguese sportsmen load their guns, and was not surprised. A small handful of powder, a little grass or a leaf or two, and an equal handful of shot of all sizes; and a huge wad of any available material, from wood shavings to paper, is rammed down upon this terrifying charge. Well do I remember the awe with which I regarded my armed Portuguese companion on a certain shooting expedition. Not till I had seen the gun discharged and my companion still on his legs, after a mild, squib-like detonation, did I understand that the powder was of native manufacture, and that my fears had been groundless.

"And do your dogs never catch the wolves?" I asked.

"Never," said the priest, as positively as before—"never by any chance. They seem just going to, for the beast never hurries itself, but," he said, imitating with his hand the slow, striding gallop of the wolf, "corre, corre, e o diabo mesmo não o apanhava"—*he would leave the devil himself behind.*

This is saying a good deal for the wolf's swiftness, for these dogs are long-legged lurchers which, with a good start, will often kill a hare, and before which a rabbit will not live three minutes in the open.

I admit that I like stories about wolves. In these upland and remote parts, where sheep and goats are the farmer's principal wealth, and the snow often lies for weeks on the ground (we rode for several hours, this November day, over fetlock-deep in snow), the wolves are numerous and mischievous, and, if the peasants are to be believed, even dangerous. Talk about wolves is very common, and as the Portuguese animal is certainly a large variety of the common wolf of Europe if not a distinct species, darker in colour and fiercer in character, the Portuguese wolf-tales have some reasonable foundation in fact.

A noble race of wolf-dogs, dark, long-haired mastiffs standing nearly thirty inches in height, is bred in the great Estrella range, of which these uplands are outlying spurs, and every flock is guarded at night by one or more of these dogs, which, armed with broad, spiked collars, remain on the outskirts of the flock, while the shepherds sleep in their midst. Then, if the wolves steal down, on some moonless night, and make a rush upon the mixed flocks of sheep and goats, they have to do battle with the watch dogs. Often, I have been told, if the wolves are in number and hungry, some very serious fighting takes place, the men in the darkness and in the hurry of the fight being able to take little part, but they run up and lay about them with their quarter-staves, with, no doubt, a very pretty running accompaniment of oaths and shouts, mingled with howls and barking and growling and resounding blows of the shepherds' staves. And nine times out of ten, the wolves get off scot free, perhaps leaving a dozen of the flock half bitten to death, and the dogs limping and bleeding from their wounds, for by all accounts a wolf's bite is severe beyond that of any dog.

Of such a midnight medley the priest gave me a most lively description. The dogs, he told me, although so large and fierce, are no match for the wolves, and a single wolf will kill a single dog with ease. It is recorded that the smaller German wolf has left indented tooth-marks on a fire-shovel used as a weapon against him, and a Portuguese shepherd once showed me, on the tough ashen stock of his gun, what seemed to me such tooth marks as no dog could have made. As to their prowess against human enemies, the priest told me—and this opinion I found generally accepted in this district—that a man of moderate coolness and courage, armed either with a gun or with any cutting weapon, has nothing to fear from an encounter with a wolf, but that with his quarter-staff only, which every shepherd carries, a man would be likely to get the worst of the fight. "The strongest man," said the priest, "cannot with this weapon deal a blow that will stagger a wolf." If this be the case, it speaks volumes for the hardness of the wolf's head, for the mountaineers are as clever in the use of the staff as our own ancestors. It is common to see two peasants, on a holiday, fencing (jogando do pao) very scientifically in play, and on the only occasion on which I saw the quarter-staff used in earnest, one of the combatants was brought to the ground by as neat a knock-down blow on the crown of the head as I ever saw delivered.

In all my travels in Portugal I never saw a wolf alive or dead, often as I have put myself in the way of doing so, and I suspect that their numbers must have diminished greatly of late years since cheap Belgium and Birmingham fire-arms have flooded the country. In the wolf-abounding parts it is usual for the whole country-side to join in a hunt of the common enemy in summer time, when the cubs are young, and many are thus killed. These compulsory parish hunts, known as *Montarias*, were once common all over the country.

To an Englishman, who has never dreamt of being brought face to face with a wolf, it is curious to see how the daily life of people living in wolf-frequented countries is, as it were, flavoured by the presence of this uncanny beast. We in Great Britain may imagine what it is if we could fancy our foxes paying occasional visits to our nurseries as well as to our hen-roosts, and carrying off a plump baby sometimes instead of a fowl or goose. I have heard many a story of a wolf leaping through the cottage door at dusk, and making off to the woods with the first child. I do not believe in these tales, but the peasants in the mountain districts do, and when the mother leaves the house, she bids the children be sure to keep the door shut for fear of the wolf.

In the last century wolves were very common indeed in parts of Portugal where they are now unknown. A long period of peace, increase of population, and cheap guns, have been their destruction, but it is only within about the last fifty years that these influences have been at work. In the last century the delivery of wolves' heads was an incident of certain tenures of land, and a very common form of *personal service* was attendance at wolf-hunts; but, even then, their number was lessening, for a trustworthy native chronicler of the last century, writing of the country 100 years before, says the number of wolves in those days was "a fearful thing, principally on the seashores and the banks of the larger streams. They devoured the flocks and even the shepherds, and for this reason a *Montaria* was held every Saturday."

My companion, the priest, was riding a good horse, and upon my critical admiration of it, he insisted upon taking me out of my road to his house, to show me a colt of his own breeding. The *padre* then rode with me to the ridge beyond his village, and pointed out to me my way across the mountains as far as the eye could reach, and the last I saw of him was his cheery face, nipped and reddened in the cold north wind, and his tall, burly frame wrapped in a dark blue cloak, as he waved his slouched hat to me in a parting salute—a type of a certain class of priest not uncommon in Portugal, and not, I think, very well understood by us at home. A peasant by birth, mixing on nearly equal terms with the peasants his parishioners, and with hardly more education than themselves, farming his own land, breeding his own ponies, pruning his own vines, and planting his own garden plot, and possessed of all a countryman's taste and habits—a kind neighbour, and doing his priestly duties, as I was told, with a certain dignity and earnestness, he was a man against whom rumour could allege no scandal of an immoral life.

Such a man as this, if the standard of his life is not a lofty one, can have no influence but a good one; a tolerant man and a shrewd man, he evidently knew when he and his people were well off, and was not to be seduced into any Ultramontane vagaries. If such priests were as common in the Biscayan provinces as in Portugal, Don Carlos would never have got a party and an army. My friend's life interests were in his own parish, and he did not care to enlarge them. He seldom, he told me, went to Lamego or Viseu, and only once in his life had been to Oporto; he had never seen Lisbon. His interest in distant parts seemed to reside in their sporting capabilities, and what was sport in his eyes took a sufficiently fantastic shape in mine. About Coimbra, he informed me, there was excellent thrush shooting, —near Oporto there were crows to be got.

"Crows!" I asked, "are they game birds? You cannot eat them, can you?"

"To be sure I can; they are the best game in the world," said the *padre*, "stewed in vinegar there is really nothing so good!"

The road from Viseu to Mealhada, after a descent from the high lands about that city, and after passing through the pretty village of *Saint Columba on the river Dão,* which the Portuguese shorten into *Santa Combadão,* enters a series of rich but uninteresting valleys till the heights about Busaco are reached,— " grim Busaco's iron ridge," Scott calls this famous battle ground,—though how Sir Walter came to call this tree-covered, rounded hill-side, set in a smiling landscape, a "grim iron ridge" is difficult to say. Mealhada, near the railroad, seems to be chiefly a "station town," and like all such towns everywhere, is regular, ugly and uninteresting.

Here I take the rail, and proceeding by Coimbra and by towns already described, reach Oporto in four hours, and passing through that city, travel along the road which leads due north from it, and enter the pine forests which reach close down to the city on this side. A league brings us to the Leça river, a pretty stream winding its course, willow and alder margined, through rich meadows; a tiny river, hardly more than a brook indeed, yet more celebrated in poets' strains than perhaps any stream of its size in Europe. Half a mile down from where the road crosses is a fine fourteenth century conventual church, and the remains of conventual buildings of great interest. The place is known as Leça do Balio, a corruption of *Bailia,* a bailiwick or commandery of the Knights of St. John of Jerusalem, and an important capitular house of this great

Militant Order existed here, in this fertile valley of the Leça, from a very early date.

In the fifteenth century, the convent buildings are described as being still in perfect repair. A heavy battlemented wall surrounded an extensive range of monastic buildings,—a chapel, granges, threshing floors, and farm buildings; a square tower of immense strength and solidity occupied one angle of the inclosure. Of the ancient fortress, this tower is all that now remains. It is, without any manner of doubt, the work of men who lived in the first hundred years after the establishment of the kingdom. A grand piece of work;—not a ruin; for it stands all in its ancient formidable integrity, and the great mass of squared granite, hardly touched by the tooth of time, frowns down upon the mild ecclesiological tourist of to-day with all the warlike dignity with which it daunted the marauding Saracen of the twelfth and thirteenth centuries.

In 1330 Friar Stephen Vasquez Pimental, being then Grand Commander of the Order, and also Prior of the Monastery, began to build the church, which still remains very nearly as he left it. It was finished in 1336, and in that year Prior Stephen died.* The

* In May, 1336, or, as the fine monumental brass in the church curiously and neatly puts it, in longs and shorts,

"*Mil tercentenis et septuaginta quaternis
Hic obiit Madio mense quasi medio;*"

building of so large an edifice in six years testifies to the wealth of the Order in no slight degree. The church consists of a particularly lofty central aisle and two side aisles, divided by shapely columns with elaborately carved grotesque capitals of high artistic value. The central aisle terminates in a spacious apsidal recess, very finely groined, forming a kind of chancel. I look upon this church as being—apart from its actual beauty—the most important in Portugal from an ecclesiological point of view. The building itself, quite apart from what the records tell us, gives every evidence of being almost wholly of one period, and that a short one. The wealthy Order to which it belonged would have employed, and clearly did employ, the highest architectural talent of the period. The workmanship is indeed admirable; and a knowledge of Leça do Balio as a whole and in detail is, in my opinion, an indispensable key to the study of Portuguese ecclesiastical archæology.

The road northward from Leça lies through the

which must not, however, be translated literally, for the Christian era was not in general use in Portugal till about the middle of the fifteenth century. Till then the Portuguese usually reckoned from the conquest of the Peninsula by the Romans, B.C. 38. This fact seems to be not generally known, for I have met with some very curious chronological misapprehensions in accounts of Portugal. In all dates on Portuguese monuments or charters before 1470 or 1480, unless there is apparent reason against it, it is safe to deduct thirty-eight years.

vast pine woods which form so broad a zone along the Portuguese sea-board. The pine of Portugal is as a rule the fast-growing *Pinus maritima*, very like our own Scotch fir, and quite as ugly a tree when young. In some places the more picturesque stone pine is found, but it is of slower growth, and notwithstanding the greater value of its timber and the use as food of its filbert-like cone kernels, it is little cultivated. The commoner pine grows rapidly in poor soil, and fine trees are often seen with their roots in mere sand.

The pine forest is in general monotonous and unpicturesque, for the trees are always cut before they reach to the dignity of "two ton timber," and the side branches are lopped year after year to within a yard or two of the tree top. The traveller passes league after league of straight-stemmed pine, and wearies for the sight of a green field or a vineyard. The pine forest, too, as in other countries, is silent and deserted: blackbirds, jays and magpies are the only birds commonly seen or heard. Now and then a wood owl flits out of the shadow of an ivied tree, and the occasional tap of a woodpecker's beak, or his sudden, laugh-like cry, are sounds that a traveller feels to be a relief to the stillness. Human beings are rarely encountered, though the forest maintains its own peculiar population. Where the trees are rooted in anything but blowing sand, gorse grows; and the cutting of it once in every three years affords some profit. Gorse in Portuguese farm economy is of great value, being used for the bedding of horned cattle, while the whole of the straw of the farm is used for their food; a system that has many obvious advantages, and others that are not so obvious.

Every now and then, in the depth of the forest, a party of charcoal burners is met with, or of sawyers and carpenters, who encamp in the woods, fell and saw up the pines, and make the boards upon the spot into doors, window-frames and boxes, that are carried long distances for sale. If the forest is in the neighbourhood of towns, the fallen *needles* and cones are collected by women and children, and carried in nets on donkey-back for sale as fuel. These are the purely forestal industries—the only human life connected with it—but this dreary desert of pine wood has its oases. Wherever a brook crosses the forest the scene shifts immediately, and the watercourse is margined by narrow fields of maize, rye and wheat, or orchards of fruit trees reach on either side as far as the water can be made to flow. The stream itself is bordered with pollarded oak and chestnut trees, over which vines are trained. The water-drops work like magic under these hot suns, and the barren, dusty soil is turned by them into fertile meadow land. The silence of the forest is exchanged in an instant for a concert of woodlarks and nightingales, and the refreshing coolness of the water-laden air and the green shadow of deciduous trees are positively delicious to the traveller who has passed through the shadeless forest and breathed the dry, over-sunned air, pungent with the peculiar burnt odour which the pines give out.

In giving this account of a Portuguese pine forest, I have broken my rule of not dwelling upon scenery, for what I have described is typical of many long, weary leagues that every wayfarer in Portugal will have to travel over.

On this northward road, however, through the Minho province, the forest soon begins to break into fields, and the pines give place to some of the most highly cultivated land in Europe; not the most fertile nor the most scientifically cultivated, for the soil is, for the most part, a porous decomposed granite, of great depth, but little natural fertility. The province is densely populated, and the farmers are as a rule peasant proprietors with small holdings of from five to twenty acres.*

The system of farming is by no means unsuited to a country where land is scarce and dear, and labour plentiful and cheap,—a hilly country, full of

* Holding, as I have before explained, by the Emphyteutic tenure, which has got in process of time to be nearly equivalent to our English tenure by copyhold.

streams, springs and water runlets, and where water is the chief source of fertility.

My way northward lay through Barcellos, a charming type of an old Portuguese town. The river Cavado is here crossed by an ivy-clothed, mediæval bridge with massive arch-piers of immense solidity, and it is singular in this respect, that the water is dammed at the bridge itself and falls in a broad cascade which is used to turn the wheels of several water mills, each of which nestles picturesquely at the foot of the piers.

The town is built on rocky land which rises abruptly from the water's edge, and the grey ruins of a massive stronghold of fourteenth century work face the approach by the bridge. It is a town for an artist or an antiquarian to linger in, and willingly would I detain the reader among the Gothic churches and the remains of curious mediæval domestic architecture; but my space is drawing to a close, and a writer may do worse than remember that agreeable writing does not always make pleasant reading.

So I pass on through the streets of Barcellos to stop before an open doorway whence proceed sounds of a curious rhythmic chaunt, a refrain of childish voices, which brings to my memory jumbled associations of Sunday-school children in England, and of schools of shrill-voiced children in far-off Eastern countries; and the latter association prevails, as I walk in and see some thirty dark-skinned and bright-eyed children of from four to nine sitting cross-legged on the ground, exactly as I had seen a party of little Mahometans in Cairo or Damascus, all repeating at the dictation of a teacher, in a loud, rhythmic, sing-song tone, a sentence which, after some trouble, I made out to be part of a poetic version of the multiplication table. The whole thirty swung their bodies forward at the end of each verse, exactly as I have seen Eastern children do. The same monotonous, howling chaunt, the same cross-legged attitude, the same antiphonal mode of teaching, the solo part taken by the teacher and the repetition in the shrill voices of the children, were common to the Christian and the Mahometan school children. The children appeared to like it, their attention did not seem to flag, but then it was difficult to say how much of it was engaged; half their eyes were shut.

A young priest was teaching. An elderly one, with white hair and a benevolent expression of face, sat by. I bowed to him; he returned my salute and requested me to be covered. I told him I was a traveller, and was desirous of seeing a Portuguese school. He begged me to be seated.

He told me of their mode of education; it was an appeal, he said, chiefly to the memory—too much so it seemed to me, with my narrow British and

Protestant prejudices. "First," said the priest, "they have to learn facts; reasoning comes afterwards." The position is a strong one, and I never argue with a courteous host. "What do *they* know?" I said, pointing to a row of the eldest.

"They can read," he said, "they understand geography, they can cipher, and they have the doctrines of our Holy Church at their fingers' ends."

"It says a great deal for the system," I said.

"Would you like to see for yourself?"

I thought he was going to use the established formula—would I *take a class?* Perhaps he was, and perhaps, seeing me visibly shrink from the proposition, he refrained.

He beckoned to a pretty little girl of eight, sitting at the end of the front row. She came up, putting her head on one side, her finger in the corner of her mouth, and stood before us. The benevolent priest patted her on the head. "This gentleman is going to ask you some questions," he said.

My mind suddenly became a blank. I did not know where to begin. There came into my head a story of a school inspector, or some equally formidable person, asking under similar circumstances, a little school girl, "*When the dove returned to the ark the second time, what did it bring back?*" and being entirely puzzled and thrown off his balance by the unhesitating answer, "*Adam, sir!*" the child having by some utterly inscrutable mental process fished up our first parent from the depths of her childish puzzle-headedness.

I was afraid of being brought to shame by some similar childish vagary, and beyond eliciting from her that her name was Zefinha, which is childish for Josepha, and that she was eight years old, I did not venture further to explore her mental resources. Arithmetic is not a favourite subject with me, school theology is a dangerous one, and Mr. Forster himself might have hesitated to commit himself before a schoolful of sharp-witted foreign children and a couple of critical Catholic priests. I begged the priest to question her for me.

I am sorry to say that she broke down shamefully. With an unblushing and smiling face she made the most fearful havoc with the multiplication table, and failed so completely in her divinity that finally the priest and I and the child herself had to give way to our feelings, and laughed out fairly and loudly; and when he had recovered a little of his gravity, the good priest shook his forefinger in mock anger at Zefinha and sent the interesting little idiot back to her seat on the floor.

"What, after all, Senhor Padre," said I, using a broad and consolatory form of philosophy, "what, after all, is the value of earthly learning?"

The priest pursed his mouth together, screwed

his eyes up a little, and slowly nodded his head several times in token of assent.

"That little girl clearly knows too much," I said.

The priest again assented.

"As she grows up," I pursued, "she will begin to forget a little of what you have taught her; her facts will arrange themselves; she will no longer mix up her arithmetic with her theology, she will separate her geography from her grammar—just as —as——"

"Just as a farmer separates his kidney beans from his maize on the threshing floor," said the priest, pleasantly, and offering me his open snuff-box.

"Poor child!" I said; "one cannot expect reason from her."

"No, indeed!" said the priest; "how can any one expect reason from the poor little creatures? That is not our system at all. We make them say a thing a hundred, a thousand, ten thousand times, bawling it out, as you heard, at the top of their voices, and then they know it."

"Yes," said I, "and believe it."

"Of course," said the kindly priest, "and believe it too."

I have said, almost at the beginning of these

Travels, how the farm system of this northern corner of Portugal seemed to me to be more completely after the old Roman type than that of any other country of Europe, even Italy; and now, visiting the province again after an interval, and after seeing the other provinces of the kingdom east and south of it, it strikes me with more force than ever how close is this resemblance between the Minhote and the old Italian husbandry, and how exactly the ancient traditions have been handed down. The field instruments of modern Portugal in shape and often in name are Roman: the *arado* is the single stilted plough (*aratrum*) formed of a crooked bough; the sickle, *fauce*, the Latin *falx;* the *carro*, the solid-wheeled cart with wicker-work sides, is called after the Latin *carrus*, but is equivalent to the Roman *plaustrum;* the lighter hoe is *sacho*, from the Latin *sarculus; grade*, a harrow, is, no doubt, the Latin *crates;* and plough, cart, sickle, hoe and harrow do not merely resemble the old Roman instruments, but are absolutely identical with those which are represented on the medals and bas-reliefs of ancient Rome.

The introduction, in the sixteenth century, of maize as a cereal crop might be supposed to have interfered with the old farming traditions, but it has done so only to a small extent. The Portuguese called the New World corn *milho*, after the millet (*millium*) which they already possessed, whose tall growth it somewhat resembles, and sowed it, hoed it, and irrigated it as they had been accustomed to do with millet.

It is not, however, in such matters as the forms of tools, which are preserved in all countries through long generations, nor in their names, which are still less likely to suffer alteration, that the ancient masters of the Portuguese have left the strongest evidence of the lessons first taught by them. These are matters that the most hasty and cursory tourist can discover for himself; it is in the inner life of the farm that the old traditions are most faithfully preserved.

Columella tells us that for a farm of a little over a hundred acres, two yoke of oxen and two drivers to each, and six labourers for general cultivation, were enough; if there was much underwood, two more men were wanted. This is, indeed, a low estimate where wine and maize are grown, and where hoeing and constant irrigation are required, but in the hilly rye-lands of Portugal, with flocks of sheep and grazing land, it is a fair estimate. On the great upland plain of Chaves, a farmer whom I asked about the stock and labour for a hundred acre farm, answered me almost in the words I have quoted. To be sure, both the Portuguese and the Peninsular Roman had a very low standard of farming, and the land in modern Portugal is but half farmed, as it must have been in Iberia and ancient Italy.

Then again, there is the wine making. In a recent number of a contemporary magazine,* Mr. Matthew Freke Turner has told us how the Roman farmers made their commoner wines—their *vin ordinaire*—and the process is identical with that followed in this province. The vine is grown as a climber on pollarded trees, as the vines of Latium and the Campania were grown: the Minho province is near the sea, as those districts were: the vines are pruned exactly as they were pruned in Central Italy, the latitude is the same, and the varieties of the vine perhaps even identical. Anyone therefore who has tasted the famous *vinho verde* of northern Portugal—the thick, red, sour and astringent wine which the Minhotes delight in—may satisfy himself that he has drunk a liquid identical in every way with that wherewith the Latian farmer quenched his thirst two thousand years ago. He may even please himself by thinking that Horace himself on his Tusculan farm, in daily life, when the jars of Cæcuban, Alban and Falernian were left undisturbed in the cellar, drank such a wine as this. The scholar or the antiquarian, who is too dry-souled to amuse himself with such a mere sentiment, may

* "Wine and Wine Merchants," in the NEW QUARTERLY MAGAZINE for April, 1874.

yet drink a glass of the *vinho verde* and understand for ever after that which has always been a puzzle to students of antiquity, namely, how it was that the Greeks and Romans could bring themselves to dilute their wines with sea water, to mix them with honey or spices, or even to grate goat's-milk cheese into the wine cup. No stranger who has drunk a full draught of this really awful Minho wine but might sigh for even such adulterations as these.

It is curious, too, as further evidence of the long and faithful tradition of farm economy, that these northern Portuguese farmers deal with the drinking of the wine (they mostly keep it for farm use) just as their first masters in agriculture did before them. "Let the labourers," says the frugal Cato, "drink up the *lora*," the thin stuff made by adding water to the already pressed grapes and treading out a thin and make-shift kind of wine therefrom. "Let them drink up the lora," he says, "in the three months that follow the vintage." The Portuguese call this stuff *agua pé*—foot water—and likewise consume it in early winter. After Christmas, Portuguese farmers follow Cato's precept, and let their men have a small measure of real wine daily. In the spring, the quantity was doubled in ancient Italy, and is doubled in modern Portugal. In the long summer days, the portion is trebled for the Minhote, as Cato prescribes; and, calculating the ancient measure as well as we are able, the allowance would reach three or four gallons a month the year through. It is quite as great on a well managed Portuguese farm to this day.

Let the fact be observed, and let the reader draw from it what deduction he pleases, that this Portuguese wine is probably about three times as strong as ordinary English beer, and yet that drunkenness is very rare.

To our nicer palates it is a terrible drink, one that rasps a man's throat, fills his eyes with tears, and almost takes his breath away; but to the Minhote labourer, in the heat and burden of his long day's work, it is clearly delicious. It is meat and drink to him. He finds refreshment in its acidity, he is fortified by its austerity, revived by its strength, and finds in its œnanthic, etherous essences—beyond the reach of chemists and professors—some subtle distillation of Nature's laboratory kindly to life.

Often in travelling along the dusty highway have I watched a group of sunburnt peasants, lying under the shade of a vine-trellis or a cork-tree, taking their afternoon *merenda*—a sort of five o'clock tea, if the bull may be used—when they rest for a quarter of an hour—a tiny slice of repose out of their thirteen or fourteen hours of continuous labour—eating a handful of olives and a crust of black bread; and pleasant it is to see these hard-working, civil-spoken men, jaded with honest toil, take a long, sweet pull from the wine jar, and to watch how the wine god enters into them, restores their spirits, and renews their strength.

I am now within a few leagues of the northern boundary of the kingdom, and of the road which I travelled over in my first chapter. Braga, the archiepiscopal city, and Guimaraens, the famous seat of government of the early kings, I leave undescribed, though they lie in the country between where I now stand, and the northern frontier. I need say nothing about them, for they are well known cities, tourist-haunted, and described by worthier pens than mine.

There now remain but a very few lines to write of these Travels, and I cannot fill them better than by summarizing the experience I have gained of the Portuguese as a people.

Unless a man have denationalized himself, and parted with all the prejudices that his birth and breeding have made part of his nature—and I can claim to have made my observations from no such philosophic standpoint—unless he have become a thorough citizen of the world, all foreigners will seem to him to fall short whenever they differ from the standard which he has got to set up. In following me the reader will have had evidence enough that I am not unbiassed by the prejudices of a thorough-going Englishman, and in his wisdom he will have made due allowances accordingly. Moreover, he will remember that the fatigues, the delays, the many small worries of travel, are sore trials to the temper, and that a man is never so little of a philosopher as when he is on a journey.

I have found plenty to criticise in some phases of the Portuguese character, and I have perhaps too much followed the humour of the day in being over scant of approbation. Nevertheless, writing now calmly and at a distance of time and place, and summing up the character of a people whom I may claim to have studied carefully, I can find little but good to say of them. The heart of the nation is a sound, honest heart. Portugal is essentially an agricultural country, and in the country districts a fairly high standard of honesty and morality prevails. If this standard is not so universally reached in the towns, it is rather the inferior tradesmen and the loafers in the streets who fail to have quite persuaded themselves that "honesty is a good policy." Among such people to say of a man that he is "*muito fino*," very sharp, is high praise, and the expression comprises some very sharp practice indeed. I should say that the morality of such people was of about the looseness of that of betting men of the lower class at home—not very outrageously bad, but morality that will not bear too close a scrutiny.

On the other hand, to say of a countryman that he is a "*pé de boi*," is to pay him the greatest of compliments. Literally "an ox-foot," it of course means that he is a steady, true man, slow to make a promise, but sure to keep it. These two proverbial phrases tell their own story.

In Portugal the highest classes and the lowest classes are the most agreeable in every way to have to do with. The very highest class in a country which is almost purely agricultural is, of course, a class of country gentlemen. Countrymen by birth, by breeding, and in heart, they are for the most part men of the world who have rubbed off the uncouthness of country breeding. From this rank come many of the foremost politicians, merchants, and financiers of the country; and the high standard of honour and the educated manner which are characteristic of such a class everywhere, reach a long way down in Portugal. To be sure, the morality is a little diluted, as the social scale is descended; but of this I have perhaps already said enough. This class is a small one, and the black sheep in it are, after all, rare exceptions.

Of the working men, in town and country, it is

difficult to speak too highly. Sober, hard-working, well-mannered, frugal, light-hearted and law-abiding, the Portuguese peasant and the Portuguese workman make a class of citizens of whom any country might well be proud.

This, then, is the result of my observation of this small and, of late years, little noticed people. The geographical position of the kingdom, with the finest natural harbour on the whole western shores of the continent, its long independence under difficult circumstances, its nearness to our own coasts, the part it has taken with ourselves in great historical emergencies, the successful working in the country of a representative government not unlike our own—all these things make Portugal a country deeply interesting to the people of Great Britain.

To us Portugal is, and always has been, an important part of Europe. The nation, small as it is, is not without potentiality of influence in European affairs. The individual Portuguese is perhaps not a braver man than the individual Spaniard, but he is less of a gasconader; he is more capable of loyalty; he is more susceptible of discipline; an army of Portuguese is an admirable army. It is well known how Wellington was inclined at first to rate the Spanish troops much higher than his Portuguese allies, and how soon he found out his mistake; well fed, well led and well disciplined, they became, in the Duke's own words, "the fighting cocks of the Peninsular army;" he ranked them next only to British troops.

These facts should not be forgotten. This nation is our natural ally; the vigour, the self-respect and that peculiar sturdiness of temper which we pride ourselves upon, are also Portuguese characteristics. The nation is one friendly to ourselves, and whose interests in this continent are our interests, whose enemies in a great war are quite certain to be our enemies, and who have left their own indelible mark on the page of history by virtue of some great and rare qualities, which happen to be those very qualities which have made of ourselves a great and famous nation.

SUPPLEMENTARY CHAPTER.

Reasons for Writing a Supplementary Chapter—Influence of the Moon in Portugal—The Planting of Cabbages—Spade and Hoe Cultivation—Women's Work—Superstitious Notions—The Fattening of Pigs—The Priests' Influence—Non-Secular Education—Cheap Substitute for Newspapers—Hints to Tourists—Climate—Language — Anecdote — Philistinism — Anecdote — Manners and Morals—Management of Forests and Orchards—A Secret in Forestal Science—Flower Gardens—A Problem in Agriculture—Farm System of Portugal.

THE occasion of my writing this last and Supplementary Chapter was the allegation made by several critics in the public press who, having reviewed in no unfriendly spirit the previous portions of these Travels as they appeared in periodical issues of THE NEW QUARTERLY MAGAZINE, complained that although I had written fully of the "manners, customs, dress, architecture, painting, land tenure, government and so forth," of a little-visited country, I had failed not only to give any hints for the guidance of future travellers, but, further, that I had not "reported any facts of substantial practical utility." "Is there nothing," one of my critics asked, "in the ways of a people whom our author describes as thrifty and ingenious, which could be turned to advantage by the great mass of our own countrymen?" The same writer asked me, with somewhat greater severity (after certain complimentary remarks which I refrain from quoting) what, " beyond mere amusement and a sort of æsthetic literary interest, is to be got out of what Mr. Latouche has written?"

The good sense and justice of these criticisms struck me, and I lost no time in stringing together as many hard and practical facts concerning Portuguese ways of life as I could bring to my recollection, setting them forth so seriously and so plainly that I am sure no critic whatever, be he ever so unæsthetic and anxious for solid information, will have occasion to quarrel with me any more.

The Portuguese are a shrewd people and an acute people; they love to look into the nature of things that concern their daily life. They will reason soundly, and (when they can forget the influence of the moon) to good purpose, not indeed on such themes as—

"Providence, foreknowledge, will and fate,"

but on those lesser and yet not unimportant laws of Nature which concern the planting of cabbages, the fattening of pigs, the curing of bacon, wine-making, farming and the domestic treatment of diseases.

It is not to be expected that a true-born Englishman, strong in his many wholesome convictions and prejudices, should admit for a moment that in any one of these matters he has anything to learn from a Portuguese; but he may be instructed by the blunders of the foreigners, and now and then he can take note that there are sometimes two ways of doing the same thing, and that it is just possible that the English way may not be the best. I will illustrate these two propositions by the above-mentioned simple operation of planting cabbages. Our gardeners plant them with a spade, the Portuguese with a strong, broad-bladed hoe. Now, it is a demonstrable fact that while the spade plants two cabbages, the hoe, stirring the soil as deeply and as effectually, and distributing the manure more deftly, will plant three. The same comparison applies to potato planting; and an English civil engineer in Portugal once gave it to me as his opinion that the hoe as a navigator's tool (supplemented by a basket carried on the head) was in some respects superior to the spade—or rather to the pick and shovel of the English navvy. The pick, shovel and barrow, in the hands of a strong navvy, were certainly, he said, the most efficient means of doing navigator's work, but where the best male labour was not procurable in sufficient quantity, it was found that the cheaper labour of women, and even of children, with hoe and basket, was very efficient.

I will observe, in passing, and as a small contribution to the great "Woman's Work" controversy, that in rural Portugal the women work as hard in the fields as the men, both sexes beginning as mere children; and further, that in health and a generally buxom, contented appearance, the peasant women of Portugal compare favourably with peasant women the world over. No representative exists in Portugal of the pale, care-worn, slatternly labourer's wife of our English cottages; she is replaced by a cheerful, robust, sunburnt, gaily-dressed woman, who on festivals wears from five pounds to twenty or thirty pound's worth of gold jewelry round her neck and in her ears.

To return to the planting of cabbages:—if the Portuguese gain by planting them better and more quickly than we can, they lose by failing to understand that the plant dwindles if it is grown continuously in the same plot of ground, and, so planted, only thrives at all by being preposterously manured. In this matter, then, we may learn from the Portuguese to plant our cabbages more quickly, and if we do not choose therein to better our ways, we can at least be thoroughly confirmed in our own wisdom, which teaches us never to plant them two years running in the same ground.

There is another matter in which our good sense is not very particularly apparent, and is yet far above that of the natives of Portugal. In remote parts or Great Britain certain mischievous superstitions still lurk, and in districts of our native land not remote, the moon still governs the actions of men. Belief in witchcraft and similar folly is continually cropping up at home, but it is as nothing to the similar credulity that is prevalent in Portugal. If a man were minded to write a paper on the folly of superstition, —on superstition as a hindrance to human welfare— nowhere could he do so with greater ease and profit than in this small kingdom. All manner of innocent and of nasty plants are thought to be sovereign in various diseases, if only they are culled at some particular age of the moon, carried in a particular manner by a church door, or even laid for an instant on the altar. An ox or a sheep dying of active inflammation, poisoned by yew leaves, or henbane, or foxglove, has an incantation muttered over it, is drenched with a decoction of some generally innocuous but sometimes hurtful herb, and often gets no other treatment whatever.

The credulity that prevails in rural Portugal respecting the ways of birds and beasts is marvellous,—an ignorance which the people might be supposed able to correct by common observation. Their strange distortion of facts quite within every-day knowledge governs their practice, and is found—best proof of its acceptance—in their very proverbs.

The common people express sudden, rapid and complete action by a proverb which implies that it is the habit of the weazel, on occasion, to jump down the throat of the toad! The screech owl haunts graveyards in Portugal, and digs up the bodies of the dead; not content with which, this bird acts the same ghoul-like part towards newly-sown peas and beans. The hedgehog sucks the milch cows, as with us at home, and I have been told that snakes and the larger lizards do the same by goats and ewes. The wehr-wolf belief is almost universal in northern and western Portugal, and the existence of witches and warlocks and *revenants* of every kind is established on evidence more than sufficient to convince Mr. Wallace of spiritualistic celebrity.

Such innocent superstitions, as these, however, amuse the people, and do them, so far as I can tell, no material harm. The actual damage to their interests is inflicted in a much more prosaic manner, and a statistician might profitably employ himself in calculating the actual money loss suffered by a nation which allows itself to be ruled by the moon rather than by its own senses. To take one instance;—the market gardeners and farmers near the two principal seaports of Portugal grow quantities of the large and valuable onions which are exported to many European countries. The climate, together with very careful and skilful cultivation, brings these onions to a size and flavour not to be obtained elsewhere. As may be supposed, the crop is a precarious one at best. The seed is sown in about October, and the young onions transplanted in the following April. Now, every farmer or gardener would see the paramount importance of choosing moist, warm, and showery weather to sow the seed. Not so the Portuguese: he will let the most favourable weather pass if the phase of the moon be not favourable as well, and will sow in a frost or an east wind if only his almanack bids him. It is quite certain that this stupidity is sometimes equivalent to the loss of more than half of this important crop.

To take another instance from rural domestic life:—With an agricultural population, pig-fattening is necessarily an important matter. No Portuguese, high or low, rich or poor, old or young, is, I am inclined to believe, quite happy who does not possess a pig in process of fattening. Autumn comes round, the pigs get fatter, but not rapidly. The breeds of Yorkshire and Berkshire are unknown; the Portuguese animal has the length of leg, the leanness, and nearly the speed of the English greyhound. He will not be hurried into presentable bacon; his fattening is a slow and precarious process. Nevertheless, fat or lean, the last new moon before the winter quarter must be fatal to him. A fortnight more might make a respectable

"Martinmas pig" of him; but the popular belief is that if he is not killed before the hunter's moon has waned, salt will not pickle him, nor wood-smoke cure him. It would be curious to speculate how much the nation loses every year through this superstition alone.

I have not, in the course of these Travels, had occasion to say much of the religion of the country. In ninety-nine rural parishes out of a hundred the priest is the best informed and most rational man in it, and, as a general rule, gives no countenance to such " old wives' tales " as I have mentioned above. It is not necessary, however, to go to Portugal to learn how even a slight superiority of education removes a man in some sort from the sympathies of his fellow men, and lessens his influence for good or evil. The most reasonable of priests can make little head against a parish full of superstitions. It is not the clergy who are to be blamed, but, as I believe, the system of education. Without presuming to enter into a comparison of religions, or venturing too far into a most dangerous question, it may at least be asked whether it be good for any people that its school teaching should be so entirely non-secular as that of most Roman Catholic countries, and that the purely literary element in the "reading" of the rural classes should be scrutinized and hindered by the priests of a religion jealous of intellectual enlightenment in its mildest form. This I put modestly as a question; but what I do think past being considered as a question, and as being a very unquestionable and deplorable fact is that, chiefly in consequence of this clerical education and clerical scrutiny, it should come to be that a traveller should never by any chance find in the hands either of yeoman-farmer or peasant any non-religious book whatever, always excepting almanacks, in comparison with which, that of the late Zadkiel would appear a sober astronomical treatise. The rural population is the backbone of the kingdom, and it is a real misfortune for the country that it should be destitute of any sort of literature. It is said that when an American farmer emigrates westward beyond the reach of posts and railways, there will be found in his log-house, nine times out of ten, besides his Bible, a Milton or a Shakespeare or, at the very least, a stout " Encyclopædia of Domestic Economy." A man would have to travel long through Portugal to find anything equivalent to such a library as this in a Portuguese homestead.

It is one of the chief objects of foreign travel to stimulate the traveller to bring the results of his observations to bear upon the solution of political and social problems in his own country, and everyone knows how the critical tourist may stumble, when he least expects it, upon food for most valuable reflection and generalization.

The Portuguese are, as I have already said, in regard to a national press, very much what we were a hundred and fifty years ago. The immense development of journalism in our own country is, no doubt, fully appreciated by us in most of its phases; but has it quite come home to all of us that it is one of the consequences of our possession of that priceless boon, a free and cheap press, that we have the wherewithal to light our domestic fires? Not only are the law reports and the police news and the proceedings of Parliament disseminated, but an admirable, cheap, and, in fact, an indispensable fuel is equally distributed among the public. In Portugal, this is not so. A taste for reading is rare, newspapers are scarce and small, and the people do not possess this easy mode of rekindling the fires on their kitchen hearths. Under these circumstances, what do they do? They grow a plant called *carqueja*—a sort of broom—they dry it in the sun, and it is then carried to all the large towns and sold to housekeepers at a farthing for three bundles. This natural fire-lighting material fortunately grows on waste land, with little and often with no cultivation. If the time ever comes when our daily and weekly journals cease to circulate —their influence has already aroused the indignation of some of our demagogue politicians—it will be well to remember that the botanical name of the *carqueja* is *genista bidentata*.

I began these Travels by remarking that Portugal was no country for the mere tourist; but I understand that this enterprising and nearly ubiquitous personage has, since this warning was written, turned his attention to the capabilities of Portugal for his particular purposes. A peaceful country, free from brigands, and with a civil and hospitable population, might seem to invite invasion of this sort, but I compress my advice to such intending immigrants into the dissuasive " Don't." They will find reasons for it in nearly every chapter I have written. The real traveller, the patient, inquiring and serious person, will indeed find in Portugal "fresh woods and pastures new;" but though he need not possess the physique of a Livingstone, he will require qualifications such as the traveller of the idle, amateur kind does not possess.* He must be

* Portugal, and especially Lisbon, enjoyed at one time a reputation as a winter residence which it has lost for no good reason that I am aware of. The winter climate of Algarve in the extreme south might probably, if meteorological statistics existed, be shown to bear competition with any South of Europe climate whatever; but in no town of Algarve could the invalid find any sort of comforts; nor would he find such comforts, or English and French speaking people anywhere but in the two principal cities of the kingdom. There are several good hotels in Lisbon, in all of which French and English

a linguist, a born linguist, if he is to make any head with the crabbed language of the country in a reasonable time. Very intelligent men are often poor language learners, and many a rare fool is a good linguist, so that a man need not think much the better of himself for his fluency in a foreign tongue.

and even German are spoken. The charges are moderate, the cooking and attendance good. The best are the Braganza and the Central, and Madame Durand's hotel, the latter, kept by a Swiss and his English wife, is particularly comfortable.

The winter climate of Lisbon, to my thinking, resembles that of Naples. The mean annual temperature of Oporto is a few degrees lower than that of Lisbon; but the alternations of heat and cold are not so great. The Northern Capital is surrounded by vast pine forests, and these clearly moderate both the extreme heat and the extreme cold, and the winter temperature is probably higher than that of Lisbon. The climate of Oporto may be compared to that of Rome, in whose latitude it lies; but I suspect that a comparison of meteorological observations would show Oporto to be the more genial and healthy climate of the two.

At Oporto the hotels are not quite so good as at Lisbon, but they are good enough. There is, as at Lisbon, a Protestant place of worship, and at Oporto is an important and numerous and, I should add, hospitable British colony, the most important, perhaps, in Southern Europe. There is also an excellent English physician. Portugal is within easy reach of Great Britain. Overland, viâ Madrid by rail, Lisbon can be reached in 6, Oporto in 7 days. By sea, the fast mail steamers from Southampton reach Lisbon in $3\frac{1}{4}$ days. Smaller, slower, but very safe and comfortable boats, leaving London and Liverpool once or twice every week, reach Lisbon in 5 and Oporto in $4\frac{1}{2}$ days.

This is, I believe, a fair statement of the capabilities of Portugal as a winter residence. I do not advise mere sight-seeing or sporting tourists or confirmed invalids to go to Portugal; but to persons who simply wish to escape the English winter, I think the country may safely be recommended.

Still, the accomplishment is a *sine quâ non* in all real foreign travel; and if we ever come to live under a purely paternal government, it may suggest itself to some future Bismarck (if we are ever blessed with one) as a useful reform, and one much to the furtherance of British prestige abroad, to compel intending travellers on the Continent to pass an examination in languages before they step on board the steamboat at Folkestone or Dover. Our national prestige does unquestionably suffer from our peculiar linguistic shortcomings; and, in sober seriousness, is it not a mistake for the members of a proud nation to place themselves, as we do, at a signal disadvantage with almost every foreigner they encounter? The English certainly speak worse French than any European nation; and it is probably a great surprise to most Englishmen, travelling on the continent for the first time, to find how completely this language has become a *lingua Franca* among educated classes in all parts of Europe.

A traveller should do even more than speak French fluently, he should be able to discriminate between the accents and idioms with which other European nations speak it—no very difficult matter, and ignorance of which once brought the present writer into a somewhat awkward predicament.

It was on the occasion of finding myself on board a large ocean steamer. My cabin companion was a very lively foreign gentleman, whom I set down as a Swiss. We talked upon things in general, and the conversation falling, as it often will fall between chance acquaintances, upon the characteristics of different nations, my new friend descanted with some humour upon this subject, and I followed suit as well as I could. We had expended the small artillery of our ridicule upon the foibles of the people of nearly every country, excepting always England and Switzerland—as I thought, our respective fatherlands; we had said smart and foolish things about Frenchmen, Germans, Russians and Danes, Italians and Spaniards; and as for Dutchmen, I said they would be a great nation, in spite of their canals and even their trousers, if it were not for that story of the wooden nutmegs; it has made them absurd, and shown them to be rogues the wide world over. "*Sir*," said my acquaintance, with a sudden accession of dignity, "*I was born at Rotterdam!*"

If I say that a man going to Portugal for any other purposes than travel should learn to speak Portuguese, I may seem to utter a truism. Yet I am by no means persuaded that the advice is good. The intending traveller must, as I have said, speak the language correctly and fluently. He who goes to a country intending to live in it permanently, perhaps to trade in it, may indeed wisely hesitate before he condescends to master its idiom. A stranger who permits himself to be fluent in a strange tongue, loses some of that ascendancy which a contemptuous indifference to native customs and native forms of speech always gives him. Doctor Johnson was wrong, probably, after all, when he insisted upon speaking Latin instead of French to his French acquaintances. To have heard so learned a man break down in his French genders and his auxiliary verbs, must infallibly have both mortified and impressed the Parisian philosophers.

The judicious impertinence of our resident countrymen abroad, who will neither speak the language of the natives nor let them speak English, but who contrive a barbarous *lingua Franca* between the two, is, on the whole, therefore, a successful mode of convincing foreigners of our superiority,—always assuming that it does not make them laugh. Of this, however, there seems to be little danger; even the Pigeon English which is used in China, most ridiculous of spoken dialects, and the broken-down Hindustani of our people in India (itself a speech born in camps and bazaars), never raise a smile among Chinamen or Hindoos. The Portuguese of Englishmen in Portugal has some of the "pigeon" element in it, and the less educated the speaker the more barbarous does the dialect become, till in extreme cases Philistinism culminates in refusing altogether to learn the language of the country. I once came across an old working man, whose schooling had probably been of the slightest, and whose pride of race would not allow him to compromise his dignity by condescending to speak Portuguese at all. "These natives understand English well enough if they choose," he said to me, "it's only their confounded obstinacy, sir; *if you talk loud enough they always understand!*"

There is something more than a new language to be learnt by some of our countrymen before they travel in Portugal. The natives of the country retain the ceremoniousness which was more or less universal in Europe a hundred years ago. The ceremoniousness of the better bred Italians is as nothing to that of the Portuguese. The punctiliousness and formality of their social converse exceed those even of the Castilians. In Spain a man may safely use the title *Usted* (your Worship) in addressing every class and rank, short of Royalty itself. Not so in Portugal. He shows his ignorance and makes himself simply ridiculous if he fails to distinguish at least six different classes, with their different forms of address. A little beggar boy or girl he will speak to, impatiently or charitably, as the case may be, but always in the second person singular, "*Vai te embora,*" Go thy way; or "*Pega n'isto,*" Take this. If the same boy or girl has grown to years of discretion, more ceremony must be employed in the refusing or the bestowing of alms, "*Não pode ser,*" It cannot be; "*Va com Deus,*" Pray go off (in the third person, let it be observed).

A working man takes rank with our magistrates at home, and is literally his Worship. *Vossemessê* is itself a contraction of *Vossa Mercê*, and when the dignity or the age of an interlocutor hardly entitles him to so much honour, the word is contracted to *Vossê*. Little street boys are to each other in their play together their Lordships or their Worships: "your Lordship is cheating," "your Worship has stolen my kite," and so on. A tradesman is "The Lord," *O Senhor*, or " Your Lordship," *Vossa Senhoria*, and these titles are applicable a good way up and down in the social scale. "Your Excellency," *Vossa Excellencia*, is reserved for persons of noble rank or high official position, and every lady below the rank of the Queen may also safely and properly be addressed as Your Excellency.

All these various titles of course require the use of the third person singular, as in Italian. The second person of the plural, formerly used by the Portuguese, has now for several generations been almost confined, in "polite" Portuguese at least, to prayers and addresses to the Deity.

The forms used in letter-writing are endless. How to begin and how to end, what margin to leave, where to sign one's name, when to write one's address as *A Casa de Vossa Excellencia*, Your Excellency's *own* house, and when to avoid this inexpensive kind of generosity; when to end with the formal *Deus guarde á Vossa Excellencia*, May God preserve your Excellency, and when to assure your correspondent, as is the common form, that you venerate him, and are the most devoted of his servants—all this is a necessary part of the education of a traveller who desires to pass for a well-bred and courteous person. There is a formula for almost everything, and in circles of not the very highest class this sort of social culture is, as might be supposed, most excessive.

In the remoter parts of Portugal a curious form of salutation prevails, and prevails almost universally; a man meeting his acquaintance, or even a perfect stranger, says, "*Louvado seja Nosso Senhor Jesus Christo*," Praised be Jesus Christ our Lord; and the answer is always, "*E para sempre seja louvado*," And praised for ever and ever. It is still customary in most parts of Portugal to say "*Viva!*" May you live! when a man sneezes, equivalent to the "God bless you," which prevails among certain homely folk with us under similar circumstances. But in good society this custom is no longer fashionable, though one's Portuguese friend, if one happens to sneeze in his presence, will sometimes say the word half under his breath, and with a slight deprecatory smile, as if to convey—"I know, my dear sir, that it is not quite the thing to say *viva!* but my interest in you is so strong that I infringe *les bienséances*, to show how much I wish you well."

A Jewish acquaintance, whom I have already mentioned, told me of a curious Talmudian legend to account for this singular practice, as old as Homer, and common, I believe, to every branch of mankind, of blessing a man who sneezes. When human beings were first created, the legend runs, they were very loosely put together, and a man's first sneeze would shake him so completely to pieces as to be followed by his immediate break-up and dissolution. In process of time, however, the bodies of men growing more substantial—the molecular particles perhaps, as Professor Tyndall would argue, more firmly compacted—sneezing was not invariably accompanied by instant death, and bystanders, seeing a man sneeze with impunity, would express at once their astonishment and their congratulations by some such formula as *Viva!*—God bless you! and so forth. If our modern atomic philosophers can bring themselves to believe in this theory—and they can hardly be looked upon as men of a very sceptical habit of mind—they will no doubt thank me for this addition to the fabric of a cosmogony which they are industriously building up for our benefit.

To return to Portuguese manners, it might be imagined that so courteous a people, and one whose communication with each other was so hedged about with formal observances, would be very little given to the use of "naughty words" in conversation. It is sad to say that this is not the case. They are terribly hard swearers on occasion, but a connoisseur in conversational blasphemy would find little to approve in the range of oaths used by this small nation. The Portuguese is neither so free nor so frequent a swearer as the Spaniard, and he is not nearly so ingenious a one as the Italian. Like all southerners, his oaths have a tendency to be gross or indecent; and many of these people, when they are impatient or excited, use expressions that would shock an English bargee, and raise blushes in the mess-room of a cavalry regiment.

The inefficacy of blasphemy as a mode of expression, must, I suppose, have come home to every practiser of the art of swearing. An imprecation may start by being as profane or as abominable as it can be, and yet with a little use it rubs off its wickedness or its grossness and therewith much of its point. Gentlemen in Spain with some claim to decent manners, and even women (not ladies) of quite respectable morality, use expressions which are absolutely untranslatable; and, to come nearer home, that fierce and exceedingly inappropriate epithet which our fastidious newspaper reporters print *bl——dy*, has been so weakened by use, that a recent French Dictionary-maker renders it quite correctly " *adj.*, fam. *très, fort.*"

There is, it must be admitted, something singularly startling and bloodthirsty, at first hearing it, in the shouted "*Morra!*" Let him die!—of a riotous Portuguese mob; but the generally good-humoured crowds of a Portuguese city are no more desirous of the death of the momentary object of their evil wishes, than an angry English election crowd would really like to see Mr. Disraeli guillotined, or Mr. Bright brought to the gallows.

This whole subject of swearing is one to which literary men and philosophers have, perhaps, as yet hardly done full justice. An old Scotch lady has been heard to lament the decline in these islands of this once fashionable practice; it was she contended, "a great set-off to conversation." No one can deny that oaths, to some extent, take the place of ideas. If I were further from the necessary end of these Travels, I should be glad further to moralize on this delicate theme; I must instead content myself with a comparison. As contrasted with almost every European nation, we are monotonous in our oaths, and the art, it seems to me, is getting with us more and more confined to the less educated and intelligent among us; but I will boldly assert, for the honour of my countrymen, that after some experience of the blasphemy of foreign nations, there is no oath so mouth-filling, so complete in every way, so simple, and so utterly stupid (for this is a great recommendation in swearing), as the fine, sounding imprecation which is uttered ten thousand times a day at home, and has prevailed in these Islands since the time of Froissart.

We have extracted a practical lesson or two from the Portuguese kitchen-garden. There is nothing to be learnt from their treatment of flowers, and but little from their management of orchards. They possess, indeed, many fine orchards of fruit trees, and groves of oranges and lemons, of olives and mulberries, and extensive forests of pine, chesnut, and cork-trees, but they are far behind the Germans in forestal science, and the French—the masters of us all—in pomology. The Portuguese oranges grown in the interior are as large and good as those from St. Michael's, but the oranges which come from the seaboard districts—the only ones ever exported to Great Britain—are poor in quality; for which I can give no reason except bad cultivation, seeing that the best oranges in many other countries grow within reach of the sea breezes.

The olives of Portugal—an important food of the people—are gathered riper than in Spain, France, or Italy, and are small and dark coloured. They are probably more wholesome, and, in my opinion, far better to eat, than the olives of any other country; so good, indeed, and so cheap that it is a wonder they are not brought to this country in place of the hard, half-ripe and expensive olives of France. The oil made from them is generally badly made, but when properly purified it is quite as good, though by no means as saleable, as the fine oils of Italy.

The climate of Portugal appears to be identical in many respects with that of Japan; and many Japanese shrubs and flowers, which dwindle and fail in the open air in France and England, grow magnificently in Portugal. Chief among them is the camellia, brought, it is said, about ninety years ago from Japan, and often seen in Portugal of the size of a full grown apple-tree. The camellia seems to require a rather damp climate, and perhaps a granite soil, for the tree is a weakling in the dry air of Lisbon, but thrives close by at Cintra, and still better at Oporto, where many new and beautiful varieties are grown,— among others the sweet-scented kind,* of whose

---

* A variety, if I am not mistaken, of *C. myrtifolia*. It has a beautiful, compact, rose-coloured blossom, with very close, regular,

existence no English gardener or botanist to whom I have spoken seems to be aware. Lovely as the flowers of the camellia are singly, the tree itself, in full bloom, is by no means an attractive sight. A camellia-tree with a thousand flowers on it might be supposed, with its compact growth and its shiny leaves of rich green, to be an exquisitely beautiful object, but it is nothing of the sort. The flowers, as they begin to fade, get to be of a dingy brown, and hang a long time on the tree, and a camellia-tree in full blossom has by far the largest proportion of its flowers withered and ugly. As a flowering shrub the camellia is not comparable to the poinsettia, which blossoms to perfection in the Algarve provinces, with its mass of intense scarlet bloom looking like a richly-coloured silken drapery hung on the branches of the tree; or to the white datura. A datura shrub in full bloom, with its thousands of pendent flower bells reflected in a pool of water, is a thing not soon to be forgotten.

In their treatment of trees the Portuguese have a practice which, if I could be quite certain of its efficacy, I should not hesitate to proclaim to be an invention of singular value and importance. It was while travelling through the eastern part of the Province of Alemtejo,—the great province which lies

waxy and rather pointed petals. The flower has a faint, honey-sweet scent.

immediately to the south of the river Tagus,—that I one day came upon a farmer boring a hole with an auger into the very heart of a large cork-tree. Having driven the instrument about a foot into the tree he took from his pocket a small bottle, and was proceeding to pour its contents into the hole he had made. At this juncture, my curiosity overcoming me, I dismounted and asked him what he was about. He showed me the bottle, which contained about a spoonful of quicksilver, and told me that this being poured into the hole, the tree would eventually die. He told me that a few drops of quicksilver so applied were enough to destroy the largest and most flourishing tree. Cause and effect seemed to me—and still seem—strangely disproportioned, and I cannot speak from any actual observation of the results as to the efficacy of this curious method of killing trees; nor, assuming that it is efficacious, can I account in any rational way for the destructive effects of so small a quantity of mercury. Perhaps it permeates the tubes of the vegetable tissue; perhaps it mechanically arrests the ascending sap; perhaps, combining with the chemical constituents of the sap, it forms some powerful mercurial salt, poisonous to vegetation; perhaps the hole in the heart of the tree is itself fatal to it. I can only say that the practice, as I have described it, is not confined to one part of Portugal, and is at least believed in by the Portuguese. It might be worth while to try the experiment. If it be true that a tree can be so easily and cheaply destroyed, the value of such a fact to a colonist in uncleared forest land would be simply incalculable. I give the receipt for what it is worth. I do not vouch for it. I do not even believe in it. "It may be true," as a Welshman says in one of our old comedies, "but it is very impossible."

As farming is, in an agricultural country, the most important and interesting of subjects, I will bring this Chapter to a conclusion with a few words upon the matter. It is needless to say that farming in Portugal is the reverse of scientific. The owners of great estates in the midland districts of the country are, indeed, at last turning their attention to the cultivation of their lands by machinery and by steam; but Portuguese agriculture in general is quite two hundred years behind what it is in our own country. For instance, the rotation of crops involves a simple principle which I could never get a Portuguese farmer to entertain. He could perfectly understand exhaustion of the land, but not that certain constituents only of the soil could be taken out of it; not that it could be exhausted for one crop and not for another. In practice, indeed, the Portuguese disregard the great principle thus involved; and they disregard it with curious impunity. On farms suitably situated for irrigation, fair crops of maize have been raised, summer after summer, for over a hundred years. Jethro Tull himself could never have proposed to carry his famous and fallacious principle so far as this.

How, then, it may be asked, can the Minho farmer do what the English theorist failed of accomplishing; how can he fly in the face of organic chemistry and all experience, and secure a valuable grain crop year after year from the same field?

The answer is a curious one, and the solution of the problem is in perfect accordance with scientific law. Baron Liebig himself would have admitted its soundness. Every Minhote farm has adjoining it a piece of poor land occupied with gorse; it is usually a part of the pine forest. I have already described how the gorse growth is cut every three years. The cutting is a root and branch operation, effected with the strong country hoe. The gorse is literally scraped up, and with it are cut mosses, bent-grasses, gentians, ferns, and a liberal portion of the surface earth itself. All this is thrown into the cattle byres, into which no particle of straw (as with us at home) is ever cast; and this system naturally results in three very appreciable advantages. First, a much larger quantity of manure is made than with the straw-fodder system, and, all the straw being used as food, the land of course "carries more stock." Secondly, the seeds of plants taken from the forest patches are of species whose seed will not germinate in cultivated land, or having germinated will not thrive, and the fields are not in consequence made weed-dirty. Thirdly, these forest perennials of slower growth and development are fuller of enriching ingredients—phosphates, carbon, alkalis, and I know not what besides—than straw-fodder, and benefit the land accordingly; they put into it probably what it never had before; and the earthy particles which go with them are a direct transfusion, as it were, of fresh blood into the veins of the soil, emptied and exhausted by successive grain crops. This is the explanation of the mystery, and it is for our farmers at home to say whether they think the plan worth adopting. It is not, I think, science that will try to dissuade them.

To return to the farm system; the growing of maize (the chief bread corn) and the fattening of cattle bred in the highlands of the interior, are the two chief operations of the farmer, where the small farm system prevails. The oxen are stall-fed, because it would be wasteful to let them tread down the tiny fields in feeding themselves. During the summer they are given the male flower pannicles of the maize, and the thinnings of the maize fields, and straw of various kinds; in winter they get clover, rye and other grasses, and maize straw—a comparatively sweet and fattening food.

Instead of mowing the grass fields with scythes, which will cut from half to three quarters of an acre a day, the Portuguese use tiny saw-toothed hooks that will cut but the fourth or sixth part of that area in a long summer's day. The grass thus painfully and slowly reaped is carried on men's or women's heads often the distance of a mile; and yet, wonderful to say, cattle so fed and fattened, can be sent to England, pay freight and insurance, and sell at an excellent profit; and this exportation begun some twenty years ago, has reached large proportions, and has had much to do with the enrichment of the farmers of the northern Provinces.

The common plough in Portugal is formed of a crooked branch, and is so small that a man can carry it on his shoulder, and the friable soil is rather scratched than ploughed. The maize is sown broadcast, and hand-hoed two or three times in the course of the year, and irrigated with little driblets of water led to its roots with all economy of the precious fluid and a skilfulness which it is pleasant to watch,—the bare-footed labourer quickly cutting out with his hoe narrow channels for the flowing water, and stamping out a little basin round each plant.

A Scotch or English farmer would, I have no doubt, laugh at the clumsy ploughs and harrows, the absence of labour-saving machines, and the seeming waste of manual labour; but it may be questioned whether, looking to the smallness of farms and the abundance of labour, the ridicule would be altogether justified. The Portuguese farmer makes his farm pay—and pay well—and, after all, this is the surest test of farming. Until quite recently he has had, in the North at least, a wonderfully prosperous time; but changes are taking place even in Portugal, and I doubt whether the old system and the old order of things will continue long unmodified and unreformed. Mines and railways compete with the farmer for his labourers, and emigration to Brazil is going on rapidly. The wages of day labour have nearly doubled in thirty years. Already farms are less fully cultivated than they used to be. The prices of cattle and Indian corn cannot continue always to rise in sympathy with the rise in wages, for cattle must follow the prices of the London market, and if maize gets much dearer, it will be cheapened again by importation. One of two things must therefore shortly take place: either the non-cultivation of the poorer lands, or a reform in Portuguese agriculture.

So it is that even the yeoman farmer on the remote hills of Portugal makes part of the great commercial system of the world, and gains or loses by a rise or fall in the price of corn in Chicago and Odessa, or of butcher's meat in Leadenhall Market.

THE END.

Simmons & Botten, Printers, Shoe Lane, Fleet Street.

THE NEW QUARTERLY MAGAZINE

Published April 1, July 1, October 1, and December 1.

A SOCIAL AND LITERARY PERIODICAL.

Price 2s. 6d.;

Annual Subscription, 10s.; Free by Post, 11s.

THE NEW QUARTERLY MAGAZINE differs from all existing Magazines:—1. In admitting none but signed contributions; 2. in each Number being complete in itself; 3. in containing considerably more printed matter than any other Magazine published in Great Britain; 4. in the fact that two completed Stories, by Authors of established reputation, are contained in each Number.

Contents of last Number of

THE NEW QUARTERLY MAGAZINE,

Published on July 1.

DE QUINCEY. By the EDITOR.
AFFONSO HENRIQUEZ AND THE RISE OF PORTUGAL. By OSWALD CRAWFURD, H.M.'s Consul at Oporto.
THE MODERN STAGE. By ROBERT BUCHANAN.
DARK CYBEL. By Mrs. CASHEL HOEY, Author of "Only an Episode," etc.
LORD BUTE THE PREMIER. By Rev. F. ARNOLD.
THE TOWN MOUSE AND THE COUNTRY MOUSE. By FRANCES POWER COBBE.
BY THE LAW. By E. LYNN LINTON, Author of "Patricia Kemball," "The Mad Willoughbys," etc.

CONTENTS OF NO. 9,

Published October 1, 1875.

VILLAGE ORGANIZATION. By RICHARD JEFFERIES.
PHILIP MASSINGER. By GEORGE BARNETT SMITH.
NINO BIXIO. By EVELYN CARRINGTON.
NO SIGN: A NOVEL. By Mrs. CASHEL HOEY, Author of "The Blossoming of an Aloe," &c.
THE ARTISTIC SPIRIT IN MODERN POETRY. By J. W. COMYNS CARR.
THE DOLOMITES OF THE TYROL. By G. F. GODDARD.
THE SUMMERFIELD IMBROGLIO: A TALE. By MORTIMER COLLINS, Author of "Frances," "Sweet and Twenty," &c.
TENNYSON'S QUEEN MARY. By the Rev. T. H. L. LEARY, D.C.L.

LONDON: WARD, LOCK, & TYLER, PATERNOSTER ROW.

www.ingramcontent.com/pod-product-compliance
Lightning Source LLC
Chambersburg PA
CBHW020304240426
43673CB00039B/701